RELIGION AND DEMOCRACY
IN TAIWAN

RELIGION AND DEMOCRACY IN TAIWAN

CHENG-TIAN KUO

STATE UNIVERSITY OF NEW YORK PRESS

Published by
STATE UNIVERSITY OF NEW YORK PRESS
ALBANY

For information, contact State University of New York Press, Albany, NY
www.sunypress.edu

Production by Marilyn P. Semerad
Marketing by Michael Campochiaro

Library of Congress Cataloging-in-Publication Data

Kuo, Cheng-tian, 1957–
    Religion and democracy in Taiwan / Cheng-tian Kuo.
        p. cm.
    Includes bibliographical references and index.
    ISBN-13: 978-0-7914-7445-7 (hardcover : alk. paper)

    1. Taiwan—Religion.   2. Democracy—Taiwan.   I. Title.

BL1975.K84 2008
322'.10951249—dc22   2007033219

10 9 8 7 6 5 4 3 2 1

Contents

Illustrations

FIGURES

TABLES

Preface

Many religious elites and scholars have encouraged and escorted my adventure into this new territory of research. Among the numerous supporters for this work in the past five years, except for those who requested anonymity, are Christopher Achen, Christie Chang, Chen Lu-hui, Thomas Gold, Dennis Hickey, John Hsieh, C. Julia Huang, Guo Wen-ban, André Laliberté, Leng Ze-gang, Li Feng-mao, Lin Ji-wen, Emerson Niou, David C. Schak, Shen Xin-yuan, Robert Weller, and Joseph Wong, who read different parts of the manuscript and offered constructive comments. The two anonymous reviewers of the SUNY Press provided insightful and practical revision suggestions, including adding "sights, sounds, and smells" to the otherwise esoteric analysis.

The faculty members and graduate students of the Graduate Institute of Religious Studies and the Political Science Department of the National Chengchi University helped me to tighten the loose ends of my arguments. So did the participants in Thomas Gold's graduate seminar and in the Center for Chinese Studies at the University of California–Berkeley, where I spent my sabbatical leave and finished the first draft of the book.

Special thanks are due to Rev. C. S. Song and Kuan Ping-yin. Although we disagreed strongly with each other on theological and political issues, Rev. Song made my sabbatical leave at the Pacific School of Religion (2004–2005) very productive. Kuan Ping-yin, a sociologist at the National Chengchi University, patiently updated my statistical knowledge. He carefully walked through with me the statistical programs and results I generated. Without his help, the sometimes uncooperative data could not have been tamed, and many of my case studies could have been misled by the qualitative data that other scholars depend on. In appreciation of his critical contribution, I list him as coauthor of chapter 5.

Lan Yu-chen, Liao Bin-zhou, and Wu Zhen-jia provided excellent research assistance to this project. Generous financial funding came from the National Science Council of the Taiwan government (NSC 90-2414-H-004-004 and

92-2414-H-004-018), National Chengchi University, and the Chiang Ching-Kuo Foundation for International Scholarly Exchange. However, the views presented in this book do not necessarily reflect those of the aforementioned people and institutions.

Finally, no one else deserves more appreciation than my dear wife, Lee Chin-jung, who has replaced black-and-white with flying colors in both my academic and real life. Therefore, she shares with me both the merit and responsibility for this book.

CHAPTER 1

Introduction

It was in the chilly morning of 3 March 2004, hundreds of men and women nervously waited in a magnificent ballroom. Outside the building, more than ten thousand men and women patiently lined up in preparation to welcome their distinguished guests. When presidential candidate Lian Zhang and vice presidential candidate James Song arrived, the crowd's emotion exploded with thundering applause and repeated shouts of: "*Lian-Song, Dongswan!*" (which means "winning the election" in Taiwanese dialect.) Joyful tears ran down on their faces like waterfalls. The solemn host rose and made an inspiring welcome speech. He vehemently accused President Chen Shui-bian for his miserable economic performance, disasterous social policies, acrimonious ethnic maneuvers, violations of religious rights, sabotage of democracy, and provocation of war in the Taiwan Straits. Fists clenched, he spoke loudly and with exaggerated body language. Bitterness, anger, and frustration permeated the air and the crowd's mind. "Only Lian Zhang can save us from these political, social, and economic disasters," he emphatically concluded. During his speech, the crowd echoed every sentence the host said with deafening applause and "*Lian-Song, Dongswan.*"[1]

This might have been any of the ordinary campaign gatherings during an ordinary election in an ordinary democracy. But this campaign was anything but ordinary. The hall was not at the headquarters of any political party but at the center of a newly constructed Buddhist temple worth US$ 300 million. The emotional men and women were not devoted party workers or representatives, but monks, nuns, and sincere believers of the otherwise tranquil temple. And the host was certainly not an ordinary convention organizer, but the abbot of the largest Buddhist organization in central Taiwan, proclaiming a membership of over five-hundred thousand.

1

The scene is changed to a different place and a different time. On 25 May 2006, President Chen Shui-bian attended the Sixth National Prayer Breakfast, hosted by the major Christian denominations in Taiwan. He seemed a little bit disoriented when he stood among the jubilant pastors on the platform. He had reason to be disoriented, because his son-in-law was just arrested for insider trading, his wife was implicated in a bribery case, and he himself was involved in a looming case of corruption.

The convention host, Presbyterian pastor Gao Jun-ming, walked to the podium to deliver a sermon and pray for the president. President Chen squeezed a comforting smile on his face. After all, Pastor Gao was a long-time and ardent supporter of him. Their relationship was as cozy as those of American evangelist Billy Graham and President Richard Nixon—at least before the Watergate scandal broke out. The president expected to hear something cheerful in the pastor's prayer and sermon. To the president's great dismay, however, Pastor Gao looked straight into the president's eyes when he sternly quoted, word by word, from I Timothy 6:10, "For the love of money is a root of all kinds of evil." The smile on the president's face suddenly vaporized as Pastor Gao went on elaborating upon the verse. After the sermon, the president emotionlessly delivered a short speech without responding to Pastor Gao's comments and left the convention in a hurry.[2]

When religions resurface elswhere in national politics and world politics of the twenty-first century, we might want to ask as well: does religion matter in Taiwan's democracy? The two aforementioned scenes seem to provide an affirmative answer to this question. However, despite voluminous research on Taiwanese religions in both Chinese and English literature, little of that research deals with the subject of the relationship between religion and state; even less discusses the transformation of this relationship during and after the political democratization of the 1980s. No study has yet compared the relationships between democracy and all major Taiwanese religions. There-fore, we have not been able to answer the following important empirical and theoretical questions about the relationship between religion and democracy in general and in Taiwan in particular: If religions matter at all in Taiwanese democracy, do Taiwanese religions contribute to or hinder the establishment and consolidation of democracy? Do different religions and religious groups support different political parties? Do various religions and religious groups have varying support for democratic values and behavior? And are Christians more democratic than believers of traditional Chinese religions?

In the process of answering these questions, this book will make three original contributions to the study of the relationship between religion and democracy in general and in Taiwan in particular. First, it provides a the-oretical framework for the analysis of these relationships by examining the democratic theology and democratic ecclesiology of religions as well as their interaction with the state. Second, in contrast to the lack of comparative stud-ies in current literature, it compares nearly all major religions and religious groups in Taiwan. Finally, it utilizes both case studies and statistical methods in order to verify theoretical hypotheses and to correct misperceptions in the current literature based solely on case studies.

THEORIES OF RELIGION AND DEMOCRACY

Many scholars regard democracy as incompatible with religious revivalism.[3] The incompatibility thesis is built on one or more of the following elements: democracy cherishes pluralism, accountable leadership, tolerance, compromise, separation of state and religion, peace, gender equality, and respect for human rights, while religious revivalism, particularly religious fundamentalism, espouses a dominant value system, charismatic leadership, intolerance, dogmatism, unity of state and religion, violence, male chauvinism, and disrespect for human rights (Marty and Appleby 1991: 817–835).

Major historical and contemporary events seem to support the incompatibility thesis. St. Augustine's "correction of heresy" was used to justify the burning of witches and sorcerers in the Middle Ages. The "Holy War" was used by Crusaders to justify the slaughter of Muslims, heretics, and pagans. Six million Jews were massacred by the Nazis because of their ancestors' alleged religious crime of crucifying Jesus, although Hitler had planned to abolish all religions including Christianity (Steigmann-Gall 2003). The "White Man's Burden" was regarded as a sacred mission to save the people of the Third World through military, cultural, and/or economic means. In Asia, the integration of Confucianism, Daoism, and Buddhism with politics prevented the birth of democratic ideas in China for 2,500 years (Zhang Hao 1990). In prewar Japan, state Shintoism helped deify the emperor and sanctify the military's attempt to create an Asian coprosperity zone (Hardacre 1989). But it has been the global ascendance of religious fundamentalism since the 1980s that has elevated the incompatibility thesis to the academic altar.

In 1993, Samuel P. Huntington warned of a "clash of civilizations" in the prestigious journal *Foreign Affairs*. Although Islamic fundamentalism seemed to be his major concern, Huntington also cited evidence of severe conflicts among and within the eight major civilizations (Western, Confucian, Japanese, Islamic, Hindu, Slavic-Orthodox, Latin American, and African) sponsored by religious fundamentalists (Huntington 1993: 26). The September 11 terrorist attacks in the United States seem to give credence to his thesis and contributed to worldwide sales of the book version of "The Clash of Civilizations" (Huntington 1996). In the meantime, the American Academy of Arts and Sciences along with the McArthur Foundation provided generous funding to the Fundamentalism Project (Marty and Appleby 1991; 1993a; 1993b; 1994; 1995), documenting the history, environment, strategies, and development of various fundamentalist movements. In general, the conclusion of the Fundamentalism Project seems to reconfirm the incompatibility thesis.

Borrowing heavily from the findings and conclusions of the Fundamentalism Project, Gabriel A. Almond, R. Scott Appleby, and Emmanuel Sivan define religious fundamentalists as "militant and highly focused antagonists of secularization. They call a halt to the centuries-long retreat of religious establishments before secular power. They follow the rule of offense being better than defense, and they often include the extreme option of violence and death." Furthermore, "a fundamentalist 'family trait'" is "the defense and consolidation of patriarchy as the divine plan for the moral ordering of society" (Almond, Appleby, and Sivan 2003: 2, 11).

However, the incompatibility thesis has encountered theoretical, empirical, and philosophical criticisms. Many theoretical and empirical works have suggested important linkages between democracy and religion in general. In the early nineteenth century, Alexis de Tocqueville and Max Weber explained the establishment and consolidation of American democracy in terms of Protestant theology and practices (Tocqueville 1969; Weber 1978). The establishment of democracy further led to the "democratization of American Christianity" in the first fifty years of the new country (Hatch 1989).

The connection between democracy and religion attracted renewed interest from academia in the 1970s when Catholic democracies in Latin America and Southern Europe fell like dominoes. From these and other cases, scholars concluded that democracy seems to prosper better in Protestant countries than in Catholic, Confucian, or Muslim countries. Nevertheless, in the "Third Wave of Democratization," religion, especially the Catholic Church, played a critical role in establishing democracy in Poland, South Korea, the Philippines, and Latin American countries, while some Confucian countries and most Muslim countries continued to resist democratization (Huntington 1991; Ostrom 1997; Jelen and Wilcox 2002; Gill 1998; Monsma and Soper 1997; Diamond and Plattner 2001; Tamadonfar 2002). Rejecting the secularization thesis he championed in the 1960s, Peter L. Berger (1967; 1999: 14) has recently been impressed by the compatibility of Evangelism and democracy in many Third World countries and now argues that "the Evangelical resurgence is positively modernizing in most places where it occurs. . . . [It serves] as schools for democracy and for social mobility."

Even regarding Muslim countries, Abdou Filali-Ansary (2001: 40–41) points out that Islam has several features that are compatible with modern democratic values, such as utilitarianism, individualism, egalitarianism, republicanism, and rule-based governance. John L. Esposito and John O. Voll (1996) argue that Islamic fundamentalism is not necessarily incompatible with democracy; it depends more on strategic calculations of major political and religious groups than on theological doctrines or values. Mark Tessler (2002) has found statistical evidence that, contrary to American academic perceptions, there is strong popular support for democracy in Egypt, Jordan, Morocco, and Algeria, where fundamentalist movements are significant political forces. Steven Ryan Hofmann (2004) surveys Muslims in eight other countries and reaches a similar conclusion that Islam and democracy are compatible at the micro level.

Philosophical challenges to the incompatibility thesis are represented by the research of social philosopher José Casanova (1994) and political philosopher Peter Berkowitz (1999). Casanova argues that the "deprivatization of religion" can contribute to democracy when religion gets involved in politics to protect all modern freedoms and rights, to question and contest the absolute lawful autonomy of the secular spheres, to protect the traditional lifeworld from administrative or juridical state penetration, and to open up modern discursive ethics (Casanova 1994: 57–58). After reexamining the works of Hobbes, Locke, Kant, and Mill, Berkowitz (1999) argues that these political philosophers regarded liberal institutions and virtues as inseparable, and that religion, among other private institutions such as family, school, and social organizations, could play a critical role in promoting those virtues that facilitate the smooth functioning of democracy.

The question remains, however, how does religion actually influence democracy or vice versa? Most literature tends to focus on the theological side of religion. Protestant theology emphasizes "covenant," "the priesthood of all believers," and "the freedom of conscience," based on which government accountability, individual freedom, and political equality in modern democracy are built (Locke 1683, 1993; Morgan 1965; Shields 1958; Paine 1776, 1995; Witte 2000; Eidsmoe 1987). By further mixing Catholic teaching with Marxism, the progressive Catholicism that emerged after the Second Vatican Council (1962–1965) advocated human rights and launched the Latin American liberation theology (Sigmund 1990; Gutiérrez 1988). These Protestant and progressive Catholic theologies have provided religious legitimacy to democratic movements in various countries.

Important as it is, theology alone does not necessarily lead to behavioral change on the part of believers (Gill 2001: 128). There may be limits to the political influence of the clergy's public speech (Greenberg 1999; Djupe and Gilbert 2000). Furthermore, even if liberal theology may explain the establishment of democracy, it still needs to find expression in concrete institutional forms in order to explain the consolidation of democracy. After all, democracy is not just a system of ideas but also a way of life.

When Max Weber and Alexis de Tocqueville analyzed Protestantism, they discussed not only the theological component but also the institutions that translated abstract democratic theology into concrete democratic practices. For instance, in America, abstract democratic theological arguments like the idea of a covenant with God, freedom of conscience, the priesthood of all believers, and original sin all found concrete expression in institutional forms within many Protestant churches. These include the protection of the freedom of speech, congregationalism, and checks and balances between the clergy and the laity (Clark 1994; Nettels1963; Schlesinger 1968). In this book, I call a theology that includes key components of democratic theories a *democratic theology*, and a religious institution that resembles key institutions of democracy a *democratic ecclesiology*. The exact criteria for what constitutes a democracy will be elaborated further on.

The differentiation between the ideational level (democratic theology) and the institutional level (democratic ecclesiology) is useful in explaining the relationship between religion and democracy in Taiwan. Fundamental to a democratic theology are the promotion of human rights, the theological transformation from spiritual equality to political equality, and an assertive attitude toward the relationship between religion and state. Key elements of a democratic ecclesiology include the rules and norms that provide institutional checks on religious leaders, relatively equal power between clergy and laity, and the autonomy of local religious organizations.

Theories of social capital have advocated the importance of civic organizations to the development of democracy. Civic organizations cultivate values of trust, duty, norms, and social networks, which are essential to the functioning of democracy (Bourdieu 1986; Coleman 1990; Putnam 1993; Wuthnow 2002). However, both logical and empirical gaps seem to exist between social capital theories and theories of democracy. Logically speaking, do the values of trust, duty, norms, and social networks necessarily lead to the democratic values of checks and balances, regular leadership turnover, voter sovereignty, fair election, freedom of speech, and other democratic values? Empirically speaking, the proliferation of civic organizations in modern authoritarian societies, such as prewar Japan and contemporary Singapore, not only failed to contribute to democracy but, on the contrary, helped to consolidate their authoritarian regimes. Therefore, in addition to the provision of social capital, civic organizations (including religious ones) must also cultivate norms and rules that are directly related to the functioning of a democracy.

According to the aforementioned criteria, one would suspect that most Taiwanese religions—folk religions, Daoism, and Buddhism—lack either a democratic theology or a democratic ecclesiology to exhort their believers to respect democratic values and to learn democratic behavior. To varying degrees, they are all affected by the traditional Chinese culture, particularly Confucianism. Many scholars have suggested that certain characteristics of Confucianism are inimical to the functioning of democracy: dependence on authority and hierarchy; reliance on a benevolent ruler rather than on governing institutions; fear of chaos; loyalty to collectivity over individual rights; emphasis on consensus over open conflicts to resolve disagreements; low social trust toward out-groups; and governance based on particularism instead of universalism (Pye 1985; Ling and Shih 1998; T. Shi 2000; Hwang 1988; Rozman 2002; Solomon 1971).[4] Most Taiwanese Christians, with the exception of Presbyterians, are also weak in democratic theology and ecclesiology, although they might have a head start in these two analytical dimensions because they have been less affected by traditional authoritarian culture. All of these aspects might explain the low level of commitment to democratic values shown by Taiwanese elites and by the general public almost two decades after the lifting of martial law (T. Shi 2001).

A few scholars have noted the connection between religion and democracy in Taiwan. But most of them have either concentrated on one particular religion or a few sects of a religion, or have not fully captured the significant transformation of the relationship between religion and state after the Democratic Progressive Party took over the government in 2000. In particular, they have focused more on the external relations between religion and democracy than on the interaction between democratization and the internal institution/theology of religion, which this book will systematically examine and compare.[5]

RESEARCH METHODOLOGY

The research design of this book consists of both "between-systems" (religions) and "within-system" (religious groups) comparisons.[6] The between-systems design allows us to find systemic similarities or differences among different religions. The within-system design enables us not only to find variation among religious groups but also to make comparisons across religions. Therefore, a combination of between-systems and within-system research designs may verify general theoretical arguments across both religions and religious groups without the deficiencies that arise when each design is employed alone (Przeworski and Teune 1970).

Following the between-systems design, I select Buddhism, Daoism, Christianity, and folk religions for comparison. Buddhists constitute about 28.3% of the Taiwanese population; folk religion believers, 25.5%; Daoists, 21.3%; and Christians (including Catholics), 5%; together they constitute 78.1% of the population.[7] For within-system design, I choose the largest and/or the most representative sects of each religion. In Buddhism, I include the Buddhist Compassion Relief Ciji Foundation (about 4,000,000 members), Buddha Light Mountain (*Foguangshan*, about 1,000,000 members), Dharma Drum Mountain (*Fagushan*, about 1,000,000 members), and Zhongtai Zen (Chan) Monastery (about 400,000 members). The representative cases in Christianity include the Presbyterians (about 227,000 members), Baptists (about 24,000 members), and Local Church (*Jiaohui Juhuisuo*, about 91,000 members). Within Daoism and folk religions, Way of Unity (Yiguandao, about 1,200,000 members) is chosen as a representative case, although it is a syncretic religion of Buddhism, Daoism, Confucianism, Christianity, and Islam. The Mazu belief (about 6,000,000 worshipers) is a syncretic folk religion of Buddhism, Daoism, and Confucianism with a strong Daoist flavor. Other smaller sects of each religion are also briefly discussed for illustration.

As other scholars have found, the aforementioned numbers of believers and worshipers are usually exaggerated and can be best treated as references only. The Buddhist numbers are estimates based on my interviews with these

Buddhist organizations and cross-checked by other sources. The Buddhist Association of the Republic of China reported the total number of Taiwanese Buddhist believers to be 4,485,000 in 1999 (Ministry of the Interior 2001: 3–4, 13). The basic qualification of Buddhist membership, which the Ministry of the Interior adopts, is to have completed the initiation ceremony of "taking refuge in the three gems" (*guiyi sanbao*)—Buddha, Buddhist law, and the clergy. Age qualification varies across Buddhist sects. In 1999, the Ministry of the Interior reported a much smaller number (187,260) of Taiwanese Buddhists who had completed the three-gem ceremony (Ministry of the Interior 2000: 28).[8] Apparently, most Buddhist organizations include not only initiated members but also volunteers, worshipers, or family members in their membership rosters.

Like the Buddhist figures, the numbers for Christian believers are not very reliable either. The Presbyterians, the Local Church, and the Bread of Life Church (*Lingliangtang*) all accept teenagers or young children for baptism, while the Baptists set a higher age for baptism. But since these Christian denominations belong to "strict religions" in the sense that they impose a certain level of discipline on their members, the Christian numbers are more reliable than the Buddhist ones. They could be more influential politically than their Buddhist counterparts (Campbell 2000). In 1999, the Ministry of the Interior reported the number of baptized Christians to be 378,025 (Ministry of the Interior 2003: 28).

Members of Yiguandao usually require believers to complete the initiation rite of "transmitting the three treasures" (*chuan sanbao*)—pointing to the mystic portal, the hand seal, and the true sutra.[9] Some local branches also include visitors and family members in the membership rosters that they report to the Yiguandao headquarters. The Mazu belief has no initiation rite at all. Therefore, most believers are considered worshipers. Some believers join the affiliated but independent organizations of Mazu temples.

The research methodology of this book consists of two parts: case studies and statistical analyses.[10] For case studies, in addition to secondary sources, we conducted more than seventy interviews with the clergy, theologians, senior lay believers, and ordinary lay believers of these religions and religious groups. Interview questionnaires consisted of open-ended questions divided into three categories: democratic theology, democratic ecclesiology, and interaction with the state. These three categories of questions overlap substantially with Robert Dahl's criteria of democracy and Robert D. Putnam's criteria of a civic community. These criteria include: elected major officials, free and fair elections, inclusive suffrage, right to run for office, freedom of expression, alternative information, and associated autonomy (Dahl 1989; Putnam 1993). Questions posed to respondents were almost the same, differing only in terms of respective religious jargons. Each interview usually took about one hour. Many of the names of respondents and their branch organizations have been modified in this book in order to protect their anonymity.

In addition to the case study method, this book also employs statistical methods to verify the observations and arguments raised in these case studies. The statistical results not only confirm some qualitative arguments, and reject others; they also generate some surprising findings of their own. These methodological advantages confirm Evan S. Lieberman's (2005: 435) promulgation of his "nested analysis" for comparative research by combining case studies with statistical analysis. The merit of this methodological combination is that "not only are the advantages of each approach combined, but also there is a synergistic value to the nested research design." The details of the statistical methodology are explained in chapter 5.

CHANGING POLITICAL AND RELIGIOUS ENVIRONMENT

In order to analyze the relationships between religion and the state in Taiwan, it is useful to understand the political and religious environment in which these relations are embedded. This section briefly compares the political and religious environment of the martial law period (1949–1987) and the post–martial law period (1987–present).[11] The comparative criteria are: political regime, religious community structure, state control of religion, religious response, and cohesion within a religious group. The major differences are summarized in table 1.1.

Before explaining the differences, a few caveats about the division of the two periods are in order. First, the change in the political and religious environment in Taiwan was a progressive process that culminated in the lifting of martial law in 1987. The lifting of martial law brought about dramatic legal and normative changes in the relationships between the state and religious organizations as well as within religious organizations. Second, there are substantial variations among religions as well as among sects of the same religion with respect to these criteria. But the political regimes do set broad constraints on the behavior of the state and religious organizations.

TABLE 1.1 Changing Political and Religious Environment

	MARTIAL LAW PERIOD (1949–1987)	POST-MARTIAL LAW PERIOD (1987-PRESENT)
Political Regime	Leninist state	liberal democracy
Religious Community	semi-corporatist	pluralistic
State Control of Religion	strong	weak
Religious Response	submissive or isolationist	multiple choices
Religious Cohesion	strong	weakening

After being defeated by the Chinese communists in China in 1949, the Kuomingtang (KMT, the Nationalist Party) government found sanctuary in Taiwan. Upon arriving in Taiwan, the KMT government declared martial law on the island in order to stop the communist advance. The martial law government was not an ordinary authoritarian government, as seen in other developing countries. It was a Leninist state in the sense that the political party (KMT) and the state formed a symbiosis with an overlapping leadership at the top of both bureaucracies.[12] Once the party-state was established in 1950, it began to penetrate the society by setting up corporatist associations and implanting party cells in all large social organizations.[13]

However, there were substantial variations of party-state control across social organizations and within each category of social organization.[14] The KMT state's control of the religious community reveals similarities and differences. Under corporatist law, only one national umbrella religious association was allowed to exist for each religion to represent the interests of its clergy and believers. For instance, at the national level, there were the Buddhist Association of the Republic of China (*Zhongguo Fojiaohui*), the Daoist Association of the Republic of China (*Zhonghuaminguo Daojiaohui*), the Chinese Regional Bishops' Conference (*Tianzhujiao Zhongguo Zhujiaotuan*), and the Confucian Association of the Republic of China (*Zhongguo Rujiaohui*). No other similar associations of the same religion were allowed to challenge these state-sponsored associations. Although most Christian denominations had their own national associations, such as the Presbyterian Church in Taiwan, the Chinese Baptist Convention, and the Local Church, there was no national umbrella association for all Christian denominations. This was probably due to the decentralized nature of Protestantism and the foreign connections of most Taiwanese denominations. The KMT government probably did not want to upset these Western Christian denominations, whose missionaries were powerful lobbying groups in the United States, by imposing a state-controlled umbrella organization on them.

Under the KMT regime, the state was able to control religious groups through both formal and informal means. In addition to general martial law regulations restricting free movement, information, and speech, the major formal instrument was the Law Regulating Temples and Shrines (LRTS, *jiandu simiao tiaoli*) enacted in 1929 in China. The LRTS enabled the state to regulate religious activities and punish religious leaders if they broke the law. Strangely enough, the LRTS did not apply to Christians, Catholics, and practitioners of folk religions. Possible explanations include the fact that the first two presidents of the nation were Christians, that Taiwan relied heavily on American military support, and that Taiwan needed the symbolic support from the Vatican in the international community. In contrast, folk religions were too small and numerous to attract the eyes of the bureaucrats.

The KMT government tried several times to tighten its control over religion through attempted revisions of the LRTS. However, all attempts failed due to strong opposition from the major religious organizations. The major controversy was less about the external political relationship between religion and the state but more concerned with the state's attempt to put lay believers above the clergy in the governing structure of religious organizations. Since these changes would seriously undermine religious freedom and the vested interest of the clergy, religious groups vehemently opposed these revisions (Y. Ye 2000: 188–199).

More effective forms of state control over religion came from various state intelligence-gathering agencies, such as the local police, the Garrison Command, the Investigation Bureau, the military intelligence office, and the National Security Bureau. They often paid surprise visits to religious leaders involved in controversial political activities. Some religious leaders were barred from traveling abroad, including President Jiang Jie-shi's court pastor, Rev. Zhou Lian-hua, who was involved with the Presbyterian political movement in the early 1970s. The more serious offenders were put in jail without the protection of due process of law.

In addition to the supervision of state bureaucracy over religious organizations, the KMT also implanted party cells in large religious organizations. These party cells assumed at least three functions: to recruit party members from within the religion, to monitor religious organizations' political activities, and to elect party members to lead national religious organizations. The KMT central coordination center was the First Office of the Social Works Department.[15] In general, party members in religious organizations were not very active in recruiting other believers or clergy to join the KMT. It just seemed awkward to implement such a secular task in a spiritual environment. Thus, political monitoring seemed to be the major function of the KMT cells in religious organizations, which individual party members usually did in secret. Unlike in other social groups, the KMT did not set up tight and active party organizations in religious groups. There was a loose party caucus (*dangtuan*) set up in the Buddhist Association of the Republic of China, but no smaller party cells existed in the monasteries or temples. No evidence shows that formal party organizations existed within Christian denominations. Individual party members performed only the function of political monitoring, not of recruitment or of election campaigning.[16]

Because of the dual supervision of the state and party machinery, most religious organizations during the martial law period had no choice but to adopt either a submissive position or a strictly isolationist attitude toward the state. During national holiday celebrations and in national representative bodies, patriotic priests and believers dressed in different religious garb were routinely put on display. When the opposition movement questioned the government's legitimacy, some religious groups would openly defend martial law and eulogize the supreme political leaders as being bestowed with a heavenly mandate. Most of the religious groups, however, decided to uphold the principle of absolute separation of state and religion. Their teaching and learning concentrated on spiritual aspects and they rarely commented on political issues, particularly those related to democracy. Even where their religious activities involved social welfare, they refrained from interacting with the state as much as possible.

Finally, due to the authoritarian cultural and political environment, most religious organizations were able to maintain internal cohesion through authoritarian norms and structures. Religious leaders with charismatic personalities or perceived magic powers governed their religious groups in a way similar to the methods by which the supreme political leaders led the Taiwanese.

Taiwan's political and religious environment transformed in the early 1980s when the supreme political leader's health was deteriorating. The opposition movement made great progress in attracting supporters by combining democratic ideals with Taiwanese nationalism. Under pressure both from a formidable opposition movement and from the Democrat-controlled American Congress, which repeatedly put pressure on the KMT government to improve its human rights record or face the termination of arms sales, the KMT government lifted martial law in 1987.[17] Subsequently, most laws and regulations violating human rights were rescinded, and new laws promoting human rights were instituted. Most important among these new laws were the revised Law on the Organization of Civic Groups (*renmin tuanti zuzhifa*) and the Law on Assembly and Parade (*jihui youxingfa*), which guaranteed Taiwanese the same freedom of association and movement as citizens in other democratic countries. This meant that the increasing pluralism of religious organizations that began in the early 1980s was finally legally endorsed by the state. The corporatist structure of religious groups soon yielded to the mushrooming of all kinds of national religious association independent from the old religious associations.

In the post–martial law regime, the state bureaucracy has tried to maintain its close supervision of religious groups, but its intentions and methods are very different from those of the martial state. The increased freedom of association brought about the burgeoning of "new religions" (*xinxing zongjiao*), which combine the traditional religious practices with the personal ideologies of new religious leaders. At the same time, however, sexual and financial scandals in these unregulated new religions have been exposed from time to time. Partly due to the concern over their collective image and partly due to strong competition for membership and financial donations from these new religions, most religious groups support the government's effort to regulate all religions.[18] But the content of the proposed law aroused heated debate not only between the state and religious organizations but also among the principal religions concerning accounting procedures, property management, building construction, and internal governing structures. After decades of negotiation, the bill has been watered down to keep state intervention at a minimum while allowing maximum religious freedom.

Nevertheless, the bill has still not been approved by the legislature due to the conflicting and ever-changing demands of various religious groups. Meanwhile, the state has been very reluctant to intervene in religious affairs unless serious crimes are committed.

With the lifting of martial law, party cells in religious organizations lost their political legitimacy and political monitoring function. Even the campaigning function has now become counterproductive as most religious groups assert their political autonomy and are resentful of an interventionist state.

The increased political autonomy of religious groups is evidenced in several ways. With the help of economic prosperity, new religious groups have mushroomed outside the state-controlled religious associations (Katz 2003: 395; Paper 1996: 105). Religious support of the KMT government and politicians has declined. Many religious leaders now receive politicians from various political parties. State and local elites compete for votes by supporting local religious traditions (Katz 2003: 412). In turn, religious organizations solicit support from different political parties in order to maximize government funding for religious affairs. More and more religious organizations support candidates to run against KMT candidates. Furthermore, some clergy run for public offices under different party banners. However, many religious organizations decide to maintain their isolationist position or maintain equal distance from all different political forces.

It was not clear whether or not the religious belief of different political leaders had a significant impact on these changes of state-religion relationships. Jiang Jie-shi was a regular churchgoer but kept all religions on a tight leash. No religion or religious denomination received privileged treatment from the government.[19] Although his son, Jiang Jing-guo, was also a Christian, there was very little evidence revealing his religiosity. Li Deng-hui was a devoted Presbyterian, but he did not forget his duty as the national leader to pay regular visits to holy places of various religions and participate in their religious ceremonies. Chen Shui-bian was an initiated member of Yiguandao. Nevertheless, he never publicly acknowledged his religious belief. Probably because of the syncretistic nature of Yiguandao, Chen has payed his respects to all religions on their important holidays. In sum, there were complaints about the interventionist state by various religious groups over the decades, but there were few grudges about religious discrimination in Taiwan.

Finally, the increased pluralism in the political and religious environment challenges the cohesion of religious groups. Lay believers have more choices of religious groups to join. Differing political preferences among lay believers have prompted religious leaders to refrain from strongly endorsing a particular political party or candidate. Otherwise, they would face a great loss of membership and financial donation. Furthermore, democratic ideas and reforms are introduced gradually from the bottom up. More decision-making power is delegated to or shared by lay believers or junior clergy.

Having said this, however, it is important to notice that large variations remain not only among religions but also among sects of a single religion. Sometimes the variations between sects can be larger than those between religions. This is the focus of the following chapters of this book.

CHAPTER 2

Taiwanese Buddhism

One night in the early February 1912, a senior monk surreptitiously led several dozens of muscular monks and monastery workmen carrying knives and clubs to launch a blitzkrieg on the headquarters of the Association for the Advancement of Buddhism located inside the monastery. About twenty staff members of the Association were seriously wounded and driven off of the property. The senior monk and five or six other attackers were later charged and imprisoned for their offenses.

One month earlier, the famous Chinese Buddhist leader Ven. Taixü had just won an election held in the monastery to establish the association for the purpose of turning the monastery into a Buddhist educational school. The two hundred plus resident monks were outnumbered by three to four hundred lay guests clandestinely mobilized by Ven. Taixü and lay leaders. Ven. Taixü had told the monastery's monks that these lay guests came only to attend an academic conference and mentioned nothing about his intention to turn the vast monastery into a school. The resident monks vehemently refused to let the laymen take over their property and staged the aforementioned assault.[1]

This episode was later named in modern Chinese Buddhist history the Fracas of the Quinshan Temple (*Danao Qingshansi*). In retrospect, this episode not only represented the modernization pains of Buddhism in China but also became the prologue to the establishment of various humanistic Buddhist *(Renjian Fojiao)* empires in Taiwan. Short-lived in China, the humanistic Buddhism pioneered by Ven. Taixü has flourished in Taiwan and provided a potentially fertile ground for democratic learning. This chapter elaborates this intriguing development.

GENERAL DESCRIPTION

Although Taiwanese Buddhism had its roots in the Qing dynasty or earlier, the most important Buddhist organizations existing in Taiwan originated from pre-1949 Chinese Buddhism.[2] Their Chinese heritage is reflected in four areas: leadership, theology, ecclesiology, and political connections. First, among the four largest sects of Taiwanese Buddhism—Buddha Light Mountain, Dharma Drum Mountain, Zhongtai Zen Monastery, and Buddhist Compassion Relief Ciji Foundation—the first three sects were created and are still led by monks born in China. Although the abbot of Ciji is Taiwanese, she is a disciple of the eminent Chinese monk Venerable Yinshun, who passed away in June 2005. Ven. Yinshun was the favorite disciple of Ven. Taixü.

Second, Taiwanese Buddhist theology and ecclesiology follow that of Chinese Buddhism, which belongs to the school of Mahayana (Great Vehicle) Buddhism and adopts an authoritarian ecclesiology. Within the Great Vehicle school, the theology of humanistic Buddhism is the most popular among Taiwanese Buddhists.[3] Ven. Taixü and his disciple Ven. Yinshun were the major founders of this humanistic theology.[4] The theology's departure point was to replace the individualistic view of salvation with a socially oriented view. Humanistic theology extensively discusses the application of Buddhist principles to family relationships, financial management, health, career development, environmental protection, office relationships, affection and love, and international relations. However, due to the sensitivity of politics in an authoritarian environment, humanistic theology has rarely touched on political issues (Laliberté 2001: 120).[5] On the rare occasions where it did discuss politics, the discussion would be based on purely Buddhist theology rather than a combination of Buddhist theology with democratic ideas (Y. Chen 1990). Humanistic theology proposed that Buddhists "participate in politics, but not govern" (*wenzheng bu ganzhi*), meaning that the clergy should not take up administrative positions in the government, although representative and consultative positions were allowed. The laity could take up both types of positions.[6]

In 1954, Ven. Yinshun was almost arrested by the KMT government. Some Buddhists from opposing sects in the Buddhist Association of the Republic of China (BAROC), reported to the state security agency that Yinshun had written an article promoting communism, in which, in fact, Yinshun talked about a utopian Buddhist community that existed in ancient India (H. Yang 1993: 19–29; Z. Song 1989: 52–54; Y. Ye 2000: 226–227). To avoid further persecution, Yinshun unwillingly wrote a confession letter to the BAROC and to the government about his religious "mistakes" (Hou 2003: 9–13). After the Yinshun incidence, supporters of the humanistic theological tradition imposed self-restraint, agreeing to discuss everything humanistic except for politics. They did not emphasize or reinterpret the original meaning of "participating in politics, not governing" until after the lifting of martial law.

Why did humanistic Buddhism but not other Buddhist sects flourish in Taiwan? Most scholars correctly attributed the success of the sect to the very nature of this-worldliness of humanistic Buddhism that strengthened the theological and organizational links between temples and lay believers. The implementation of the Buddha way (*xingpusadao*) was no longer restricted to studying esoteric classics, chanting sutras, and performing meditation rituals at remote temples but included the application of Buddha's cosmic love in the believer's daily life such as charity works, maintaining good family relationships, and promoting work ethics. The rapid economic growth, social transformation, and technological progress of Taiwan in the 1970s and 1980s helped fuel the expansion of humanistic Buddhism, which provided practical social, psychological, and spiritual services to the needy.[7] Furthermore, a virtuous cycle was formed between the supply and demand of humanistic Buddhism: the more humanistic services it provided, the more resources (both in terms of knowledge, donation, and manpower) it could get, and the more humanistic services it could provide.

Third, in terms of ecclesiology, the first Buddhist group (*sangha*) established by Buddha 2,600 years ago adopted a very egalitarian decision structure. Decisions were made collectively and usually by consensus vote (Shengyan 1979: 71–88; Shengyan 1999: 119–124; N. Shi 2003: 42–44).[8] However, this egalitarian governing structure gradually yielded to an authoritarian structure as the Buddhist group expanded. After Buddhism was introduced into China, it adapted completely to the authoritarian and class structure of the Chinese political and social environment (M. Zhang 1979; Song 1989: 30–58; Ministry of the Interior 2001: 3–4). During the early republican era in China, some Buddhist reformers such as Ven. Taixü made an alliance with lay believers in order to implement his reform programs. But the traditional clergy as well as many liberal clergy reacted strongly against sharing power with lay believers. As a result, Taixü's reform program in ecclesiology largely failed in China (Welch 1968: 28–34). Deriving from the Chinese Buddhist tradition, most Taiwanese Buddhist temples abandoned the more egalitarian structure of the native Zhaijiao tradition. Instead, they reconstructed the ecclesiology to govern their internal affairs according to three principles: supreme mastership, the superiority of the clergy over the laity, and centralization.

The principle of supreme mastership holds that the founder of the religious group is the supreme leader. Followers believe that the master can do or say nothing wrong in either spiritual or secular affairs. If there is a difference in opinion between the head master and other clergy, it must be the mistake of the other clergy whose thinking is tarnished by insufficient religious training or experience. In Taiwanese Buddhism, the supreme master is not just one of the three gems;[9] she or he embodies the three gems as one, a Buddhist trinity (Zhong 2001).

The second governing principle is "the clergy decide clergy business" (*sengshi sengjue*), which means that the clergy lead the religious group with laity serving only as an auxiliary arm. The clergy may delegate some power to the laity to handle nonclergy-related business (such as temple cleaning, maintenance, accounting, and charity works), but the laity must obey the commands of the clergy. As for purely clerical matters (such as the recruitment and promotion of clergy, the hosting of religious ceremonies, and sermons), the laity is largely excluded from these functions.[10] Ven. Taixü painstakingly elaborated this division of labor between clergy and laity in order to pave the institutional foundation for the implementation of humanistic Buddhism in republican China (J. Hong 1995: 250–254).

Chinese Buddhism holds that there are nine classes of Buddhists ranked by their spiritual status and training, despite the general claim that "all living beings are equal" (*zhongsheng pingdeng*). The lowest class consists of men and women just admitted to Buddhism. Those with more commitment to Buddhist laws are ranked higher. Those with full commitment to Buddhist laws are the highest in the ranking, that is, the monks and the nuns (Shengyan 2001b: 40; Welch 1968: 206). Therefore, equality among Buddhists is a theological assumption that is diluted by the aforementioned class differentiation in practice.

The final governing principle is centralization in decision-making. Local temples or chapters of a Buddhist organization have very limited autonomy over religious matters, finances, and personnel management. The headquarters defines "correct" religious interpretations, collects and allocates financial resources, and makes important decisions concerning the promotion of the local clergy and laity.

Despite the traditional Chinese authoritarian structure, Taiwanese Buddhism contains a great deal of leeway in the learning of democratic values and allowing the practice of democratic behavior by both the clergy and the lay believer. This space is created by the theology of humanistic Buddhism. Although containing self-imposed political restrictions, humanistic Buddhism justifies the lay believer's participation in the religion's newly expanded activities on social issues. Not only do lay believers need to learn the democratic values of respect, compromise, and coordination in order to mobilize other believers for volunteer social work, the clergy also need to respect, coordinate, and make compromises with lay believers regarding those social works in which the clergy have no expertise. The more humanistic missions a Buddhist organization assigns to itself, the larger the relative space for democratic learning, and the more influential the lay believer is within the organization.

The enlarged space created by humanistic Buddhism does not necessarily imply a harmonious relationship between the clergy and the lay believer, or among lay believers. When Ven. Taixü promoted an enlarged role for the lay believer in temple management, he received violent protest from the clergy, epitomized by the infamous Fracas of the Qingshan Temple (*Danao Qingshansi*) in 1912 (Welch 1968: 29–33). However, one way or another, lay believers actively or passively participate in decision-making and implementation of temple activities connected with social issues, in which democratic values are learned and practiced.

The fourth connection between Chinese and Taiwanese Buddhism is political. Almost all of the major Buddhist organizations in Taiwan established friendly relationships with the KMT government during the period of martial rule. In fact, prominent Buddhist leaders such as Baisheng, Xingyun, Weijue, Wuming, and Dongchu were high-ranking KMT members (Y. Ye 2000: 219). On national holidays, they routinely criticized the Chinese communists for their atheism and eulogized the KMT government for its protection of principal Buddhist organizations.

In 1949, in fear of the communists' atheism, many Chinese Buddhist clergy fled with the KMT government to Taiwan. Unfortunately, the KMT government suspected they were communist agents disguised as monks and nuns. Many Chinese clergy were arrested by the KMT government in Taiwan for conspiracy or for being "unemployed street people" (*wuyeyoumin*). In order to protect these Buddhist clergy, Chinese monk Ven. Dongchu reconvened the Buddhist Association of the Republic of China (BAROC) to represent the interests of Buddhists and to detect any possible communist elements in Buddhist disguise for the government (Jiang 1995b: 518; Jones 1999: 176; Hou 2003: 5–7).[11] The BAROC was organized according to the corporatist principle in the sense that it was the only national-level Buddhist association (Yang 1993: 35–36; Ministry of the Interior 2003: 12).[12] Under the BAROC were local chapters corresponding to the government's administrative hierarchy, and only one such chapter was allowed to be established at each level. All Buddhist temples and organizations had to be members of these local chapters. Lay believers could apply for individual membership in these chapters, but ordained monks and nuns had to join these chapters. In fact, before the lifting of martial law, the BAROC held the exclusive right to ordain monks and nuns under the government's order. It also held the exclusive right to rescind clergy status if serious violations of Buddhist regulations were found.

The BAROC was under the strict control of the KMT. The KMT set up a party caucus within the BAROC that was responsible for screening out any antigovernment Buddhists and for electing the director-generals of the BAROC (Jones 1999: 176–177). During martial law, the BAROC actively cooperated with the government in anti-communist policies as well as in domestic politics. For instance, it publicly condemned the opposition movement associated with the Formosa Island Incident of 1979 and later opposed the lifting of martial law (Hou 2003: 24–31, 36).

After 1987, the monopoly of the BAROC was shattered by the four largest Buddhist organizations, which established their own hierarchy from the local to the national level. The BAROC was also challenged by more than a dozen new national Buddhist associations such as the Buddhist Youth Association of the Republic of China (*Zhonghuaminguo Fojiao Qingnianhui*, 1989), the Modern Buddhist Association of the Republic of China (*Zhonghuaminguo Xiandai Fojiao Xuehui*, 1990), and the Chinese Buddhist Temple Association (*Zhonghua Fosi Xiehui*). These organizations share ordaining power with the BAROC, although the BAROC always sends representatives to attend the ceremony sponsored by these sects (Y. Ye 2000: 270–271; Jones 1999: chap. 6).

During the martial law period, Taiwanese Buddhists supported the KMT government with differing degrees of enthusiasm. Initially, some supported the government through harsh criticisms of the Chinese communists. When the democratic movement progressed rapidly in the 1970s and 1980s, some Buddhists supported the government by criticizing the democratic movement (BAROC 1983: 1). Most Buddhists, however, chose to espouse humanistic Buddhism with an almost total exclusion of political concerns. They maintained a safe distance from the democratic movement or social protests.

After the lifting of martial law, Taiwanese Buddhists scrapped their anti-communist rhetoric in order to establish religious connections with Chinese Buddhists. On the domestic front, the adjustment process was protracted by a series of trials and errors. The Foguangshan actively supported an independent candidate in the 1996 presidential election. The Zhongtai Chansi bet its organizational reputation and resources on the 2000 and 2004 presidential elections. Both organizations suffered a great deal in terms of membership and donation loss after their candidates lost. By contrast, the Dharma Drum Mountain and Ciji decided to keep communication channels open to both the KMT and opposition parties. But at the time of election, they refrained from endorsing any candidate and political party. In the 1997 legislative election, the BAROC director-general Ven. Jingxin openly endorsed KMT candidates by saying that "if other political parties are in power, I am not sure whether all the religions can keep what we have."[13] But after the 2000 election, he also toned down his support and kept his distance from the KMT.[14] In sum, most Taiwanese Buddhist leaders are reducing their KMT affiliations and trying to keep a delicate balance among competing political forces.

Some radical Buddhists emerged after the lifting of martial law, but their influence has been limited (Jiang 1995b: 163–172; Song 1989; Song 1990). For instance, a couple hundred of progressive Buddhists organized a Buddhist Movement of Safeguarding the Nation and Constitution (*Fojiao Jiuguo Jiuxian Yundong*) in support of a student demonstration in 1990 (Chen, Li, and Lü 1990: 9–11). The organization did not receive much attention in the news media. In 1992, the Ten Thousand Buddha Association (*Wanfohui*) organized a political party and sent five lay believers to participate in the first democratic election of legislators on the island. They all lost the election (Jiang 1995a: 170). Ven. Zhaohui, Song Ze-lai, Jiang Can-teng, Chen

Yi-shen, and Yang Hui-nan were among the few Buddhists or Buddhist scholars to criticize the political and religious conservatism of principal Buddhist organizations. But few Buddhists in the four largest organizations would publicly echo their views.

THE BUDDHA LIGHT MOUNTAIN
(*FOGUANGSHAN*: HEREAFTER, FGS)

Without the embarrassing short remark, the dinner hosted by Ven. Xingyun could have been perfect by all standards. The dinner was held on 4 October 2006 at the FGS's Taipei headquarters in honor of distinguished Chinese visitors, the chief and officials of the Religion Affairs Bureau of the Chinese government. The dinner guests also included the deputy chairman and officials of the Mainland Affairs Council of the Taiwanese government, plus a couple religious leaders and scholars, including me.

It was one of the best diplomatic dinners one can expect: the vegetarian dishes were luxuriously delicious, and everyone delightfully concurred on the necessity of expanding religious exchanges between China and Taiwan. Both the Chinese and Taiwanese officials echoed every comment made by Xingyun by saying, "Thank you for your wise revelation (*kaishi*)."

Toward the end of the dinner, however, suddenly coming from nowhere, Ven. Xingyun spoke gently to the guests: "The reason why I urged President Chen Shui-bian to resign from the presidency a few weeks ago was because I sympathized with the predicament he had gone through. It was not worthwhile for him to endure all the humiliation and accusation about his corruption." Although our Chinese guests would probably like to see President Chen step down immediately, they made no comment, no "thank you for your wise revelation," or any approving gesture. Neither did the officials from the Taiwanese government; they probably dared not do so. The dishes on the table seemed suddenly frozen by the extremely quiet and discomforting atmosphere in the room. After thirty seconds of embarrassing silence, Ven. Xingyun realized that he might have brought up something he shouldn't have and wisely changed the subject back to religious exchanges. Everyone felt great relief and pretended that Xingyun had never made the remark. A tropical breeze came back to the room to defrost the dishes. Yes, it was the flamboyant style of Ven. Xingyun, a well-respected Buddhist leader with a persistent interest in political affairs. Even America's major mass media learned about his political devotion when his Los Angeles branch made a controversial campaign contribution of US$ 10,000 to Democratic presidential candidate Al Gore in 2000.[15]

Ven. Xingyun (or Hsing Yun) established the FGS in 1967 to promote humanistic Buddhism, which he had studied under the guidance of Ven. Taixü (Laliberté 1999: 83). He was one of the Chinese monks who fled to Taiwan in 1949. After building a religious base in a remote northeastern county, he moved down to southern Taiwan to establish the FGS. With the help of local elites, the FGS soon developed into an international religious empire consisting of hundreds of temples, museums, libraries, publishers, hospitals, high schools, universities, and welfare organizations, with more than one thousand clergy and about one million registered believers across five major continents (Foguangshan 2002: 8).[16]

Ven. Xingyun's writings rarely touched upon political issues. Among the few comments on politics and politicians, his democratic jargon is often fused with authoritarian interpretations. In a book published in 1987, before the lifting of martial law, he said, "We are in the democratic era. We care about democratic politics, but we don't need opposition parties. Liberal democracy has moral standards. . . . How can a few [opposition] politicians serve us as well as the hundreds of thousands of KMT members can?" He equated the politics of Kharma Emperor with a liberal democracy (Z. Lu and Liu 1987: 282–283).

In a long essay expounding upon humanistic Buddhism, Xingyun included a section on the Buddhist political view. He proposed that "politics needs assistance and enlightenment from Buddhism, and Buddhism needs protection and assistance from politics." He cited the close relationship between Buddhism and the state in ancient India and China to support his argument. He argued that Buddhists have a responsibility to protect human rights and to promote social welfare. He further urged Buddhists in a democracy to abandon the old isolationist view and adopt a more assertive interpretation of "participating in politics, not governing" (Xingyun 2001). In another short pamphlet, he briefly criticized the corrupted public officials of the new democracy (Xingyun 2002: 250–252). Both statements, however, are derived more from Confucian or Buddhist standards of self-discipline in public officials than from democratic values or institutions.[17] Except for these few works by Xingyun, none of his one thousand clergy teach or write anything about politics (Foguangshan 2002: 112–120).

In contrast to the slow development of a democratic theology, the FGS began to develop a nascent democratic ecclesiology in the early 1990's (Jones 1999: 191–197). The Organic Law of FGS (OLFGS, *foguangshansi zuzhi zhangcheng*) was promulgated five years after the FGS was established. Although more democratic and institutionalized than its counterparts in other major Buddhist organizations, the OLFGS and other practical norms specify a number of traditional organizational principles. First, the status of Xingyun is unique and supreme. He was the founder and abbot of the religious empire from 1967 to 1985. Even after he voluntarily resigned from the abbot position, he is still the de facto supreme commander in the FGS system. He appoints abbot successors and makes decisions on major organizational affairs, such as the hosting of ceremonies for ordaining clergy and admitting laity (Foguangshan 2002: 58–74). His published works are required reading for all clergy and believers. In the eyes of his followers,

Ven. Xingyun can say or do nothing wrong.[18] Therefore, even though the "monastic order strives to function according to a set of fixed rules rather than following a charismatic style of leadership" (Laliberté 1999: 88), the practice has lagged far behind its ideals.

The OLFGS established a nine-member Religious Affairs Committee (*Zongwu Weiyuanhui*) as the governing body of the FGS.[19] The abbot is elected from the nine members of this committee, who in turn are elected by all clergy with at least ten years of residency. Although this is a more democratic structure than that of other Buddhist organizations in Taiwan, the actual operation of the procedure is not as democratic as one might expect. Xingyun was the abbot for three consecutive terms, facing no competitors in the elections. In 1985, after serving three terms as abbot, Xingyun appointed Ven. Xinping as his successor. Since the nine committee members were the same until the election of 1990, and Xingyun was still the real decision maker, there was no competitor during Xinping's election.

Democratic elements were introduced in the elections of committee members in 1990, 1994, and 1997. Not only were the elections held more frequently, but younger clergy were also elected. Although the election of the abbot was still influenced by Xingyun, the general clergy possessed more autonomy than before. When Ven. Xinping died unexpectedly in 1995, Xingyun appointed Ven. Xinding as his successor through a hastily convened committee meeting. The appointment of Ven. Xinding aroused some controversy among the clergy. Before the appointment, reelection of the committee members and the abbot was conducted in 1997 before their terms expired. In this election, five of the nine senior members withdrew and were replaced by younger clergy. Ven. Xinding received the largest number of votes (332) in the election of nine committee members but was closely trailed by Ven. Huikai (319 votes), a nun who, among other outstanding religious records, held a Temple University PhD in religion. The nine committee members then elected among themselves the abbot. When asked about the election of the abbot, one senior nun voiced her reservation by saying that "nuns in our organization are very competent, but some senior clergy still prefer to have a monk to head the organization."[20] In fact, the FGS "comprise 1,000 nuns and only 300 monks, and all five heads of departments within the order are women" (Laliberté 1999: 106).

In 2004, a replay of the 1997 abbot election was carefully orchestrated when the forty-year-old (or young?) monk, Ven. Xinpei, was elected to succeed Ven. Xinding. For unknown reasons, Ven. Xinding stepped down before his second six-year term expires in 2009. The second runner in the 1997 election, Ven. Huikai, was not even elected to the nine-member committee. The nine members, then, elected Ven. Xinpei as the new abbot. In his inauguration ceremony, most of the guests never heard of him before. His short credentials included "knowledgeable in rules and rituals" and experience as a superintendent within the system but not as an abbot of a local branch, which the previous abbots had included in their resumes. When asked by a news reporter about his opinion on the credentials of the new abbot, one guest replied: "I heard that he was an excellent hymn singer."[21] It seems that the FGS's formal democratic structure is still held at bay by undemocratic practices.

In terms of the power relationship between the clergy and the laity, FGS made some progress after the lifting of martial law. According to the OLFGS, the FGS local temples follow the principle of "clergy decide clergy business." The first article of the first chapter of the OLFGS prescribes that FGS "be led by the clergy and assisted by the laity." The laity assume only an auxiliary and subordinate role and do not share decision-making power with the clergy.

In the early 1990s, limited democratic reforms were introduced into the FGS system. First, after the reform in 1992, a female lay believer was elected to the Religious Affairs Committee in 1997, although only as an alternate member. More important was the establishment of the Buddha's Light International Association (BLIA) in 1991. The BLIA gave the laity a more active role in managing association affairs, including delivering sermons, which traditionally was regarded as an exclusive privilege of the clergy. But the clergy still hold key positions in the BLIA (Laliberté 1999: 103), thus limiting the spread of democratic norms and practices within the organization. In 1993, the BLIA passed a constitutional law to establish the Lay Dharma Teacher/ Lecturer system (*Tanjiaoshi/Jiangshi*). By 2002, the system had generated 7 teachers and 133 lecturers (BLIA 2001: 55). Lay Dharma Teachers and Lecturers may deliver sermons in BLIA member temples. However, one Dharma Teacher, a professor at a major university in Taiwan, told me that he does not know much about what goes on in the BLIA. He only gives lectures when he is occasionally invited to do so. As far as he knows, Lay Dharma Teachers have little influence in the BLIA. At the local FGS temples, the clergy maintain prime leadership roles, with the laity serving only as auxiliary arms. The clergy, not the laity, conduct all important religious ceremonies.[22]

Closely related to the supreme mastership and the dominance of the clergy over the laity is the centralization of decision-making in the FGS system. The FGS headquarters provides a standardized minimum wage of no more than NT$ 500 a month, to all clergy (D. Zheng 2002: 77). Except to cover routine maintenance work at local temples, all donations are to be submitted to the headquarters. Properties under the care of local temples and chapters all belong to the headquarters, despite the fact that some of the larger temples have registered separately with the Ministry of the Interior. Local abbots are rotated between different temples to prevent the emergence of warlordism. A strict hierarchy has been established for the clergy, with grades and ranks based on seniority and performance. It "operates more like a military review board than a monastic system of the past," Charles B. Jones perceptively comments (1999: 193). Personal interpretations of Buddhism are to be based on that of Ven. Xingyun, and are not allowed to differ from those of the headquarters.

In terms of the interaction between state and religion, FGS played a submissive and supportive role in relation to the KMT government prior to 1987. Ven. Xingyun was arrested by the KMT government in China once and was arrested again in 1949 on an espionage charge after the KMT government moved to Taiwan. He took the advice of other prominent clergy to join and support the KMT in order to avoid any future suspicion and harassment from the government (Hou 2003: 33–35; Laliberté 1999: 101). Afterwards, KMT candidates were able to deliver political speeches and distribute campaign fliers via the FGS system. Ven. Xingyun was elected director or executive director of the state-sponsored BAROC from 1952 to 1993.[23] Furthermore, he was a KMT member and elected to an important advisory position in the party in 1988 (Jiang 1997: 23). After the lifting of martial law, FGS began to take a more autonomous role in political affairs. Within the FGS system, free discussion about politics was allowed. Any FGS laity who was a candidate for public office or supporter of other candidates was permitted to conduct limited political advertisements at religious gatherings. In 1995, Ven. Xingyun publicly endorsed independent presidential candidate Chen Lü an, who was a former minister of defense, a devoted Buddhist, and a disciple of Ven. Xingyun.[24] Chen did not get the expected support from the rank and file of the FGS system nor from other major Buddhist organizations, and performed poorly in the election, receiving only 8% of the total votes (Laliberté 1999: 94–96). This electoral loss led to a sharp drop in the FGS's membership and financial support, which prompted Ven. Xingyun to "seal the mountain" (*fengshan*) in May 1997 to consolidate its financial structure and to reformulate development strategies (Jiang 1997: 15–17). Adding insult to injury, the local government began to harass the FGS over zoning violations of its buildings (Laliberté 1999: 97). The FGS did not reopen until 2001.

However, the "sealing of the mountain" did not spell the end to the FGS's contact with politics. After a few months of recuperation, Ven. Xingyun rebuilt his relationship with the KMT by incorporating important KMT politicians into the BLIA. A KMT vice chairman (Wu Boxion) was BLIA's president for two terms, and another vice chairman of the KMT (Wang Jin-ping) was a member of the board of directors for two terms. Many other important KMT politicians were members of the governing board of the BLIA (BLIA 2001: 98–103).[25] With a successful coalition strategy that crossed party lines, the FGS pushed a petition through the legislature to make the birthday of Buddha a national holiday (Y. Ye 2000: 268). In 1998 and 2002, the FGS also hosted two extravagant Buddhist ceremonies to welcome Buddha's relics to Taiwan. Distinguished politicians from all major parties attended the ceremonies. When the FGS reopened its mountain in 2001 it warmly welcomed the Democratic Progressive Party president in order to reconcile with the new government. In the 2004 election, the FGS continued to favor the KMT/People First Party slate, but did not do so publicly.[26]

BUDDHIST COMPASSION RELIEF CIJI FOUNDATION (HEREAFTER, CIJI)

The founder and current leader of Ciji is Ven. Zhengyan (or Cheng Yen). Born in 1937 to a movie theater owner in central Taiwan, she learned the skills of business management before Ven. Yinshun ordained her in 1963. In 1966, she established the Buddhist Hardworking Ciji Gongdehui (*Fojiao Kenan Ciji Gongdehui*) and started her systematic efforts in charity works. Ciji membership did not grow rapidly until after the Ciji hospital was completed in 1986. Over the next twelve years, Ciji developed into a giant Buddhist philanthropic corporation with more than 2.6 million members (D. Zheng 2002: 53). Unlike other Buddhist groups, these members do not need to perform the three-gem ceremony of monastic vows. They become members after making continual donations to Ciji or after passing a home interview by a commissioner (*weiyuan*). Most Ciji members are relatives or friends of commissioners (D. Zheng 2002: 58; Huang and Weller 1998: 386).

Ciji differs from other major Buddhist groups in one major aspect, which also affects the composition of its theology and ecclesiology. The organization started not as a religious organization but a charity, and was registered with the government as such. However, this does not mean that religious activities, such as prayer, reading Buddhist texts, chanting Buddhist hymns, and Buddhist rituals, are absent from the organization's routine works. It is the overwhelming emphasis on nonreligious activities that makes Ciji different from other major Buddhist organizations from the beginning. Hence, the organization's activities place more emphasis on charity works than on the study of Buddhist theology (Laliberté 1999: 122–124; Weller 2000: 491–493). Ven. Zhengyan's favorite Buddhist text is *Fahuajing*, but Ciji members are encouraged to read her *Still Thoughts* (*Jingsi Yulu*). As a result, the number and the roles of the clergy are reduced to a minimum, leaving the laity to take full control of the organization. There are only about 110 nuns and a handful of monks living at Ven. Zhenyan's residence, performing maintenance and making souvenir candles.

As a disciple of Ven. Yinshun, Ven. Zhengyan follows the theology of humanistic Buddhism, but adopts a more restrictive version than her master did. Since the majority of Ciji members are women, Ven. Zhengyan upholds traditional values of submission, caring, and endurance. (H. Lu 1997: 106; Huang and Weller 1998: 380–381; Weller 2000: 493). These values are applicable to all aspects of social life, including politics. She disapproves of social activism, because "a sense of responsibility is more important than a sense of justice. If everyone acts this way . . . then there is a possibility that society will become even more fair and just."[27] This submissive style will partially explain, as discussed in chapter 5, that even though Ven. Zheng-yan insists on political neutrality, her followers prefer the KMT to the more flamboyant DPP.

In contrast to other followers of Taixü or Yinshun, who proposed the principle of "participating in politics, not governing," Ven. Zhengyan for-mulated the "Three-No Rules" to discourage her members from participat-ing in politics; these are "not running as a candidate, not assisting election campaigns, and not recommending any candidates."[28] One of the Ten Pre-cepts prescribed for male members is "no participation in demonstrations or political campaigns" (H. Lu 1997: 103).[29] Instead, she proposed the prin-ciple "care about but do not get involved in politics (*guanxin dan bu jieru*)" (Laliberté 1999: 124–125). Other than an occasional reminder of voting at election times, she has never openly commented on political matters or poli-ticians, nor has she lobbied on behalf of those who receive her help (Lalib-erté 1999: 118).

Like other Buddhist groups, the ecclesiology of Ciji is based on the supreme mastership of Ven. Zhengyan (Laliberté 1999: 114–115). Ciji mem-bers address her as "Shangren" (the supreme person) and treat her as such by kneeling down before her or even when receiving phone calls from her.[30] The uncommonly thin Buddha statue at the Ciji headquarters looks very much like Ven. Zhenyan. English translations of Ciji publications often address her as "him" to imply that she is no longer carrying the inferior female body but is a superior male Buddha with the appearance of a woman. Her lectures and writings guide all Ciji members, particularly her collected works, *Still Thoughts* (Huang and Weller 1998: 380–381; Weller 2000: 383). The motto of Zhengyan's disciples is: "The Master's resolve is my resolve, the Buddha's mind is my mind" (Jones 1999: 206). Ciji has successfully persuaded many primary schools to adopt *Still Thoughts* as a textbook through Ciji teachers and parents at these schools. Her biography, of which more than three-hun-dred thousand copies have been published, describes her as a living Buddha with magical powers (H. Chen 2000: 59–62; Jones 1999: 211). The suprem-acy of Ven. Zhengyan is elevated to such a high place that no potential suc-cessor has been named, nor have the rules of succession been published to lead the huge religious empire, despite her occasional hospitalization caused by severe problems with her angina pectoris.

Unlike other Buddhist groups, the ecclesiology of Ciji does not place the clergy above the laity. Since Ciji is basically a charity organization rather than a clergy-training facility, there is no need to emphasize the superiority of the clergy over the laity. The only clergy superior to all Ciji members is Ven. Zhengyan. She performs the three-gem ceremony only for those who are to become Ciji staff.[31]

Ciji is a highly centralized corporation. At the center is the general management center (*zongguanli zhongxin*, established in 1990), which issues orders to all local chapters and controls the finances and personnel of Ciji through a structure resembling a modern business organization (D. Zheng 2002: 56–60).[32] Ven. Zhengyan is the chief executive officer, and is assisted by three vice executive officers (all lay believers). One of the three vice executive officers, also the second man in Ciji, Wang Duan-zheng, is a brother of Ven. Zhengyan's (Huang and Weller, 1998: 388). Local chapters have no autonomy in matters of finance, personnel management, and public relations. Many outside researchers and media representatives have shared the same experience, if not frustration, that interviews with a local Ciji chapter require prior approval from the headquarters.

Compared to the BLIA of Foguangshan, Ciji provides more opportunity for the laity to make important decisions in a religious organization, due to the lack of clergy influence at every level of this global organization. But due to the centralized structure and the emphasis on seniority, the opportunity to learn democratic values and to practice democratic behavior is still limited.

In terms of the interaction between the state and religion, Ven. Zhengyan holds a more isolationist view than other Buddhist leaders do. Unlike Ven. Xingyun of FGS and Ven. Weijue of Zhongtai Chansi, Ven. Zhengyan has never been a member of the board of directors for the state-sponsored BAROC. In fact, since by law Ciji is not a religious organization but a charity organization, it is outside the jurisdiction of BAROC (Laliberté 1999: 114). Before the 2000 presidential turnover, Ven. Zhengyan received as few KMT politicians as possible at Ciji headquarters. Opposition politicians had a hard time trying to take a picture with her.[33] After 2000, she quickly adapted to the new political reality and has maintained a delicate balance among political parties. Although occasionally reminding followers to go to the voting booth at election times, Ciji never endorses any political candidates, even those who are important members of the organization. If a member of Ciji becomes a political candidate, she or he must resign from all Ciji posts and is not allowed to mention his or her affiliation with Ciji in campaign flyers (Jiang 1995a: 171).[34] Ciji routinely issues public warnings and complaints if these rules are violated. No candidate can politically afford to ignore Ciji's warning. A public apology and revision of the campaign flyer always follows. In sum, Ven. Zhengyan and Ciji have done more than any other religious groups in Taiwan to maintain the image of political neutrality.

THE DHARMA DRUM MOUNTAIN
(*FAGUSHAN*; HEREAFTER, DDM)

The predecessor of DDM was Nongchan Monastery, established in 1975 by the Chinese monk Ven. Dongchu. Two years after Dongchu's death in 1977, Ven. Shengyan (or Sheng Yen), a Chinese monk who received his PhD in religious studies in Japan, became the abbot of Nongchan Monastery. The religious empire began to grow rapidly. In 1989, the headquarters of DDM was established in Taipei County. The DDM system consists of dozens of temples, cultural enterprises, academic institutions, and social welfare foundations, with more than one hundred clergy and about one million members spread over Asia, America, Europe, Africa, and Australia.

The theology of DDM belongs to the school of humanistic Buddhism, which includes Buddhist values regarding social welfare, family relationships, financial management, love and friendship, environmental protection, and office relationships—everything except for politics (Shengyan 2001a, 2001b). Ven. Shengyan holds a very strict, isolationist view regarding the relationship between religion and the state. He rarely comments on political issues or figures. In his early writings, Ven. Shengyan, like Ven. Xingyun of FGS, basically followed the position of Ven. Taixü, who proposed the principle of "participating in politics, not governing." The clergy's duties are self-cultivation and preaching and should not include direct involvement with the government's administrative works. However, the clergymen are allowed to vote and even become representatives in order to protect and promote Buddhist interests. As for the laity, they can become administrative officials and representatives without the clergymen's restrictions (Shengyan 2001b: 131–132).

The ecclesiology of DDM follows that of traditional Chinese Buddhism in terms of the supreme mastership and dominance of the clergy over the laity. Ven. Shengyan is both the de jure and de facto leader of the DDM system. His followers intensively study his publications. In their mind, he can do or say nothing wrong. "It is not the question of right or wrong," a lay leader defensively explained, "it varies according to people, work, timing, and place. Ven. Shengyan would sometimes scold me in public, which I did not think was justified. But he did so nevertheless in order to be considerate to the feelings of bystanders."[35]

The DDM system places the clergy above the laity. Although Ven. Shengyan has admitted that a layperson can sometimes become as good a Buddhist as a member of the clergy, he believes that on average the clergy is superior to the laity in terms of Buddhist theology, wisdom, character, and spiritual status. Only on rare occasions should the laity become the center of Buddhism (Shengyan 2001b: 241–243). This principle seems awkward in light of the fact that most organizational works of the DDM are performed by the laity, not by the clergy. Although it has a similar number of believers, DDM recruits only about one hundred clergy members, while the FGS system has more than one thousand. What the DDM system does is to place the clergy at the decision-making center of organizational works, while letting the laity implement the clergy's decisions. But in practice, due to the complexity of modern nonclerical organizations and the relatively small number of the clergy, lay believers with different professional backgrounds are in control of DDM's huge and multiple nonclerical organizations, through which they are able to learn and practice democratic values and behavior. When there are important differences in opinion between the lay leader and the clergy leader in a nonclerical organization, Ven. Shengyan makes the final decision, often in favor of the professional lay leader. Senior laity can also deliver sermons at routine DDM religious gatherings, although not in important ceremonies.[36] Similar to FGS, DDM has adopted a centralized decision-making structure. All the properties of local temples and chapters of DDM belong to the headquarters. Local abbots are assigned and rotated by the DDM headquarters.[37]

In terms of the interaction between the state and religion, Ven. Shengyan has formulated a two-track principle. He actively solicits support from politicians to expand his religious empire, but he strictly forbids his clergy and laity to bring partisan activities into the empire.[38] Unlike Ven. Xingyun of FGS and Ven. Weijue of the Zhongtai Chansi, Ven. Shengyan has never been a member of the board of directors in the state-sponsored BAROC. He encourages his followers to vote for their ideal candidates or political parties (Shengyan 1995: 123–126; 1999: 175–179), but he never reveals his political preference. Additionally, political candidates are not allowed to speak or distribute campaign flyers at DDM gatherings. If a member of the clergy or laity becomes a political candidate, he or she must resign from all official positions in the DDM.[39] The DDM never publicly endorses any particular political party or candidate. Since the turnover of the government in 2000, Ven. Shengyan has not changed his centrist position between the two political parties. In October 2005, when the compound of the headquarter was completed, Ven. Shengyan held the hands of both Chairman Ma Ying-jiu and President Chen Shui-bian in the celebration ceremony, while he stood in the middle.

THE ZHONGTAI ZEN MONASTERY
(*ZHONGTAI CHANSI*; HEREAFTER, ZHONGTAI)

I did not anticipate such a fervent response from a monk after I sent him the first draft of this chapter for verification and clarification. "Take out the whole section on Zhongtai in your chapter, or we will file a libel lawsuit against you," he angrily warned me over the phone. I patiently replied: "Please tell me where the mistakes are, and I'll be willing to correct them to your satisfaction. If you file the lawsuit, I am afraid that both of us will end up in the popular gossip magazines." He unwillingly retracted his threat but could not persuade me to cross out all the hard evidence that made his organization controversial. One week later, a political science professor of the National Taiwan University and a deputy minister of the Finance Ministry, both of them senior lay believers of the organization, came to my office to make the same request of correction. I agreed to replace some of the expressive adjectives in the sentences with milder ones but insisted on keeping the evidence intact. In the end, they concurred with my explanation. Indeed, Zhongtai Zen Monastery is unique in many interesting ways among the major Buddhist organizations in Taiwan.

Ven. Weijue (or Wei Chueh), a Chinese monk, was ordained in Taiwan in 1964. Over the next ten years, he isolated himself from the world in a small temple in Taipei County to study Buddhism. Starting in 1987, the year the martial law was lifted, he transformed his isolationist strategy into one of active expansion, with a specialty in holding short-term Zen (Ch'an) training courses for urban professionals. Over the next fifteen years, he built up a religious kingdom, boasting more than seventy temples, one thousand four hundred clergy members, one million plus believers, and several educational institutions (Zhongtai fojiao xueyuan 2001: preface).[40]

Although not a disciple of Taixü or Yinshun, Ven. Weijue's theology is much like humanistic Buddhism. Weijue has proposed to transform Buddhism into an academic, educational, scientific, artistic, and humanistic discipline (Zhongtai fojiao xueyuan 2001: 66–68). His theology teaches people how to live a peaceful Buddhist life within the network of family, the workplace, and social groups. Absent from his lectures and writings is the subject of politics (Weijue 1994). The only place where he briefly mentions politics is in his advice to believers to respect political authority (Caituanfaren Zhongtaishan fojiao jijinhui bianjizu 1998: 38).

As with other major Buddhist groups, the ecclesiology of Zhongtai emphasizes supreme mastership and the clergy's superiority over the laity. Ven. Weijue claims himself to be the authentic successor to the great Chinese Zen Buddhist Huineng. A Zhongtai slogan says, "Authentic Buddha lives in Zhongtai" (*zhenfo zhu zhongtai*), which attempts to elevate Weijue to the highest religious status not only within the Zhongtai system but also in Taiwan's Buddhist community (Caituanfaren Zhongtaishan fojiao jijinhui bianjizu 1998: 1–26).[41] His believers carefully read his writings. He can say or do nothing wrong. If a member of the clergy or laity disagrees with the lecture or writing of Ven. Weijue, it must be due to the inferior wisdom of the junior believer.[42]

In local temples, the clergy take up all the important leadership roles, with the laity serving only as consultants and lower-level administrators (Zhongtai fojiao xueyuan 2001: 28).[43] Ven. Weijue provides four explanations for the superiority of the clergy over the laity. First, the lay believers are immersed in secular desires and are thus unclean. Second, because the clergy give up secular enjoyment, they are "moral" persons. Third, the clergy have devoted their full careers to caring for society. Finally, the clergy preaches without receiving a salary (Caituanfaren zhongtaishan fojiao jijinhui bianjizu, 1998: 43–44).

The superiority of the clergy over the laity can be illustrated by an intrusion during my interview with a young abbot of a local Zhongtai temple. We sat across from each other at a table with my back facing the door of the reception room. While he was patiently explaining to me how compatible Buddhism is with democratic ideas, a female believer about fifty years old entered. She stood quietly behind my back for a while before the abbot turned his eyes to her and asked about her intention. She humbly asked the abbot whether she could pay respect to him. He gladly said yes. I thought it would not take more than two seconds to say hello and shake hands. But I was terribly wrong. She prostrated herself on the floor to pay her respect, with her feet, hands, and forehead touching the ground. The abbot said Buddhist greetings to her in return without even standing up. I was extremely puzzled by the democratic ideas he had mentioned just a few minutes ago and the humble ritual I observed thereafter. So, I posed the question to him. He replied with a very assertive smile: "This is a custom in our system. That is how we pay respect to the spiritual elders and educate the believers to be obedient." Thirty minutes later, when the female believer was leaving the premise, she performed the same ritual to him again. I asked him whether a member of the clergy would pay such respect to a lay believer. He said, "Never. It is because Buddhism focuses on what's inside, not what's outside." Other senior Zhongtai lay believers confirmed his statement and added, "The ritual is beneficial for the lay believers to learn about humility and wisdom."[44] Apparently, the ritual implies a very asymmetrical ethics and power relationship in the Zhongtai system.

Similar to other Buddhist groups, Zhongtai has adopted a highly centralized governing structure. Ven. Weijue labels this system as "one unified by five methods" (*wutong chengfa*): unification in finance, construction, education, evangelism, and spiritual training (Caituanfaren zhongtaishan fojiao jijinhui bianjizu 1998: 75–84). The brain of the Zhongtai system is the Religious Affairs Committee, headed by Ven. Weijue. The clergy receives no salary, yet the headquarters covers all their personal expenses. All the properties and donations collected from local temples and chapters belong to the headquarters. The headquarters, moreover, initiates all religious activities for the entire Zhongtai system.

In terms of the interaction between state and religion, Ven. Weijue has been more expressive in supporting the KMT than Ven. Xingyun has, although both of them were elected as the central advisors of the KMT in 1988. He was also elected as executive director of the state-sponsored BAROC from 1993 to 1997.[45] Before the presidential turnover of 2000, Ven. Weijue maintained a close relationship with KMT politicians by supporting their electoral campaigns. During the 2000 presidential election, Ven. Weijue held a clergy parade and mobilized its members to support the KMT candidate. Unfortunately, the KMT candidate lost this important election.[46] To amend its relationship with the new DPP government, Zhongtai invited important DPP politicians, including the president, to attend a ceremony marking the completion of a gigantic Zhongtai temple in 2002.[47] Some attributed this change in party lines to the fact that one third of the new multibillion-NT-dollar Zhongtai temple structure violated construction codes and faced potential demolition.[48] In fact, among Taiwan's four largest Buddhist groups, Zhongtai has generated more legal and social controversies than the others, reflecting some systemic problems within the Zhongtai governing style.[49] In 2004, Ven. Weijue broke with the DPP again by openly supporting the KMT presidential candidate in front of dozens of news reporters. He criticized the Chen administration for ethnic antagonism, deteriorating law and order, economic stagnation, and illegal plebiscites. But his critics pointed out that the lack of settlement of Zhongtai buildings' construction code violations might be one of his reasons for supporting the KMT candidate.[50]

OTHER BUDDHISTS

In addition to the four major Buddhist organizations, I conducted interviews with more than a dozen independent, liberal Buddhist scholars and abbots of smaller temples. These are liberal Buddhists in the sense that they oppose certain elements of traditional Buddhism, such as supreme mastership, Buddhist affinity with the KMT government, and gender discrimination against female clergy. Most of these liberal Buddhists agree that Buddhism and democracy are compatible, that as democratic citizens Buddhists should be more active in politics, and that there should be more equality between religious leaders and the clergy as well as between the clergy and the laity. However, they also agree that there is a lack of democratic theology and ecclesiology in Taiwanese Buddhism. They had not heard of any Taiwanese Buddhist scholar or clergy, including themselves, publishing a substantial essay on these topics or engaging in democratic reforms within the Buddhist community. The only exception is Ven. Zhaohui's feminist movement. The mainstream Buddhist groups, however, maintain a careful distance from them, leaving these liberal Buddhists with very little influence outside the academic circle or their small temples.

Although an exception to Taiwanese Buddhism, Ven. Zhaohui has set a historical precedence for other Chinese and Taiwanese Buddhists in supporting the idea that Buddhism can be compatible with democracy in theology, ecclesiology, and interaction with the state. Ven. Zhaohui was a disciple of Ven. Yinshun but has outgrown her master in enriching the democratic aspects of humanistic Buddhism. With a solid academic background in Buddhism, comparative religious studies, and legal studies, she provides a creative theological foundation to engage in direct dialogue on various modern issues, such as organ transplants, surrogate mothers, stem cell research, the death penalty, adultery, environmental protection, animal rights, and particularly gender equality both in society and within Buddhism (Z. Shi 1995). Her critical and sometimes theatrical comments on Buddhist chauvinism have enraged many Buddhist monks.[51] In 2002, she publicly challenged the discriminatory Buddhist law, the Eight-Respect Law (*Bajingfa*), by tearing apart these eight laws written on a poster in front of a large group of news reporters. Several BAROC monks immediately motioned to rescind her status as a member of the clergy. But she did not violate any Buddhist laws, nor did she directly receive ordination from the BAROC. The BAROC had no choice but to drop the motion.[52]

In terms of the interaction with the state, she has been actively involved in social movements of antiabortion, animal rights, antigambling, environmental conservation, and gender equality, among others. She does so by participating in demonstrations, lobbying the legislature, and convening press conferences. She does not avoid endorsing particular candidates, regardless of their party or religious affiliation, as long as they agree with her social agenda and meet her minimum ethical standards. She appreciates the "give and take" logic of Taiwanese democracy in order to advance her social agenda.[53]

Other potentially democratic Buddhist groups have emerged for brief periods of time throughout Taiwan's Buddhist history, but none have lasted very long. During the period of Japanese rule in Taiwan (1895–1945), there was a popular sect of the Vegetarian Religion (*Zhaijiao*), in which the laity held leadership roles in these independent Buddhist organizations. However, after Chinese Buddhists brought powerful organization and leadership to Taiwan, the Vegetarian Religion declined rapidly (J. Wang 1996; Z. Zheng 1991; Jiang 1995a: chap. 5). In 1971, a small group of activist Buddhists (numbering around three hundred) organized the pro-Taiwan independence Ten Thousand Buddha Association (*Wanfohui*, TTBA) to engage in social protests. In the early 1990s, it established the Truth Party (*Zhenlidang*) to participate in various elections, and the association's social protest strategies became more confrontational (Z. Zheng 1994). In 1995, the government sentenced the president of TTBA, Ven. Zongsheng, to eight months in jail for his alleged instigation of a riot. Ven. Zongsheng fled to the United States, not returning to Taiwan until April 2002 when the statute of limitations on his charge expired. The TTBA adopted a very low profile after their 1995 legal trouble.[54]

CHAPTER 3

Christianity

From 1971 to 1977, the Presbyterian Church of Taiwan (PCT) boldly challenged the KMT martial law regime by issuing three political statements to promote electoral reforms, religious freedom, ethnic harmony, human rights, and Taiwan independence. Except for the last goal, the great majority of Taiwanese Christians nowadays would wholeheartly support these "Christian" values. However, thirty years ago, most of the Christian brothers and sisters in other denominations, including the Catholic Church, did not rally behind the PCT's causes and decided to stay out of the dangerous controversy.

Furthermore, some chose to cast the "first stones" at the PCT by publicly accusing it and its statements as "childish and contradictory," "self-destructive," "not speaking the truth in love," "being possessed by demons," "committing indecent acts," "interfering with politics," "self-appointed prophets," and "sidetracking the church's evangelical mission."[1] The root of mutual distrust between the PCT and other Christian denominations was planted then and continues to divide the Taiwanese Christian community both politically and spiritually. Nevertheless, the close relationships between Christianity and democracy in Taiwan bear ample resemblance to that of early America as described by Alexis de Tocqueville. This is the subject this chapter turns to.

GENERAL DESCRIPTION

Taiwanese Christianity is different from Buddhism in terms of leadership, theology, ecclesiology, and political relations with the KMT government. First of all, the leaders of various denominations are composed of different mixes of both Chinese and Taiwanese. Ever since Canadian and Scottish Presbyterian evangelists came to Taiwan before the period of Japanese rule, the leaders of the Presbyterians have all been Taiwanese (Rubinstein 1991). The Local Church, the Baptists, and most of the independent "Mandarin" churches (*guoyü jiaohui*), whose spoken language in the church is Mandarin, had their origin in China (Dong 1986: 328–334), but their leaders are gradually being replaced by Taiwanese.

Second, Taiwanese Christianity is less influenced by the Chinese authoritarian culture in terms of its theology and ecclesiology than is Taiwanese Buddhism. By the time Christianity was introduced to China and Taiwan, Western countries had integrated Christian theology with liberal democratic thought. Concepts such as human rights, equality before God, freedom of conscience, the corrupt nature of man, and government responsibility were taken for granted by Western Christians and transplanted to Chinese and Taiwanese Christians via missionaries. There were theologies with different degrees of assertiveness toward church-state relations. Even the adamantly isolationist churches like the Baptists emphasized keeping the state out of church life more than keeping the church out of state business. However, this is not to say that Taiwanese Christians accepted Western liberal Christianity wholeheartedly. Due to the authoritarian environment of the martial law period, most Christian denominations (except for the Presbyterians) subscribed to the spiritual and social dimensions of Western theology but kept silent on its political components. In the post-1987 period, a few theologians began to write about Christian views on human rights and democracy (Y. Tang 1996; C. Tang 1991), however, these works generally reflect an insufficient understanding of modern democracy, and are tainted by Chinese authoritarian values.

Third, in terms of ecclesiology, Taiwanese Christianity exhibits a great variety of governing structures. Some denominations, such as the Bread of Life Church (*Lingliangtang*) and the Local Church (*Jühuisuo*), adopted the supreme mastership principle as found in Taiwanese Buddhism. Other denominations, such as the Presbyterians and the True Jesus Church, have chosen collective leadership. Still others have continuously changed their governing structure, depending on internal and external factors (Ministry of the Interior 2003: 44–218). As for the relationship between clergy and laity, substantial variations also exist across different denominations and within the same denomination during different time periods. However, the authoritarian environment did have a significant impact on the ecclesiology of Taiwanese Christianity. Even though Taiwanese Christianity exhibited more structural diversity than Buddhism did, it still tilted toward authoritarian leadership and placed clergy higher than laity in the church's governing structure. After the lifting of martial law, however, a democratic structure has gradually replaced the authoritarian one.

Similarly, the degree of centralization varies greatly in large denominations. The Methodists probably have the most centralized structure; the Baptists are the most decentralized; and the Presbyterians fall somewhere in between. Outside these large denominations, there exist hundreds of independent churches. For unknown reasons, the KMT government did not order Taiwanese Christians to establish a peak religious association similar to the Buddhist Association of the Republic of China. The KMT government had established the National Association of Chinese Christianity in China before 1949 (*zhonghua jidujiao quanguo zonghui*), but it was never reconvened in Taiwan after 1949. From 1960 to 1963, the PCT invited representatives of the Methodists, Lutherans, Episcopals, Baptists, Mennonites, and two independent churches to prepare for the establishment of a national association of Taiwanese Christianity. This private initiative was not appreciated by the authoritarian government. The Ministry of the Interior initiated the Council of Chinese Christianity (*zhonghua jidujiao xiejinhui*) in response and named Methodist pastor Chen Wei-ping as the executive director in 1963. Under the government's pressure, the PCT's effort to establish an independent national Christian association thus failed. The Council of Chinese Christianity did not do better; it was an organization only on paper (Huang 1986: 165, 250–254).

To this day, among all the religions in Taiwan, Christianity is the only major religion not under the jurisdiction of the Regulations on Temples and Shrines. Murray A. Rubinstein's analysis of the early development of Taiwan's Christian community might explain their political privilege: the Nationalist government regarded the missionaries as agents of social change, and, more importantly, as strong lobbying groups to enhance American support for Taiwan (Rubinstein 1991: 33–37). Any attempt to place all Christian denominations under one state-sponsored Christian organization would certainly antagonize these missionaries, especially the politically powerful Southern Baptists and Presbyterians.

As political democratization proceeded rapidly during the 1980s, most churches began to feel the impact of the democratic environment on their theology and ecclesiology, although varying degrees of influence already existed in some denominations and churches. In general, the democratic elements of Western Christianity have gradually been reintroduced into Taiwanese Christianity without much difficulty. Information on democratic theology and ecclesiology is abundantly available to Taiwanese Christians. Many Taiwanese clergy and deacons who graduated from Western universities and participated in Western churches are important carriers of democratic theology and ecclesiology back to Taiwan. The trend of democratization among Taiwanese Christianity has accelerated, as did the "democratization of American Christianity" soon after the democratic republic was established (Hatch 1989).

Finally, in terms of church-state interaction, the majority of Taiwanese Christians chose to take an isolationist view and rarely commented on politics before 1987. The important exception was the Presbyterians, who became the vanguards of Taiwan's democratic movement after the 1960s.

Their strong anti-KMT government attitude, however, was balanced some-what by the Mandarin churches who strongly supported the KMT. Since the lifting of martial law, the isolationists have maintained their leadership in most churches. But an increasingly large number of clergy and laity welcome a more active political role for churches.

THE PRESBYTERIANS

As a courtesy to my respondents, I always started my interview with a reminder that some of my questions are politically sensitive in nature. They had the option not to answer these questions. Many chose not to or provided me with the most diplomatic answers possible. I usually needed to work very hard to sneak behind their fences to see the truth. To my surprise, however, when I started my interview with the general secretary of the Presbyterian Church in Taiwan, Rev. Lo Rong-guang, he thanked me for my consid-erateness but corrected me frankly: "There are no 'sensitive' questions in democracy and in God's kingdom. All questions can be discussed in public." Dramatic stories about the politics within and outside the church were fully explored in our subsequent interviews, which also witnessed the development of the most democratic religious organization in Taiwan.

The Taiwanese Presbyterian churches were established directly by West-ern Presbyterians and had little connection with Chinese Presbyterians. In 1865, a Scottish Presbyterian doctor came to southern Taiwan to establish a layman's ministry based on medical services. He brought three Chinese med-ical assistants from a southern Chinese city where the Scottish Presbyterians had established a small ministry. In 1872, Canadian Presbyterians arrived in northern Taiwan to establish an evangelical-medical base. During the early period of Japanese rule, the colonial government welcomed the Presbyterian evangelists in order to provide medical and social services to the Taiwan-ese. But in the later period of colonial rule, especially after the Pacific War broke out, the government harshly cracked down on the Presbyterians for their refusal to worship the Japanese emperor and to follow other ceremonies prescribed by the Japanese national religion, Shinto (Taiwan jidu zhanglao jiaohui zonghui 2000: 3–16). After 1945, Taiwanese Presbyterians resumed evangelism via indigenous leadership, with foreign missionaries serving as auxiliary arms (Rubinstein 2001: 66).[2] This choice of indigenous leadership over foreign missionaries turned out to be critical to the rapid expansion of Presbyterian churches in the postwar period and to the invention of the Tai-wan independence theology. From 1954 to 1964, Presbyterians instituted the "Doubling Movement," which contributed to an increase of membership from 59,000 to 103,000.[3] Currently, the Presbyterians claim a membership of more than 227,900, with more than 1,200 churches, numerous seminar-ies, schools, hospitals, publishing companies, and social welfare institutions (Taiwan jidu zhanglao jiaohui zonghui 2002: 7).[4]

The Taiwanese Presbyterians did not develop a democratic theology until the late 1960s. Before then, the Presbyterians closely followed the obedient political teachings of John Calvin, who proposed that Christians take a submissive stance toward the government, even if the government is a tyranny (Calvin 1989: 670–671). In the late 1960s, a new generation of clergy and theologians emerged and took control of the central leadership of the Presbyterian Church of Taiwan (PCT). Motivated by social justice and influenced by liberal theology, they systematically transformed the submissive Calvinist theology into a liberal democratic theology, which treated human rights, political equality, and democratic institutions as being as important as personal salvation (N. Chen 2000). In their writings and sermons, they cited extensively from the prophets in the Bible to severely criticize the political leaders for their unjust policies and practices.

The Taiwanese Presbyterian liberal theology should not be treated as an offshoot of Latin American liberation theology, although both share the same emphases on human rights and social justice and developed around the same time. Major founders of the Taiwanese liberal theology, such as Huang Zhang-hui and C. S. Song, received their liberal theological training in Western countries about the same time in the late 1950s and early 1960s as the founders of Latin American theology did. These theologians of Third World countries then went back to their respective homelands in the 1960s to develop a "contextual theology" specifically tailored to their local political, social, and economic environments.[5] This explains both the similarities and differences in theological concerns between Taiwanese liberal theology and Latin American liberation theology.

The most creative and practical part of the Taiwanese democratic theology is the mixture of democratic theory, democratic theology, and Taiwanese nationalism, with the last being the guiding principle in this uniquely Taiwanese contextual theology.[6] The Bible does not necessarily support nationalism. Taiwanese Presbyterians claim, however, in a nutshell, that God has mercy on the people living in Taiwan, that all men are created equal and endowed with inalienable human rights, and that the Taiwanese therefore have the right to establish an independent government of, for, and by the Taiwanese people, not of, for, and by the Chinese on the Mainland or the Chinese immigrants in power. The Presbyterians regard themselves as "God-calling prophets," who hope to inspire the Taiwanese to build a nation of God in Taiwan (N. Chen 1991: 145–194).[7] This ethno-democratic theology turned out to be political dynamite because it simultaneously satisfied the religious and political needs of those Taiwanese believers who were exploited by the Chinese-controlled martial-law government. Hence, Presbyterian participation in the opposition movement was justified by the sacred trinity of religion, democracy, and nationalism.

After the lifting of martial law, the national association of Presbyterian churches, the Presbyterian Church of Taiwan (PCT), expanded the nationalist element in its political theology. After all, many of its democratic appeals materialized because of the lifting of martial law and democratic reforms of the national representative institutions in 1990 and 1991. Taiwan independence was made the new priority. In 1991, the PCT issued the Declaration of Independence of Taiwan's Sovereignty. The first sentence of the declaration states: "We believe that God creates men according to His image, gives men dignity and freedom in order to determine their own future. He also gives men separate land, to live peacefully." The declaration ends with a prayer: "We pray for God's help. Give us the transformative power of the Holy Spirit, so that we can establish a new Taiwan with sovereign independence."[8] After the 2000 presidential turnover, the PCT was satisfied with this democratic achievement. The pursuit of Taiwan independence became even more fervent. The PCT issued the Declaration of the Movement to Join the United Nations in the Name of the Republic of Taiwan. In this document, the PCT blamed domestic political instability, moral decay, and economic stagnation on Taiwan's lack of independence. It reconfirmed the 1991 Declaration of Independence of Taiwan's Sovereignty and appealed to the international community to support Taiwan's effort to become a member of the United Nations under the name of the Republic of Taiwan (Taiwan jidu zhanglao jiaohui zonghui 2002).

Although appealing at the beginning, the predominance of the nationalist element in the PCT democratic theology brought about unintended conflicts with other Christians. Those Christians (and Catholics) who migrated from China after 1949 felt antagonized by the theology of Taiwanese nationalism. Harsh criticisms between the two sides were exchanged in the 1970s and continue to divide the Christian community in Taiwan (N. Chen 1991: 116–118). In the post–martial law period, these controversies over Christian theology and democratic theory have been challenged by yet another new generation of clergy and theologians within the Presbyterian churches.[9] The official policy of the PCT toward the DPP government before 2005 was one of "critical support" (*pipanxing zhichi*). The PCT leadership, still dominated by the generation of the 1960s, placed more emphasis on the second word, "support," while the new generation argues that the church should emphasize the first word, "critical," that is, the church should focus on its prime mission of evangelism instead of political priesthood. They argue that Taiwan independence should not take precedence over other religious and social justice issues.[10] The stagnation or even decline in church membership in the early 2000s generated a sense of crisis at the grassroots level.[11] In particular, the aboriginal churches, which had long been staunch supporters of KMT candidates, formed an alliance with the new generation of clergy in the election of PCT leadership in 2004. In 2005, a new generation of PCT leadership was inaugurated and is expected to shift the church's major focus from political to social and religious issues. This shift has been incremental, however. The PCT continues to sponsor large rallies in support of DPP policies to

strengthen national defense, to establish Taiwan independence, and to criticize the mass media that exposes government corruption.[12]

In terms of democratic ecclesiology, Presbyterian churches had a head
start over other Christian denominations in Taiwan. Calvinism provided a
detailed description of a democratic ecclesiology, which the Taiwanese Presbyterians adopted immediately after establishing a few churches in the late
nineteenth century. Taiwanese Presbyterians have not had any supreme master and have placed the clergy only slightly above the laity. With democratization expanding in the larger environment, even the last privileges of the
clergy are under attack by the laity.

The history of Taiwanese Presbyterians does not record any supreme
master as the Buddhists do. The only "supreme master" is probably John Calvin, whom my respondents have cited more often than the Bible. Most clergy
and theologians use Calvin's works as practical guides to theology and ecclesiology. However, they would not place Calvin's works on par with the Bible,
or compare Calvin with Jesus. They are willing to challenge Calvin's works
and deeds, as they would any leader in the church hierarchy.[13] One famous
leader in the church, Rev. Gao Jun-ming, was put in jail by the KMT government in 1979 for providing shelter to political dissidents. He has earned
a lot of respect from believers. But few Presbyterians read his works and he
has never been able to dictate the church's major decisions. The polity of the
Presbyterian churches prevents the emergence of supreme mastership.

According to the PCT bylaws, the leadership of the PCT General
Assembly is composed of the speaker, vice speaker, and general secretary. As
nominal heads of the PCT, the Speaker and Vice Speaker have no real decision-making power except for hosting the biannual assembly. They are elected
by assembly representatives and serve only one two-year term. The general
secretary is the most important person in the central leadership, yet this position also has certain constraints. He is recommended by lower-level church
organizations and selected by the General Assembly, serving four years per
term with a three-term limit.[14] He can plan, coordinate, and execute PCT
activities, but only according to the decisions made by the General Assembly (Taiwan jidu zhanglao jiaohui zonghui fagui weiyuanhui 2000: 13–20).
Therefore, unlike their Buddhist counterparts, Presbyterians leaders move up
the hierarchical ladder from the bottom through a series of elections. When
they finally reach the top, their power and terms are limited.

The superiority of the clergy over the laity that once existed in Presbyterian churches was limited and has gradually been lost. The Presbyterian polity has put the Protestant motto the priesthood of all believers into practice.
The core of a Presbyterian church is the small committee (*xiaohui*), which
is composed of elders and pastors elected by the church members. The pastors are appointed by a medium-level church organization called the medium
committee (*zhonghui*). The most senior pastor chairs the small committee
and executes the decisions made by the committee. Each pastor has one and

only one vote, no more decisive than the elders in the church's collective decision. The pastor can only exercise informal influence in any attempt to have his proposals passed. To avoid offending either side of disputing parties, most pastors abstain from voting.[15] The medium committees and the General Assembly are all composed of relatively equal numbers of pastors and laity, both enjoying the same voting rights.

Very limited superiority of the clergy over the laity exists. Conducting sermons, baptisms, the Lord's Supper, and other important Christian sacraments are the exclusive right of the pastor, unless a pastor is not available at the time of the sacrament.[16] Before 1985, the chairs of the small committees, medium committees, and the General Assembly had to be pastors. After 1985, the pastor's privilege of chairing medium committees and the General Assembly was rescinded, although no laity has yet chaired these important organizations (Renshi Taiwan jidu zhanglao jiaohui bianji xiaozu, 2000: 45). In the past, the tenure of a pastor was guaranteed by the appointment power of the medium committee. In recent years, however, the medium committee has followed the majority will of small committees in recruiting or reassigning church pastors. The medium committee can hardly appoint or renew a pastor to whom the local church strongly opposes.[17]

An example of the limited superiority of the clergy over the laity is the general support for KMT—instead of DPP—candidates among aboriginal churches. Presbyterian clergy tend to be pro-DPP due to their training in the seminaries. Why haven't they made an impact on the political orientation of their believers? I asked a Presbyterian pastor and a senior elder of an aboriginal church in Taidong County in the summer of 2003. They both gave me a similar answer: the KMT has cultivated a long-term relationship with church elders through various government subsidy programs that benefited both the aboriginal tribes and these elders. Furthermore, many aboriginals felt discriminated by the overemphasis on Taiwanese nationalism on the part of seminaries and the PCT. So, when a junior pastor came to an aboriginal church and gave a sermon favoring the DPP, church elders would always warn the pastor not to do it again. In general, the pastor would comply with the warning.

The Presbyterian polity prescribes a decision-making structure that is neither highly centralized nor decentralized. Although the General Assembly is the highest decision-making body of the PCT, most of the real decisions are made in the various medium committees, which are composed of representatives from small committees. All the properties of local churches have been registered to the government under the name of the PCT. But the donations to local churches go to the medium committees, which also make decisions on church discipline, pastor recruitment, and financial allocations. In recent years, however, local churches have gained more autonomy in financial management, pastor recruitment, and political expression (Taiwan jidu zhanglao jiaohui zonghui yanjiu fazhan zhongxin 1999: 2).[18]

For instance, in my interviews with some local churches, they admitted that they would reduce the amount of required donations to the medium committees by setting up special funds for local charities, evangelical works, and construction that would not be included in the calculation of the donation quota. In terms of political expression, in recent years the PCT has suffered from "policies not being able to go outside the PCT" (*lingbuchu zonghui*), a senior consultant to the PCT told me.[19] New churches often register their properties with the government under the medium committees, not under the PCT anymore.[20]

Finally, with respect to the interaction between church and the state, Presbyterians have been unique among all Taiwanese religions. Before the 1970s, Presbyterian churches were very submissive to and cooperative with both the Japanese colonial government and the KMT government (N. Chen 1991: 80–84; Huang 1986: 264–266). The nightmares of the 2/28 Incident and the White Terror of the 1950s intimidated the postwar first-generation church leaders from thinking otherwise. Instead, they focused their attention and energy on evangelism. However, the success of the "doubling-the-church movement" from 1954–1964 generated not only self-confidence but also sociopolitical consciousness among the new generation of church leadership (Rubinstein 2003: 215, 223). The authoritarian government also became suspicious about this fast-growing denomination. In the 1970s, the PCT issued three public documents challenging the legitimacy of the KMT government. The Declarations and Suggestions on National Affairs (Dui guoshi de shengming yü jianyi, 1971) proclaimed that the Taiwanese have the right of self-determination and urged that new elections be held for national representative bodies. Our Appeals (Women de huyü, 1975) pleaded with the government to respect religious freedom and autonomy. The Declaration of Human Rights (Renquan xuanyan, 1977), addressed directly to American President Jimmy Carter and all the churches in the world, asked for the establishment of a "new and independent nation" for the Taiwanese people. These three documents were severely criticized by the KMT government and by some Mandarin churches as an act of treason and an inappropriate intervention in politics by the church. Attacks also came from within the Presbyterian churches—from those pastors, elders, deacons, and lay believers who were members of the KMT (Hu 2001: 235–236, 252, 255). Nevertheless, the majority of the Presbyterian churches stood firm.

Major confrontation between the Presbyterians and the government broke out in 1979, when the government cracked down harshly on an opposition rally. Leaders of the movement were arrested, along with some Presbyterian pastors who had participated in the demonstration (Renshi Taiwan jidu zhanglao jiaohui bianji xiaozu 2000: 40). Finally, the general secretary of the PCT, Rev. Gao Jun-ming, was arrested and sentenced to four years in prison for providing sanctuary to an opposition leader. The PCT proclaimed Rev. Gao's innocence and kept the position of the general secretary vacant until he was released from prison. He served in the position for a total of nineteen years until he retired in 1989 (Hu 2001: 291–297).

During the martial law period, the PCT supported the opposition movement with concrete actions. Pastors urged their believers to vote for opposition candidates. National and local churches cosponsored rallies and demonstrations to protest against the KMT government. The antigovernment attitude took a sharp turn in 1988 when Li Deng-hui, a Taiwanese and a Presbyterian, became president of Taiwan. The PCT supported President Li to consolidate his rule over the Chinese-dominated KMT government, while continuing to lend its support to DPP candidates in legislative bodies and in local magistrate elections (Hu 2001: 340).[21] During his administration, President Li spoke of a "Taiwanese exodus": a plan to bring Taiwanese out of Chinese political and cultural hegemony.

In the 2000 presidential election, President Li stepped down and nominated his vice president, Lian Zhan, a Taiwanese born in mainland China, to run for the presidency. The PCT leadership actively mobilized its believers to vote for the DPP candidate. After the presidential turnover in 2000, the PCT formulated the "critical support" principle in order to consolidate the new government (Rubinstein 2001: 63). Beginning in 2001, the PCT sponsored the annual National Prayer Breakfast for the DPP president and his cabinet members, despite complaints by some Christians of other denominations. The PCT continued to push for reform policies concerning social, economic, and environmental justices, with a particularly strong emphasis on Taiwan independence. In fact, the PCT did not hesitate to criticize the DPP government when it made occasional verbal concessions to the opposition parties on the independence issue. From 2000 to 2006, the PCT issued twelve public proclamations; ten of them covered political issues. The only theme that consistently ran through all ten proclamations was the clear support for Taiwan independence.[22]

Because of the PCT's political activism, it comes as no surprise that the Presbyterians have had disproportional representation in the Legislature. In 1986, eleven PCT members won seats in the Legislature and the National Assembly (Cohen 1988: 201). Among the 225 legislators elected in 2003, there were 42 Taoists (including believers in folk religions), 25 Buddhists, 6 Catholics, 21 Christians, and 45 friends to all religions; the rest refused to answer or could not identify their religion in our telephone interviews with their staff. Among these 21 Christian legislators, 15 were Presbyterians, and all of these Presbyterian legislators were DPP members.[23] This is disproportional in the sense that while Presbyterians account for only 1% of Taiwan's population, they constitute about 7% of the legislative seats. Indeed, as Rubinstein (2003: 248) correctly concludes, "the Presbyterians served as prophets and leaders during each of the four major periods of Taiwan's recent history."

The political activism of Taiwanese Presbyterians bears resemblance to that of their Korean counterparts. According to the Asian Barometer dataset,

Christians constitute 18.5% of the Korean population. Among these Christians, the overwhelming majority are Presbyterians. Korean Christians are proud to mention that Korean churches were established by Koreans themselves, not by missionaries. They were actively involved in politics ever since their introduction to Korea in the late eighteenth century. In the late nineteenth century, they helped consolidate the power of the prince who promulgated the country's modernization over the objection of traditional aristocrats. During the Japanese colonial rule, the Christian community became divided into two political camps between those who subordinated to the new ruler and those who fought against the colonial government. After the war, the first type of churches continued to subordinate to the aristocratic and military regimes, while the second type of churches maintained their prophetic role in criticizing the authoritarian regimes. They organized antigovernment societies, held demonstrations, published critical statements, and were harshly repressed by the authoritarian regimes (Kang 1997; Lancaster and Payne 1997).

The religious foundation of the Protestant opposition movement was the Minjung Theology. It took side with the people (*minjung*) who were exploited by capitalism, authoritarianism, and patriarchy (Suh 2001; Park 1993). These people were filled with *han* (resentment, regret, and alienation) caused by these injustices. Jesus was regarded as a political liberator to free these oppressed people, and Korean Christians were the chosen disciples to implement this political program.

THE BAPTISTS

Compared to the Taiwanese Presbyterians who had little connection with Chinese Christians, Taiwanese Baptists had a stronger connection with the Chinese Baptists, although not as strong as Taiwanese Buddhists had with Chinese Buddhists. The American Southern Baptists built up a sizable ministry in northern China in the 1930's. In 1948, an American evangelist came to Taiwan to establish a ministry in Taipei with the help of a few Chinese Baptists. Over the next few years, a few more Chinese pastors and American evangelists arrived and contributed to the rapid expansion of Baptist churches in the 1950s (D. Huang 1993; Wu 1998: 8–15). With the long-term support of American evangelists and financial resources, the Taiwanese Baptists now have a membership of 23,700, with about 200 churches and a few publishing companies, resorts, and a seminary.[24]

The combined influence of Chinese origins and strong American guidance has left marks on the democratic theology and ecclesiology of Taiwanese Baptists. In the early years of their development, American evangelists provided the leadership in Baptist churches and institutions. Chinese Baptist pastors managed their churches under the guidance of American evangelists and targeted Chinese immigrants for evangelism. Over the years,

American evangelists gradually transferred their leadership as well as financial resources to Chinese pastors, who in turn passed them on to their Taiwanese counterparts. But in terms of language, Taiwanese Baptists have remained the largest principal denomination using Mandarin. Most believers are refugees or descendants of refugees from China. The majority hold professions as teachers or military or government employees (Wu 1998: 106; D. Huang 1993: 48).

The theology of Taiwanese Baptists is based on a strictly isolationist view. American Baptism is famous for its insistence on the separation of church and state. But the original American version was to prevent the state from intervening in the church, not necessarily vice versa. American Baptists fought for American independence as patriotically as other denominations did, and Southern Baptists have been the backbone of the American fundamentalist political movement since the 1980s (Leonard 2003). In the Taiwanese context, however, even this active isolationist view was revised into one of passivity. Since most of the first-generation pastors were Chinese and most of the believers were government-related employees, they decided to take a passive view of separatism. The Chinese Baptist Convention, the national association of Baptist churches, writes in its constitution: "This convention insists on the separation of church and the state" (Chapter II, Section 4, Subsection 8). An official document of the convention explains the doctrine in more detail. The doctrine is said to have its origin in the time of Moses' establishment of the priest system and to be sustained by the cases of Saul and Uzziah (I Samuel 13:8–14; II Chronicles 26:16–20). Jesus reconfirmed the principle by saying: "Give unto Caesar what is Caesar's, and unto God what is God's" (Matthew 22:21). Therefore, citizens should obey the government unless government law violates God's law (Education Committee of Chinese Baptist Church 1985: 33–34). With this passive Baptist theology in mind, pastors were not supposed to comment on politics in sermons, Sunday school, nor in private. They did pray from time to time for those "governing authorities" as stated in Romans 13:1 and I Timothy 2:1–3, but rarely did they touch on the more politically sensitive books of the Prophets.

Traces of a democratic theology did not emerge until the late 1990s, when a new generation of pastors found increasing difficulty in answering political questions raised by their church members. They began to look for professional advice from both within and outside the Taiwan Baptist Seminary.

The ecclesiology of the Taiwanese Baptists follows that of the American Southern Baptists, with some influence from Chinese culture. Church documents claim that Baptists churches are "democratic, self-governing, spiritual groups ruled by God," and "the rights and status among pastors, deacons, co-workers, and believers should be equal" (D. Huang 1993: 34). Although no supreme master among the Taiwanese Baptists has emerged, little masters existed in various local churches at different times. Since American Baptism strongly upheld local autonomy, there was substantial variation among the local churches. Most of the Baptist churches emphasized strong leadership, giving the chair pastors almost unlimited powers. The strong leadership emulated those American evangelists who helped build up Taiwanese churches with their superior theological training and financial resources. Most lay believers did not feel uncomfortable with strong leadership, because they served in government institutions led by authoritarian leaders. Democratic church constitutions were either ignored or simply nonexistent.

In the early 1980s, a democratic ecclesiology began to surface in some churches after the leadership passed from American evangelists to Chinese pastors and then to Taiwanese pastors. Church members no longer regarded their Chinese or Taiwanese pastors as being as omnipotent as their American predecessors had been. They began to formulate church regulations in order to limit the power of the pastors. Some charismatic pastors succeeded in overcoming this democratic trend, while others succumbed to this wave of democracy. With the lifting of martial law, the democratic trend only accelerated. Many young pastors who graduated from the Taiwan Baptist seminary have complained about the large discrepancy between the democratic churches they serve (not lead) and the strong leadership they learned from the seminary. They learn firsthand what being God's "servants" really means.[25]

Related to the declining authority of the "little masters" in Baptist churches is the declining superiority of the clergy over the laity. As strong supporters of "the priesthood of all believers," American Baptists have put this principle into practice in Taiwan. Although pastors are normally responsible for conducting baptisms, Sunday sermons, and the Lord's Supper, the laity can, on occasion, deliver Sunday sermons and conduct baptisms and the Lord's Supper when a pastor is not available (Wu 1998: 168). In the Chinese Baptist Convention, to be discussed further on, the number of the clergy representatives cannot exceed that of the laity (Zhonghua jidujiao jinxinhui lianhui 2000: III–4).

In recent years, more and more churches have come to regard pastors not as omnipotent leaders, but as church employees who need to be regularly evaluated by the laity. Many Baptist churches have promulgated new rules or revised old rules in order to keep the pastors at bay in church polity. The collective leadership of the board of deacons has gradually blurred the distinction between the clergy and the laity in decision-making. Increasingly large numbers of the laity, who often receive graduate degrees from American universities, are beginning to challenge the clergy even on the theological battlefield.[26] Due to the growing conflicts between the clergy and the laity, reports are increasing about pastors being forced to resign, including the chair pastor of Taiwan's largest Baptist church (Zhonghua jidujiao jinxinhua lianhui 2000: II–2).[27]

American evangelists also brought with them the Baptist decentralized polity. Before 1949, the American Baptists had established the Chinese Baptist Convention. It did not move to Taiwan. The American evangelists established the Taiwanese Baptist Convention in 1954, which was later renamed the Chinese Baptist Convention (CBC). Similar to the early American Baptist Convention, the CBC was a very weak national convention, short of power, money, and personnel. There were structural weaknesses to start with. The CBC chairman and vice chairman served only one-year terms that could be renewed only once. As nominal heads of the organization, they were elected by "messengers" (*huichai*) from local churches. These messengers were appointed by local churches but could not represent local churches. Their opinions and votes in the CBC did not represent those of their churches, and therefore, the CBC decisions had no binding power over local churches. Frequent bitter arguments and occasional fistfights among the messengers often paralyzed Convention meetings (Wu 1998: 105).[28] The CBC could provide financial and consulting assistance to local churches but could not intervene in their internal affairs unless the latter requested it to do so. Furthermore, the CBC did not have many financial resources, as the American evangelists did. As in the Presbyterian Church in Taiwan, the General Secretary of the Baptist Convention took charge of the daily routine. But unlike the Presbyterian Church in Taiwan, the Baptist General Secretary served shorter terms, with little power to influence local churches.

The most influential organization of the Taiwanese Baptists before the 1990s was the Taiwan Mission of the American Southern Baptist Convention (TMASBC, Meinan Jinxinhui Taiwan Chaihui, established in 1951), which was composed of the American evangelists sent by the Southern Baptists. The association owned most of the property of Taiwanese Baptist churches. It provided financial resources to the Chinese Baptist Convention and local churches and initiated major evangelical works in Taiwan, including the management of the Taiwan Baptist Seminary, resorts, and publishing companies. Therefore, American evangelists often held the upper hand when the Chinese Baptist Convention or local churches made major decisions against their wishes (Wu 1998: 17, 97–101).[29] Among the American evangelists, Rev. Charles L. Culpepper Sr. provided the strongest leadership during the thirteen years (1952–1965) of his mission in Taiwan. He established the Chinese Baptist Convention and chaired the convention for the first year. At the same time, he built up the Taiwan Baptist Seminary and chaired the seminary until he retired in 1965. Most of the Baptist properties in Taiwan were purchased during his tenure (Wu 1998: 21, 86–88).

In retrospect, the TMASBC's dominance in general and Culpepper's strong leadership in particular were more of an obstacle than a contribution to the development of Taiwanese Baptism. Although American evangelists laid down the physical foundation for Taiwanese Baptism, their insistence on using Mandarin as the spoken language of the church and using American theology as well as hymns in church services was not appealing to average Taiwanese or Chinese immigrants. When the Presbyterians implemented the "doubling movement" in the countryside and in the mountainous regions in the critical years of the 1950s and 1960s, American and Chinese Baptist leaders were living comfortably in the urban areas. Even the Local Church and the True Jesus Church, which originated in China, successfully adopted indigenization strategies to attract average Taiwanese believers, without the guidance of foreign missionaries.

In the 1990s, due to the prosperity of the Taiwanese economy, American evangelists decided to help Taiwanese Baptists become independent in finance, management, and evangelism.[30] In the late 1990s, they transferred the ownership of church properties to the CBC. American evangelists became partners instead of supervisors to Taiwanese Baptist churches (Wu 1998: 183–184). With its newly acquired financial and management power, the CBC strengthened its coordinating function a little bit in 1997, when it revised the CBC constitution to change the term "messengers" to "representatives" in the hope that CBC decisions would be more legitimate in the eyes of local churches. However, it has not put a large dent on the long-lasting tradition of local autonomy, which the Baptists are proud of.

In terms of the interaction between the church and the state, Taiwanese Baptists have taken a submissive and isolationist role toward the state. Before the lifting of martial law, they resolutely refused to discuss politics on church compounds. They never publicly supported any political party or candidate. Even during the acrimonious debate between the Mandarin and Presbyterian churches about the latter's political statements of the 1970s, Taiwanese Baptists chose to keep silent.[31] Probably due to the isolationist character of the Baptists, President Jiang Jie-shi hired a Baptist pastor, Rev. Zhou Lian-hua, as his court pastor. Rev. Zhou intentionally avoided political subjects in his sermon to the president (Zhou 1994: 199).

In fact, Rev. Zhou was both an example of and an exception to the rule of Baptist separatism. When the Presbyterian Church in Taiwan issued the first political document, The Declarations and Suggestions on National Affairs, Rev. Zhou contributed a large part of its content. Although Chinese in origin, Rev. Zhou was very active in the movement for the indigenization of Christianity in the 1960s and 1970s, despite vehement protests from American Baptist missionaries. He had earned the trust of many Presbyterian leaders (Zhou 1994: 158, 279–283). Because of his activism in the movement, he was on the government black list, constantly monitored by secret police. An officer of the secret police confided to Zhou decades later that "one of our team members once suggested to assassinate you, the trouble-maker. But I was afraid that the public would immediately know about it when the pastor of the President did not show up at Sunday's pulpit. So, we postponed the operation."[32] Tired of his political activism, the committee of deacons of Rev. Zhou's church, the Grace Church (*Huaientang*), the largest Baptist church in Taiwan, finally issued him an ultimatum that he either stay out of politics or stay out of the church. He chose the first and transferred his energy to purely religious matters thereafter.[33]

In the post–martial law period, most Baptist churches and theologians have not dramatically changed their isolationist stance. Because of their Chinese connections, about two-thirds of the Taiwanese Baptists support the pan-blue parties.[34] However, supporters of the DPP constitute about one-third of the church membership, according to my random surveys and interviews with Baptist pastors.[35] Due to this division in party orientation, most pastors find reiterating the fine tradition of Baptist separatism to be a safe political position to take. At the same time, they urge believers to vote and tolerate church members circulating campaign flyers privately. They do not hesitate to contact local representatives or officials to apply for funding for the church's community services.[36] These are small steps away from passive separatism.

In 2006, Rev. Zhou Lian-hua distributed thousands of free copies of his pamphlet, *The Call of the Epoch* (*Shidaidehusheng*), to Taiwanese Baptists. In this pamphlet, he expressed strong disappointment with the performance of the government. "This is an important epoch, a chaotic and dangerous epoch, an epoch without values and morals, regardless of their ethnicity, gender, age, income, education, and social status." He asked everyone in the society to rise up to transform the politics and society. He backed up his prophetic words with deed by joining the three-hundred thousand-strong crowd of the anti-Chen-Shui-bian demonstration held in September 2006. Television cameras followed him closely. His showing inspired many Baptists to participate in the demonstration. A new political activism is on the rise among Taiwanese Baptists.

THE LOCAL CHURCH

Ni Tuo-sheng (or Nee Watchman) was the founder of the Local Church (*Jiaohui Jühuisuo*, or the Little Flock) in China in the 1920s.[37] Although influenced by Western evangelists in his theological training, Ni developed an indigenized theology critical of the principal churches but accessible to ordinary Chinese. In 1949, Ni Tuo-sheng sent his right-hand man, Li Chang-shou (or Witness Li), to build up a ministry in Taipei both to regroup Local Church members who migrated from China and to preach the gospel to other immigrants. The Local Churches constitute the majority of the seven million Christians in China and include a membership of 91,000 Taiwanese associated with more than 170 churches in Taiwan. The Local Church is the second largest Christian denomination in Taiwan.[38]

One can hardly find any trace of democratic theology in Local Church publications. The Local Church takes an extremely isolationist view toward church and state. Neither Ni nor Li were very interested in political issues. They never encouraged their church members to vote, organize political parties, become government officials, or join the army. The only connection between the church and the state was the Christians' prayer and their total submission to government laws (J. Li 2001: 288–293). Although the Local Church claimed that their submission to government laws was under the condition that the secular laws did not violate biblical laws, they have never publicly challenged any secular laws, including pro-abortion or pro-divorce laws.

The ecclesiology of the Local Church was a mixture of supreme mastership, equality of all believers, and a centralized decision core with strong local autonomy. Ni was the supreme master of all church members, including Ni's successor, Li Chang-shou, who served Ni as his own son. Ni's writings were the main, if not the only, instructional materials in Bible study sessions. His leadership and biblical interpretation was beyond challenge by his members; those who dared to question were driven out of the church. He appointed all elders in local churches. After Ni's death, Li succeeded him to supreme mastership. In addition to inheriting all the supreme powers Ni had, Li's writings, especially the Recovered Version of the Bible (*Huifuben Shengjing*) he edited, have replaced those by Ni in the church's Bible study sessions.

Except for the supreme leaderships of Ni and Li, the relationships among believers and between the clergy and the laity are much more equal than those in the principal churches. Being critical of the principal church, the Local Church discards the position of pastor altogether. Elders govern local churches collectively. The headquarters of the Local Church has training programs for full-time "workers" (*gongren*), who are rotated among Local churches and serve only as coordinators, theological consultants, or messengers between the headquarters and local churches. They have no decision-making power in local church affairs. At Sunday worship, witnessing and spiritual sharing by all believers have replaced the clergy's sermon. Qualified elders take turns hosting baptisms, the Lord's Supper, and other important religious ceremonies.

The Local Church abhors the pyramid structure of some Western denominations. Therefore, they refuse to establish a formal central organization like the Presbyterian Church in Taiwan or the Chinese Baptist Convention (Ministry of the Interior 2003: 183). However, the Local Church has an informal headquarters, composed of the supreme master and a dozen senior elders representing local churches. All the properties of local churches are registered collectively under the headquarters; all the donations of local churches are also passed on to the central body. The Local Church headquarters makes important decisions about church activities and personnel. Local churches cannot but obey; otherwise, they would be excommunicated from the church, as occurred in the 1960s. Among the various charges against these saboteurs, Li mentioned that they challenged his leadership in general, including refusing to sing the eighty-five new hymns composed by Li for all member churches. These saboteurs were first suspended of their elder positions and left the Local Church one year later to establish independent churches (C. Li 2001: 37–43). The Living Stone Church (*huoshi jiaohui*) in Taipei is one of the remnants of this split.[39]

However, as the very title of the church implies, the Local Church headquarters has given local churches as much autonomy as possible with regard to church affairs, management, and finance. Conflicts between the headquarters and local churches are usually resolved by continuous negotiations, unless the supreme master intervenes.[40]

Li Chang-shou died in 1997. No other supreme leader has succeeded him. Therefore, the Local Church is now governed via collective leadership with remarkable cohesion and efficiency. The theology and ecclesiology developed by Ni and Li continue to bind the churches together. A new class of clergy emerged in the 1980s and has since grown stronger in terms of their spiritual and administrative influence in local churches (B. Yü 1994). Nevertheless, with a new generation of believers growing up in a democratic environment and with the supreme master gone, more diversity in theology and ecclesiology has developed in local churches.[41]

In terms of interactions between church and state, the Local Church kept itself entirely out of politics before 1987. Church members never commented on politics nor participated in any political movement. In fact, they were not even interested in non-evangelical charity activities or community services, which they regarded as secular matters. "We absolutely abhor political and nonbiblical activities on the church's premise," one elder categorically commented.[42] Therefore, they did not find it necessary to apply for government funding to perform such services. In recent years, some local churches have begun to challenge this extremely isolationist policy by not mentioning the isolationist teachings of Ni and Li at church gatherings. Participation in community services and low-level elections are reported. Nonetheless, even as compared to the isolationist Baptist churches, the Local Church is moving at a snail's pace toward interacting with the state.

OTHER DENOMINATIONS

In addition to the Presbyterians, the Baptists, and the Local Church, Taiwan's large Christian groups include the True Jesus Church (*Zhenyesu Jiaohui*, about 48,000 members), the Bread of Life Church (*Lingliangtang*, 22,000 members), and the Catholics (300,000 members). Due to the lack of either a democratic theology or a democratic ecclesiology, none of these large Christian groups have made a significant contribution to Taiwan's democratization either in theology or in practice.

Until recently, the True Jesus Church (TJC) embraced a strong isolationist view regarding church-state relations, as did the Baptists and the Local Church.[43] They adopted a democratic ecclesiology mixed with "all the advantages of the principal denominations" (Ministry of the Interior 2003: 106). By comparison, the TJC is very similar to the Local Church in terms of clergy-laity parity, centralization, and local autonomy, except that the TJC has not had a supreme leader and the rotating clergy has had the exclusive power to conduct baptisms and other sacraments.[44]

The Bread of Life Church (BLC) was a small Chinese church that moved from China to Taipei. In 1977, a charismatic Taiwanese pastor, Rev. Zhou Shen-zhu, became the chair pastor and implemented a series of reforms within the church in both theology and ecclesiology. The BLC expanded rapidly as a result. Until recently, it has held a strong isolationist view toward church-state interaction. In terms of ecclesiology, the BLC abandoned the early collective leadership by deacons and opted for a strong leadership after Rev. Zhou Shen-zhu came to the church (Ministry of the Interior 2003: 195–198). He did so by gradually replacing the old deacons with new ones he appointed. The committees of deacons of local churches, if they exist at all, serve only as consultants to the pastors, who hold spiritual and practical superiority over the laity. The BLC headquarters holds considerable influence over the finances, management, and personnel of local churches. But the influence is based more on Rev. Zhou's leadership and informal persuasion than on a formal mechanism like the Presbyterians have.[45]

In recent years, Rev. Zhou Shen-zhu has changed his mind about abstaining from politics. He began to endorse political candidates, especially those of the KMT, New Party, and the People First Party, by offering prayers at their campaign offices.[46] The BLC members followed suit and have supported their favorite candidates (who might be running against Rev. Zhou's choices). Complaints by the laity about a pastor's strong leadership at local churches are more frequent than before.[47] In 2006, a major confrontation between the deacons and pastors broke out in the largest branch of the BLC in southern Taiwan—the Gaoxion Lingliangtang. The pastors had secretly reinvested the fund for building a new church to a high-risk business, without prior approval from the deacons. The investment turned sour and the deacons found out. The committee of the deacons relieved the duties of the chair pastor, who was the founder of the church. The other two pastors left the church for the reason of "irreconcilable differences with the deacons." The entire BLC is beefing up the checks and balances between deacons and pastors.[48]

Finally, the Taiwanese Catholics did not develop a democratic theology or a democratic ecclesiology before the lifting of martial law, despite the popularity of liberal theology in Latin American and in the Presbyterian Church in Taiwan. But in recent years, the larger democratic environment has had some impact on its theology and ecclesiology.

The Spanish Dominicans introduced Catholicism to Taiwan in 1859. After 1949, Chinese Catholics moved to Taiwan in large numbers. Due to the Second Vatican Council's indigenization policy, the number of Taiwanese Catholics increased rapidly in the 1960s.[49]

Chinese Catholics had been strong supporters of the KMT government because of the Chinese communists' insistence on atheism. Taiwanese

Catholics inherited this Chinese legacy and were staunch supporters of the KMT government. During the martial law period, they stood firmly behind government policies, including the suppression of the opposition movement. For instance, when the Presbyterians published three political statements in the 1970s, Taiwanese Catholics called these documents "childish, inconsistent, and violating national principles" (N. Chen, 1991: 118). The liberation theology of Latin American Catholics found very little audience in Taiwan's Catholic community during the 1970s.

In addition to the spiritual antagonism between monotheism and atheism, the Taiwanese Catholic Church had ardently supported the KMT government because the Beijing government insisted on the sovereignty of appointing bishops and cardinals, as well as on intervening in the internal affairs of the church. The KMT government never offended the Vatican on these grounds. Church leaders, therefore, often resorted to this contrast to justify KMT's martial rule.[50]

The Second Vatican Council of the 1960s brought only minor changes to the church's ecclesiology, by allowing lay believers to participate in the discussion of church affairs through the church's board of directors (*lishihui*) or management committees (*guanlihui*).[51] Nevertheless, the lay believers served only as consultants to the clergy. The priests remained the predominant figures in the spiritual and administrative affairs of local churches. The Second Vatican Council did not alter the centralization attribute of the church polity, but more autonomy was given to the church organization at the parish level (*jiaoqü*). Local churches had no autonomy in finances, management, theology, or personnel (Ministry of the Interior 2003: 226–227).[52]

In the late 1990s, the Taiwanese Catholic Church moved closer in line with its counterparts in Western countries in terms of the role of social critics. They began to criticize both the KMT and DPP governments' policies of constitutional revisions, legalization of gambling and of abortion pills, nuclear power plants, and other social issues. Although it has encouraged believers to vote, the church has refrained from endorsing any political party or candidate in elections.[53]

In terms of church polity, the superiority of the clergy over the laity has remained intact despite the influence of the democratic environment. However, the laity become more vocal in church affairs when they disagree with the priests. The church has advised local priests to be more patient in resolving their differences of opinion with the laity.[54]

CHAPTER 4

Daoism and Folk Religions

After showing three segments of a religious DVD to my students in the undergraduate class Religion and Politics, I asked them: "Guess who held the most important religious position among these three rituals worshiping goddess Mazu?" The DVD was a documentary film about a folk-religion Mazu parade held one month before the 2004 presidential election. All the important politicians and candidates participated in the ceremony. Three political figures representing the three major contending political parties respectively hosted a ritual during the ceremony.

Some students chose the first ritual, in which DPP president Chen Shui-bian delivered a speech and initiated the whole religious ceremony. "Good guess," I said, "because it was the president hosting the ritual and it was the initiation of the ceremony. It must be the most important position, right? Wrong, the guess is wrong." Those students who chose the first one were somewhat disappointed.

Other students confidently chose the second ritual in which the speaker of the Legislative Yuan, vice chairman of the KMT Wang Jin-ping, representing presidential candidate Lian Zhang, did not talk much while he performed the inititation ritual of the Mazu parade. Wang helped carry the icon of Goddess Mazu into a sedan chair. "Good choice," I said, "because Wang was able to literally touch the most precious and holy icon of Goddess Mazu and initiated the parade. It must be the most important position, right? Wrong again, sorry." Those who chose the second ritual were more disappointed than were the first group of students.

Only a few of the students chose the third ritual, but without much confidence. In the third ritual, the vice presidential candidate and chairman of the third largest political party in Taiwan, James Song of the People First Party, was assigned to hand-carry the Mazu sedan chair and to walk a few hundred yards. Surrounded by hundreds of thousands of devoted believers, Song could hardly move his steps and his breath was almost suffocated by the bad smell of sweat and cross-firing firecrakers. "This was a dirty job," I said, "and it couldn't be the most important position in the ceremony either, right? Wrong, it was the most important ritual in the whole ceremony. Why? It was because James Song not only got the most prolonged attention of the media (which lasted for hours and has viewed by millions of Mazu belivers), but he also had the broadest and closest contacts with the believers/voters. It was a free political advertisement. Only the best friend of the parade organizer could get this spotlight position, and James Song happened to be the best friend of the parade organizer, Yen Qing-biao, who had little affection for either Chen Shui-bian or Lian Zhang. Furthermore, politicians of lesser status were not allowed to carry the sedan chair, although they could ask to crawl under it in order to receive blessings from Mazu." My students finally understood the justification for adding to their transcripts this course, Religion and Politics. Indeed, Daoism and folk religions have played important roles in the democratization process of Taiwan, for better or for worse. This chapter examines the evolutionof these roles.

DEFINITION

Daoism is both the largest and the smallest religion in Taiwan, depending on how it is defined. Various sources estimate the number of Taiwanese Daoist believers at around six million and Daoist temples at about ten thousand, that is, 60–70% of all Taiwanese temples (Lai 1999: 18–20).[1] Ironically, however, in our interview with the executive director of the Daoist Association of the Republic of China (DARC), Zhang Sheng, he commented: "There is no authentic Daoist temple in Taiwan."[2] A DARC document also agrees with the criticism that Taiwan's Daoist temples are "Daoist temples without Daoism" (Daojiaohui 2000: 5). Not only do Daoist scholars disagree with Daoist clergy on the definition of Daoism, Daoist clergy also disagree with one another as well as with lay believers (Kohn 2000: xi–xiii). At the heart of this debate is the relationship between Daoism and two other major Chinese religions—Buddhism and Confucianism—as well as the relationship between Daoism and Chinese folk religions. The fact that "Daoism has no single founder . . . nor does it have a single key message" makes the debate even more complicated (Miller 2003: ix; P. Gong 1998: 15–21).

Some define Daoists according to the theology, rituals, and organization they first practiced at the end of the second century. Although objective criteria are necessary, there is no Daoist in Taiwan when measured against these ancient and stringent standards. For instance, Gong Peng-cheng (1998: 27–33) argues that Taiwanese Daoists are different from traditional Daoists in at least three aspects. Tradition Daoists emphasized moral values, promoted spiritual cultivation, and refrained from fortune-telling and funeral services, while Taiwanese Daoists emphasize mercantilism, promote deity worship, and extensively practice fortune-telling and funeral services. Gong's definition intends to make a clear separation of Daoism and folk religions. But it falls into the recurrent debate between two major denominations of Daoism: Zhenyi (Orthodox One) and Quanzhen (Complete Perfection). While the former denomination is famous for its expertise in various rituals, the latter emphasizes those religious values and practices that Gong elaborates. This is not a new debate. In 1912, when the Complete Perfection clergy organized the first national Daoist association in China, it proclaimed that "those who equate Talisman-Register (*fulu*) with the Way [*Dao*] are Daoist thieves; those who equate dietary practices with the Way are Daoist devils; and those who equate physical exercises with the Way are Daoist obstacles" (Qing 1996: 428). In their view, the true Daoists were disciples of the Complete Perfection.

Russell Kirkland (2004: 13) provides a practical cross-denominational definition of the Daoists. The "self-identifying Daoists [are] the people whose ideas, values, practices and institutions are expressed in the writings that have been included in the vast, amorphous collection called the Daozang (Daoist canon), its predecessors and later continuations." The Daozang is commonly regarded by Daoist clergy as the bible of Daoism. It went through various revisions after its introduction in the pre-Tang dynasty. Its current edition was edited in the Ming dynasty, around 1445 (Miller 2003: xviii). With 5,485 volumes of various subjects, the Daozang included the theologies and rituals of all major Daoist denominations of the time (Lai 1999: 14; S. Zhang 2001: 34). The majority of Daoist priests in Taiwan can still trace their theology or ritual to the Daozang.

However, this definition still does not resolve the debate concerning the relationship between Daoism on the one hand and Buddhism, Confucianism, and folk religions on the other. Since its foundation as an institutionalized religion by Zhang Dao-ling, also named Zhang Ling, in 142 CE, Daoism has transformed its focus from a philosophy serving intellectuals to a religion serving common people (S. Zhang 2001: 25; Miller 2003: 8; Thompson 1996: 88–89).[3] The institutionalization was based on an integration of family and community norms with theology and religious rituals (Lai 1999: 292; Lee 1997: 311). During the Song dynasty, Confucian scholars and Daoist priests integrated teachings of Daoism, Buddhism, and Confucianism (Ching 1993: 217). In the Ming and Qing dynasties, various deities worshiped by folk religions also found their ways into Daoist theology and temples (Lai 1999: 15).

One example of the difficulty of differentiating Daoism from other Chinese religions is the classification of whether the worship of Guanyin (Avalokitesvara) belongs to Buddhism or Daoism. Guanyin originated in Buddhism and has been worshiped as a Buddha. But ever since Emperor Huizong of the Song dynasty ordered the integration of Daoism and Buddhism (*zhao-foguidao*), Guanyin has also been a Daoist deity and has been worshiped as a great mistress (*dashi*) by the Daoists (Daojiao zongmiao 2003: 12–13; Lai 1999: 249). Therefore, a self-proclaimed Buddhist worshiping Guanyin at a Daoist temple might incorrectly be categorized as a Daoist; while a self-proclaimed Daoist worshiping Guanyin in a Buddhist temple could also be put in the wrong religious category. Guanyin worship was particularly important for the survival of Daoist temples during the late Japanese rule. In order to avoid confiscation by the colonial government or being taken over by Buddhist monks, many Daoist temples claimed Guanyin to be the temple deity and joined the state-sponsored Buddhist association. Zhinangong, a major Daoist temple in northern Taiwan, is one example (Kang 1995: 39).

More complicated examples include the two Taiwanese religious systems studied in this chapter: Yiguandao and the Mazu belief. Yiguandao characterized itself as the unity of five major religions of the world: Daoism, Confucianism, Buddhism, Islam, and Christianity; while various temples of the Mazu belief have provided different stories and rituals based on folk religions, Daoism, or Buddhism.

This book adopts a minimalist definition of the Daoists. In addition to Kirkland's criterion, we also include those self-proclaimed believers in other religions whose theologies or religious behaviors are traceable to Daozang but exclude those who worship nonhuman objects, such as animals, plants, and stones. This definition is consistent with the synthetic nature of Daoism that most Daoist scholars have recognized. It is also consistent with actual religious behaviors in Taiwan, namely that most Daoist temples also include deities of Buddhism and folk religions, while very few Buddhist temples worship Daoist deities (Daojiao zongmiao 2003: 12).

The advantage of this minimalist definition can be illustrated by the Temple of Five Fortune Gods where we conducted an interview. The abbot is an authentic Daoist priest in the sense that he is a descendant of the famous Daoist priest Xun Xü and received a priest certificate from the DARC. He performs Daoist rituals at the temple and at occasions of birth and death in nearby villages. But the main deities in the temple, whom the temple is named after, are five fortune gods that originated from a Chinese folk religion (Shiding Wulucaishenmiao Xinjianweiyuanhui 2002: 5). These deities are not listed in the deity roster published by the DARC (Daojiaohui 2000). The abbot admits that these five fortune gods are not typical Daoist deities and that it is somewhat inconsistent with Daoism to encourage believers to pray for wealth. Nevertheless, the abbot insists that his temple is a Daoist temple.[4]

DAOISM

Daoist deities were brought to Taiwan by immigrants from Fujian and Guangdong provinces in the late Ming dynasty. Daoist priests followed (Lai 1999: 9–11). The Ming dynasty promoted Orthodox One temples in southern China. During the rule of Zheng Cheng-gong in the early Qing dynasty, Zheng further promoted Daoism in Taiwan to challenge the religious legitimacy of the Qing dynasty, which was ruled by a non-Han tribe (Daojiao zongmiao 2003: 10–11). Historical records also reveal that most Daoist priests performed religious ceremonies such as exorcism, destiny change, and community rituals for the people. These ceremonies fell into the realm of expertise of Orthodox One priests.[5] During Japanese rule, the colonial government adopted religious policies to promote Buddhism and suppress traditional Chinese religions.[6] Many Daoist temples joined Buddhist associations but retained their Daoist deities and rituals. In 1949, Zhang En-pu, the sixty-third patriarch of the Orthodox One denomination, moved from the historical headquarters in Jiangxi Province to Taiwan and helped consolidate the dominance of Orthodox One in Taiwanese Daoism. Despite their strong Daoist lineage, all of the major Daoist temples in Taiwan, such as Zhinangong in Taipei, Sanqingong in Yilan, and Daodeyuan in Kaohsiung, combine Daoism, Buddhism, and Confucianism in their worship halls and in their scripture study programs.

Daoist Democratic Theology

The most influential text on Daoist political theology is probably the Scripture of the Great Peace (*Taipingjing*), edited in the late Han dynasty (25–220 CE). It contains at least sixteen short articles elaborating Daoist political theology. The Scripture of the Great Peace places the emperor as the pivotal mediator between nature and the masses.[7] If the emperor performs his role well, there is peace in the nation and harmony between nature and human beings (L. Yü 2001: 11, 13, 33; Kirkland 2004: 81). How can the emperor perform his role well? The emperor should keep a peaceful mind, rule the nation by moral teachings, and respect his officials (L. Yü 2001: 31–33, 181). But it is also very important that the officials, sages, ordinary people, and slaves perform their roles well so that the emperor can have a peaceful mind (L. Yü 2001: 13, 84, 85). The emperor is the son of heaven, the heart of the nation, and represents the yang; while officials are the body and represent the yin (L. Yü 2001, 33, 50, 186–187). Officials should be loyal and obedient to the emperor (L. Yü 2001: 13, 32). Since ordinary people are usually chaotic and ignorant, they should concentrate their will on managing agricultural affairs (L. Yü 2001: 84).

Like its Chinese predecessor, Taiwanese Daoist political theology is very conservative. Built on the principle of cosmic harmony, rulers should promote moral values and safeguard their subjects, while the subjects should be loyal to the rulers and perform their duties (Miller 2003: 89). The political role of Daoist priests was to advise all rulers and subjects on proper behavior and to perform cleansing rituals when they did not behave properly. Although seemingly a mutual obligation, Daoist political theology stressed the subject's loyalty more than the ruler's responsibility. "Be loyal to the emperor" was a major ethic imperative commonly seen in Daoist writings (S. Zhang 2001: 37; Daojiao zongmiao 2003: 2; Zhinangong 1998: iv).[8]

Reinforcing conservatism was the Daoist ideal of the amalgamation of Daoism and the state. Daoist writings frequently cite the glorious eras from the Six Dynasties to the Yuan dynasty (250 to 1250 CE), when Daoism was institutionalized in national ceremonies and the bureaucracy. Daoists have also claimed that Daoism is the only native religion among all the religions in China. Therefore, it should enjoy a privileged status in the state (S. Zhang 2001: 36–39).

Daoist scholars often cite Daoist eschatological (or millenarian) movements as evidence of Daoism's revolutionary character (Ching 1993: 115; Miller 2003: 78–83; Yang 1961: 111–113). Based on the Scripture of the Great Peace, Daoism stipulates that when human beings commit massive sins, heaven will punish human beings collectively, mostly through wars. This is called a tribulation (*jie*). But the punishment is for a good purpose, because Heaven appoints a messiah to rescue human beings from the tribulation, leading to the establishment of a new era of peace and justice (Lee 1997: 303–307). Rebellions carrying Daoist banners dated back to the establishment of institutionalized Daoism in the late Han dynasty. While Zhang Dao-ling established Daoist religion in west China, the Yellow Turbans led a revolutionary war against the Han dynasty in east China, claiming a newborn messiah would save China from government corruption and wars. Other rebellions under Daoist banners occurred frequently thereafter.

However, the revolutionary character of Daoism might have been exaggerated. As Kirkland (2004: 149) perceptively comments: "History shows that connections between Daoism and popular rebellion generally developed only when the reigning regime was demonstrably oppressive or ineffective. Whenever there seemed to be a worthy ruler, or even a plausible candidate for worthy ruler, Daoists of virtually every description seemed quite content to acknowledge the legitimacy of his authority." One such example was the patriarch of the Complete Perfection denomination, Qiu Chu-ji (also known as Qiu Chang-chun: 1148–1227 CE), at the end of the Song dynasty. While Daoists often claimed that Daoism is the most nationalist and patriotic religion, Qiu went to visit the "foreign" emperor Genghis Khan (1162–1227) of the rising Yuan dynasty and offered him religious legitimacy. After the abolishment of the Song dynasty, Qiu was appointed as the emperor's teacher (*guoshi*) by the new emperor (S. Zhang 2001: 26; Miller 2003: xviii).

Misperception or not, the Daoist eschatological theology that placed its hope in a new emperor persisted in the Taiwanese context during democratization, particularly during the 2000 and 2004 presidential elections. Talismans and registers predicting the victory of Chen Shui-bian were widely circulated among Taiwanese voters. Chen was depicted as the virtuous king or a deity reincarnated to be the new emperor of Taiwan. On the KMT side, talismans and registers were also circulated among the voters, suggesting that the inauguration of Lian's presidency would bring back the peace disrupted by former president/KMT chairman Li Deng-hui and the DPP. This eschatological theology, however, says nothing about the relationship between democratic institutions and peace. Its focus is on the messiah (Lee 1997: 327).

Daoist theology emphasizes equality not only between the clergy and believers but also between men and women. Daoist deities consist of two types: immortals (*xian*) and gods (*shen*). Immortals are those who practice self-cultivation to the highest level; gods are those who have made great contributions to the ordinary people (Daojia zongmiao 2003: 3; Miller 2003: x).[9] Unlike Buddhism, major Daoist texts rarely discriminate against women as inferior or dirty human beings.[10] Both men and women can elevate themselves to the level of immortals through self-cultivation (Gong 1998: 36). Many of the popular Daoist deities are women or have been reincarnated as women, including the Third Mistress (*Sannaifuren*), Guanyin (*Avalokitesvara*), Mazu, and the Venerable Mother (*Wujilaomu*).

The conservative political theology, state-religion amalgamation theology, and eschatological theology of Daoism all worked against the democratic values of people's sovereignty, separation of state and church, and accountability of political leaders to the electorate, not to heaven or fate. This lack of democratic theological development is partially caused by the lack of a democratic ecclesiology in Taiwanese Daoism.

Daoist Ecclesiology

Taiwan's Daoist ecclesiology consists of two types: there are monastic priests living in Daoist temples, as monks and nuns live in Buddhist temples; and there are nonmonastic Daoist priests living in households as ordinary people do. The Maoshan and Complete Perfection priests are monastic, while the Orthodox One priests are nonmonastic (Lee 2003: 125–27). Nonmonastic priests constitute the majority of Taiwan's Daoist clergy. Except for performing religious ceremonies, they live a normal life as other villagers do: they get married, raise children, and pass on religious expertise to their children or disciples.

These nonmonastic priests maintain a local monopoly (or "professional domain") in a particular village through their long-term relationships with other villagers (Lee 2003: 138–141). Priests in other villages or in remote monasteries are not able to provide as personally and culturally sensitive services as the local priests can. When a household, village, or community requires the services of Daoist priests, they contact these priests living in the neighborhood. If more than one priest is requested to perform a large-scale ceremony, one senior priest coordinates his disciples or priests in other neighborhoods to work together. These priest groups disband after the ceremony; all priests remain independent from one another. Thus they maintain both competitive and cooperative relationships (Qing 1996: 566–567; Lee 2003: 126, 153). According to Daozang, there are more than a dozen ranks among Daoist priests (Daojiao zongmiao 2003: 29–30; S. Zhang 2001: 41). Although respected, the high-ranking priests do not necessarily command more resources and privileges than low-ranking priests who work closely with the local people.

Unlike Buddhism and Christianity, Chinese Daoism never stops generating new revelations, as does Taiwanese Daoism (Miller 2003: 125–127). The wide circulation of morality books (*shanshu*) written by individual Daoist priests or lay believers has continued to enlarge the context and variety of Daoist theology. There is no central authority or sacred text to measure the "correctness" of new revelations or interpretations. The interpretive power of divine revelation falls into the hands of ordinary priests and lay believers.

Daoist temples are autonomous from one another and have not established nationwide, centralized religious empires as the four major Buddhist organizations have. Famous Daoist temples such as Zhinangong in Taipei, Sanqinggong in Yilan, and Daodeyuan in Kaohsiung do not establish subsidiaries in other counties. Some large temples practice *fengling* (the distribution of the spirit) or *fenxianghuo* (the distribution of incense powder) to build relationships between temples. When believers migrate to other counties, they can request that the home temple give them a replica of the deity (*fengling*) to be worshiped in the new place. Every year, the "subsidiary" temple sends representatives to the home temple to bring back incense powder (*fenxianghuo*) in order to rejuvenate the magic power of the replica. Once the subsidiary temple grows into a worship center, it practices *fengling* and *fenxianghuo* with further subsidiaries. The subsidiary temples pay a voluntary donation to the home temple. They may form an association to coordinate festivals, such as the birthday celebration of the home deity. But the home temple has no power to intervene in the theological, financial, or personnel matters of the subsidiaries.

A peculiar feature of Daoism is that all of its denominations can claim themselves to be different religions (*jiao*) instead of denominations: the Orthodox One Religion, the Complete Perfection Religion, and the Virtue Religion (*Dejiao*), for instance (Daojiao zongmiao 2003: 52).

Except for a few Complete Perfection temples, most Daoist temples in Taiwan are not governed by the clergy but by lay believers. They can be owned by individuals or families. The larger ones are governed by community leaders.[11] Lay believers are elected among themselves into an assembly of representatives. A governing committee is established by a vote in the assembly. Committee members are usually prominent leaders in the local political, economic, and social community. A chairman is then elected by the committee members. The governing committee supervises the daily routines of temple maintenance, festival planning, and charity activities, among others. Most temples hire Daoist priests to perform religious rituals in important festivals on short-term contracts. They may choose other priests for other festivals or for the same festivals the following year. Some temples hire Daoist priests to be stationed in the temples. In general, these priests receive only meager salaries and have no authority outside their ceremonial functions in the temple. Sometimes, at the request of the governing committee, the priests even need to make adjustments to the liturgy.

At the national level, Daoists have had difficulty establishing a strong representative association. Before 1912, Daoism was never a centralized institution despite the occasional dominance of Daoism in national politics.[12] In 1912, the Complete Perfection denomination established the first national association, the Daoist Association (*Daojiaohui*), in Beijing, to the exclusion of all other denominations. In the same year, the Orthodox One denomination established the Daoist Headquarters of the Republic of China (*Zhonghuaminguo daojiaozonghui*) (DHRC) in Shanghai, also excluding all other denominations. These two national associations functioned independently of each other. In 1936 and 1946, the leaders of both associations attempted a merger, but failed due to mutual distrust (Qing 1996: 426–435).

None of the aforementioned Chinese Daoist associations moved to Taiwan. The sixty-sixth patriarch of the Orthodox One denomination, Zhang En-pu, established the Taiwan Provincial Association of Daoism (TPAD) in 1952. In 1957, he organized the Daoist Practioners' Association (*Daojiao Jüshihui*) (DPA) to include priests of other denominations. Resembling its Chinese predecessor, most of its members were Orthodox One priests. Based on the membership of the TPAD, the Daoist Association of the Republic of China (*Zhonghuaminguo daojiaohui*) (DARC) was established in 1966 as a cross-denominational association. It claims the largest membership of Taiwanese Daoist temples among similar Daoist associations. But the DPA has maintained independence from the TPAD and the DARC in order to maintain the denominational cohesion of the Orthodox One (Lai 1999: 294; Lee 2003: 130), as have at least forty-three other national Daoist associations, including the pro-DPP *Daojiaolianhehui* established after 2000.[13]

The DARC is a weak religious association (Lai 1999: 295–296). It has no power to ordain Daoist priests, as the Buddhist Association does for monks and nuns. Some priests of the Orthodox One denomination prefer to receive their ordination from the Celestial Master House, which is independent from the DARC. Many nonmonastic priests simply pass on ordination through family practices or master-disciple relationships (Lee 2003: 131).[14] The DARC has tried to centralize ordination power, but most of its members rejected this idea. In fact, the current chairman of the DARC was de-ordained by his Orthodox One master after a dispute between the two Daoist organizations.[15] In 1991, the DARC tried to provide standardized training by establishing the Academy of Chinese Daoism at Zhinangong, one of the largest Daoist temples in northern Taiwan (Lee 2003: 143). However, only a small portion of Taiwanese priests are interested in this educational institution. Kaohsiung Daodeyuan, a major Daoist temple in southern Taiwan, which established a Daoist academy in 1977, is not a member of the DARC.[16]

The DARC adopted a democratic election system to elect its representatives from the local level to the national level. These representatives are not necessarily clergy. In the early years of the DARC, many of them were retired officials of the party, the government, or the military.[17] In fact, it was a lay believer, Gao Zhong-xin, whose incumbency as the president of the DARC made the most contribution to Taiwanese Daoism by establishing the first training school for Daoist clergy and promoting academic studies of Daoist rituals and classics.[18] He was informally nominated by President Jiang Jing-guo and approved by the DARC.[19]

From the previous discussion, it is clear that Taiwanese Daoism scores higher than other religions in terms of the sovereignty of believers, equality between believers and the clergy, and autonomy of individual temples.

Interaction with the State

The Japanese colonial government in Taiwan had suppressed Daoism, which had a strong link to Chinese culture, in favor of Buddhism, which was popular among the Japanese. Many Daoist temples were either renamed as Buddhist temples or taken over by the Buddhists, and Daoist priests were registered as monks and nuns (Lai 1999: 249). Toward the end of World War II, the colonial government promulgated the Royal Citizen movement and the Elevating Gods movement in an effort to promote Taiwanese loyalty to the Japanese emperor. The Royal Citizen movement encouraged the Taiwanese to worship the Japanese emperor and the Japanese god Kami instead of their own ancestors. The Elevating Gods movement encouraged the Taiwanese to burn their deities in the name of sending them to a better place. Neither movement achieved much result as the Taiwanese continued to follow their traditional beliefs (Daojiao zongmiao 2003: 11–12).

The Daoists had a mixed record with the KMT government in China before 1949. A major denomination of Daoism, Yiguandao, was on the Japanese side during the Second World War. But it mended its relationship with the KMT soon after the war, as will be discussed in the next section. Some Daoists supported the KMT during both the Second World War and the civil war between the KMT and the CCP. However, Chinese scholars have also cited many incidences of Daoist "patriotic" efforts to help the communists' fight against the KMT (Qing 1996: 436–443).

After 1949, Taiwanese Daoism escaped the government's attention due to its decentralized nature as described in the previous section on Daoist ecclesiology. Taiwanese Daoists could be supportive of the KMT before 1987 due to their conservative political theology. Two of the largest Daoist temples in Taiwan, Zhinangong and Sanqinggong, maintained a clear preference for KMT candidates before 2000.[20] The conservative political theology of Daoism gave the KMT an incumbent advantage. Lee Fong-mao cited a few prayers by Daoist leaders in the mid-1990s. The content of these prayers emphasized stability and harmony, while abhorring the tension caused by Taiwan independence activists (Lee 1997: 325–332). But it is more likely that KMT local politicians were routinely enlisted in the governing committees of Daoist temples, thus tilting these temples toward the KMT.

As the pace of democratization accelerated in the 1990s, many DPP politicians joined the governing committees of Daoist temples and rapidly reduced the KMT influence. Even with a DPP minority in the governing committees, most Daoist temples have decided to maintain political neutrality during elections in order to maximize donations and worshipers from both camps. They welcome candidates to worship the deities or participate in important religious ceremonies, with mass media attention beneficial to both the candidates and the temples. But they usually advise candidates to deliver their political speeches, distribute campaign materials, or receive interviews outside the temple building. They hang congratulation placards (*bian'e*) signed by leading politicians from both parties at visible places in the temples. Some temples decide not to display politicians' placards to avoid irritating politically sensitive believers.

For example, Zhinangong, the largest Daoist temple in northern Taiwan, displays only the placard signed by former President Li Deng-hui. No other placards are seen in the temple's premise. The chairman of the temple, Gao Zhong-xin, explains:

> Our major concern is that politicians have high turnover rates. Therefore, we have to keep a longer perspective and keep distance from political figures. I am a KMT member, but will not allow politics to interfere with Zhinangong's affairs. It is our motto that "all factions worship the master" (*Wanpai Chaozong*). The deities will protect everyone regardless of their parties and factions.[21]

Even when the governing committees of Daoist temples intend to influence the political attitude of believers, the effect is minimal at best. Worshipers at a particular temple are not equivalent to members of this temple. Worshipers come from all over Taiwan and do so only on specific occasions.

If Daoist temples do not have much political influence over their believers, why, then, do Taiwanese politicians always frequent these temples at election time? Most analysts would agree that it is mostly for mass media attention, which is to the advantage of both the candidate and the temple. A famous politician plus a famous temple is always a favorite headline story in Taiwan's mass media.

YIGUANDAO
(YIGUANDAO: THE WAY OF UNITY: YGD)

YGD is a syncretistic religion combining Confucianism, Buddhism, Daoism, Christianity, and Islam into one, although most of the emphasis is laid on the first three Chinese religions.[22] It believes that the same Way (*Dao*) unifies the five major religions in one. The personified manifestation of the Way is the deity called the Venerable Mother (*Wujilaomu*), who created the universe and sent her sages to establish the great religions of the world. The Venerable Mother is regarded as the same as the Glorious God (*Weihuangshangdi*) of Confucianism, the Golden Mother (*Yaochijinmu*) of Daoism, the Sunny Buddha (*Dalirulai*) of Buddhism, the God of Christianity, and the Allah of Islam (W. Lin 2001: 354).

Like Taiwan's Buddhism and other folk religions, YGD originated in China and prospered in Taiwan after 1945. They started evangelism in the lower classes, such as workers, peasants, and vendors. In the 1960s, YGD became popular among intellectuals, public officials, and weathy business people (W. Lin 1985: I–211).

Unlike other Chinese religions, however, YGD has endured a unique history of political suppression that significantly influences its political theology, ecclesiology, and interaction with the state both in China and Taiwan. Since its origin in the late Ming dynasty, it was ruthlessly suppressed by the Qing dynasty, the republican government, the Japanese occupation force, the communist regime, and the KMT government in Taiwan before 1987.

The last Great Master of YGD was Zhang Guang-bi, also known as Zhang Tian-ran, who died in China in 1947. His mistress, Sun Su-zhen, also known as Sun Hui-ming, immediately gained control of the nationwide religious organization after Zhang's death, despite opposition from Zhang's wife, Liu Shuai-zhen, his only son, Zhang Ying-yü, and their followers. Sun's faction was labeled the "mistress faction," (*shimupai*) while the followers of Zhang's wife and son were called the "senior faction" (*shixiongpai*) or the "justice branch" (*zhengyixian*) (Qin and Yan 2000: 284–289). After 1945, many YGD branches sent their senior believers, called "managers" (*dianchuanshi*), to Taiwan to recruit believers. The mistress faction commanded many more believers and resources than the senior faction did. After their arrival, YGD believers grew exponentially in Taiwan's religious market. But, just like their religious ancestors, YGD was declared an "evil cult" by both the Chinese and Taiwanese governments. Not until 1987 did the Taiwanese government approve of YGD as one of the legitimate religions.

Currently, YGD headquarters claims that the number of believers who have received the initiation ceremony is about 6,000,000 to 7,000,000, of which 800,000 to 1,200,000 are regular participants at YGD activities in Taiwan, and 1,000,000 who live overseas, spread over 40 countries on 5 continents. Unlike Buddhism and Christianity in which the clergy provides the leadership, the leadership of YGD is composed of more than 12,000 part-time religious teachers of various ranks, among which 2,000 to 3,000 are the core religious leaders called "managers." More than 15,000 YGD "Buddhist Houses" (*fotang*) associated with 200 large and medium-sized temples have been established throughout the island. YGD members own 3 nursing homes, 21 hospitals, 8 clinics, 34 nursery schools, and 30 publishing houses that print 21 major publications.[23]

Democratic Theology

YGD claims that it is not interested in politics. Zhang Tian-ran once said in 1939, "I have not gotten involved in politics in all the long years of my evangelism" (Song 1983: 39). He declared the goals of YGD to be: "Honor heaven and earth, respect deities, obey parents, respect seniors, trust friends, make peace with neighbors, be prudent with words and deeds, and rectify iniquity" (T. Zhang 1993: 6). None of these goals are related to politics. "Loyalty to the emperor," a popular goal among Daoist organizations, is not listed as one of YGD's.

These stated goals do not seem to match either their deeds or their words. The political theology of YGD is based on the theology of "the last tribulation of the third epoch" (*sanqimojie*). Human history from creation to its termination is divided into three epochs. The first epoch, called the "blue yang" (*qingyang*), is the prehistorical era; the second, called "red yang" (*hongyang*), is the dynastic epoch; and the third, called "white yang" (*baiyang*), lasts from 1911 until the end of the human history. Each epoch consists of several tribulations and every tribulation usually brings about political change. Currently, because of its sins, the human race is experiencing the greatest tribulation ever. That is why it is called the last tribulation of the third epoch (W. Lin 2001: 350).

Historically, the last tribulation theology was closely associated with revolutionary forces and disliked by the declining regime. Whenever there was a natural or man-made disaster, supporters of the tribulation theology would argue that it was a sign that the current regime should be replaced by a new regime. This theology worked well as long as the new regime eventually replaced the old. Otherwise, its supporters would be ruthlessly suppressed by the old regime or a new regime different from what they had expected.

It is this theology that got YGD into serious trouble with both the KMT regime and the communist regime after World War II. When Japan invaded northeastern China in 1937, YGD claimed that the war was the last tribulation, and the Japanese would bring about real peace not only in Asia but also in the world (Qin and Yan 2000: 253–254). After the war, both the KMT and the communist regimes accused YGD of collaborating with the Japanese regime and proclaimed YGD an evil cult.

In response to the hardships imposed by the KMT and communist regimes, YGD in Taiwan adapted its political theology. It emphasized the

Confucian virtue of loyalty to the emperor (*zhongjun*) and eulogized presidents Jiang Jie-shi and Jiang Jing-guo as legitimate successors to the apostolic line (*daotong*) of great Chinese kings. It claimed that YGD could contribute to national cohesion in the fight against communism (Song 1983: 41, 133, appendix 6; W. Lin 2001: 354). This adapted political theology helped mobilize YGD believers in support of KMT candidates before 1987 and it became the first legalized religion after the lifting of martial law that same year.

However, YGD's political theology went through yet another adaptation, from a pro-KMT to a pro-DPP theology. The turning point was the admission of Chen Shui-bian as a formal member of YGD. According to a report, Chen joined YGD a few months before the 1994 Taipei mayoral election. This new religious identity helped him to get the full support of Zhang Rong-fa, an influential YGD member and the president of the Evergreen Conglomerate, to win the election (Qin and Yan 2000: 339–340; YGD headquarters has confirmed Chen's admission).[24] During both the 2000 and 2004 presidential elections, some YGD leaders circulated the heavenly mandate that Chen was to be president. A YGD leader in northern Taiwan explained to me in detail how the heavenly mandate had chosen Chen over his competitors in the 1994 mayoral election, and 2000 and 2004 presidential elections: the strokes and qualities of Chen's name prevailed over those of other competitors.[25]

From the previous discussion, YGD political theology seems to be quite flexible in adjusting to political realities. It can be pro-government, antigovernment, or neutral, depending on the leaders' religious interpretation of the heavenly mandate.

Although it is a political theology, tribulation theology is far from a democratic theology. In fact, one senior manager commented, "Democracy is not suitable for Taiwan due to the low quality of the masses; the Singaporean model is better."[26] It endorses the proposition that the ideal polity is one ruled by a moral king, as it was in ancient China.[27] It does not address the importance of human rights, nor does it support checks and balances among governmental branches. According to YGD, heavenly mandate is the best form of governance for both itself and the nation.

Democratic Ecclesiology

Historically, the other major reason (other than its tribulation theology) why YGD and its predecessors were highly distrusted by the concurrent political regimes was its cohesive and hierarchical organization, despite Zhang Tian-ran's claim that YGD "had no organization, except for some Buddhist houses for worship or scripture study" (Zhang 1942, 1993: 9). At the top of YGD is the great master (*zushi*). YGD claims that since Bodhidharma (*putidamo*) arrived in China from India around the first century and became the first great master, there have been eighteen great masters. There is only one master for each generation. All these Great Masters have been reincarnations of

Buddha or some deities. For instance, the last Great Master Zhang was an incarnation of Jigongfo, and the great mistress was an incarnation of Yue-huipusa (Zhang 1942, 1993: 5–6, 14; W. Lin 2001: 355). Therefore, absolute loyalty to these great masters is required of all subordinates.

A great master is well versed in Confucian, Buddhist, and Daoist litera-ture. More importantly, she or he makes important decisions through a ritual of divine revelation conducted by three boys or three girls about twelve years old.[28] The most important one is called the heavenly person (*tiancai*), who is responsible for writing down on a sand box what the deities say to him or her in poems. With closed eyes, the heavenly person writes these poems hori-zontally with each character tilted ninety degrees—an allegedly mysterious behavior only a deity-inspired person can follow. Once the box is filled with words, the sand is smoothed for the heavenly person to continue writing. The second person is called the earthly person (*dicai*), and is responsible for writ-ing down on a piece of paper what the heavenly person writes. And the third is called the Human Person (*rencai*), who reads out what the earthly person writes down. Together, they are called the three persons (*sancai*).

The critics say that this ritual is subject to manipulation by the great master and his close associates, since it is they who train the children. There-fore, it is difficult to tell the difference between what the Great Master says and what the deities say (Lu 1998: 81–82, 132; Jordan and Overmyer 1986: 238). The most serious controversy over the ritual occurs when the great master fails to appoint his successor before his death. The last two succession crises involved such a controversy. Before the seventeenth great master, Lu Zhong-yi, died in 1925, he left a will appointing his sister to manage the reli-gious organization for twelve years. But Zhang Tian-ran relied on the divine revelation conducted by the three persons he had trained and claimed that the diseased great master ordained him to be the eighteenth great master. Even more controversial at the time was that the revelation commanded him to marry the widow Sun Hui-ming, of the same religion. Other senior lead-ers of YGD questioned him, "How does self-purification lead to marriage?" (Lu 1998: 11–15; Song 1983: 122; Song 1996: 56; Fu 1999: 17)

The other succession crisis occurred after Zhang Tian-ran died in 1947. He did not appoint a successor before his mysterious death. Zhang's only son had the intention to succeed his father. But Great Mistress Sun Hui-ming claimed that she was the co-great master of YGD. She also produced a number of revelations conducted by the Three Persons she had trained to legitimize her succession. She even went so far as to imply that she was the incarnation of the Venerable Mother, the creator of the universe (Qin and Yan 2000: 298; Lu 1998: 47–78; Jordan and Overmyer 1986: 219). She claimed that her adopted son, Li Wensi, would be the nineteenth great mas-ter and the king of all nations, merging religious and secular powers in one (Lu 1998: 61). She died in 1975 in Taiwan; Li Wensi was arrested in 1953 and sentenced to life imprisonment; no other successor was appointed (Lu 1988:

411).[29] Some Taiwanese believers proclaimed themselves the nineteenth great master, but the majority of YGD members disagreed with them (Mu 2002: 127–128; Song 1983: 105, 207–208). YGD is now run collectively by senior masters who belong to the mistress faction.

Under the great master are the Way masters (*daozhang*), senior masters (*laoqianren*), masters (*qianren*), managers (*dianchuanshi*), abbots (*tanzhu*), lecturers (*jiangshi*), clerks (*banshiyuan*), the three persons, and relatives of the Way (*daoqin*) (W. Lin 2001: 356–357). This is a strict hierarchy in which the superior leads the subordinates in both administrative and spiritual functions. As one YGD scholar commented: "These ranks are celestial ranks, symbolizing spiritual power. Therefore, they are not replaceable nor to be rotated" (Fu 1999: 389). Great Master Zhang personally anointed seven Way masters in China, but none of them came to live in Taiwan (Lu, 1998: 79; Mu, 2002: 31).[30] Two well-respected senior masters were also called Way masters by Taiwanese believers. Senior masters are the most senior managers who are not only senior in age and in scriptural knowledge but have also successfully recruited large numbers of believers. This title has been given to many of the Chinese managers who came to Taiwan in the 1940s and 1950s. The disciples or successors of the senior masters are called masters. They earn their titles mostly from the respect of their followers and, sometimes, from other managers. They are the leaders of YGD branches and authoritatively make the most important decisions in each branch.

The anointment of managers is called "receiving the heavenly mandate;" those below their ranks receive only a human mandate (Fu 1999: 391). This is because all the managers are thought to be reincarnations of Buddhas and celestial beings (Dong 1986: 386). Lin (1993: 289–291) describes the entire YGD system as a religion of family (*jiazuhua zongjiao*) in which managers serve as the heads of households. Except in cases of poverty, most managers do not receive a salary from their superiors or their subordinates (Zhang 1942, 1993: 14). They usually own a business to support themselves and their evangelism. Some are retired managers, civil servants, or school teachers. A manager we interviewed at the Tiantaishenggong of Gaoxion, one of the largest YGD shrines in southern Taiwan, explained:

> All the full-time staff members in this shrine are volunteers and do not receive a salary. The managers need to pay out of their own pockets for evangelism. They are supposed to be self-sufficient. For instance, I became a full-time manager only after I retired from the Formosa Plastics Company and my wife agreed to fully support me.[31]

They manage daily routines of the temple and encourage their senior believers to open their houses to other believers for weekly worship and reading courses. These senior believers are called abbots. Lecturers work with abbots to explain religious texts to believers. Clerks handle logistical works. Believers call one another "relative of the Way" (W. Lin 2001: 356–357). The three persons are part-time clergy working for the managers and those above their ranks. It seems that whoever controls the three persons has the final say in important decisions made by the organization she supervises, until another manager challenges her legitimacy with his own three persons (Jordan and Overmyer 1986: 240).

The hierarchy of YGD is reinforced by various rituals and numerous study sessions. Most public worship consists of the relatives of the Way touching their foreheads to the ground toward the managers and other senior leaders. Standing positions in worship are arranged according to seniority. The admission ritual for relatives of the Way is even more influential. The manager personally passes on "three treasures" to the new member and asks him or her to take an oath to respect the manager and the great master. Should the new member fail to do so, he or she will be punished by heaven and destroyed by lightening (*tianqianleizhu*) (Song 1983: 51–63; S. Li 1975: 67–80).[32] The numerous study sessions teach traditional Confucian values of respecting seniors and the master.[33] When there is a disagreement about scriptural interpretation between a manager and a relative of the Way, it must be due to the intellectual and spiritual blindness of the relative.[34] Lastly, there is a slight class discrimination against the poor, since 54% of the managers are either capitalist or self-employed; the writing of Zhang Tian-ran provides a religious basis for such discrimination by pointing out that poverty in this life is a result of weak self-cultivation in the previous life (Y. Li 2000: 45, 75).

There are at least nineteen branches (or lines, *zuxian*) of YGD in Taiwan, most of which were established by managers from China during the 1940s and 1950s (W. Lin 2001: 361–365). The major ones include the Foundation (*jichu*), Culture (*wenhua*), Momentum (*haoran*), Heavenly Peace (*tianxiang*), Precious Light (*baoguang*), Developed from the One (*fayi*), Emulating the One (*fayi*), and the Justice Assistance (*Zhengyi Fudaohui*) branches (W. Lin 1985: I–211–214). Only the Justice Assistance branch is part of the senior faction; others are part of the great mistress faction. Due to political suppression before 1987, each branch conducted its religious affairs independently of other branches for the sake of safety. Each believer had very limited knowledge about the major decisions and personnel of YGD. There was also competition for members between branches (Jordan and Overmyer 1986: 221; *Daxiangshandaokan* 2001: no. 7, 21).

In 1988, the National Association of YGD (*Yiguandao zonghui*, NAYGD) was established to coordinate collective actions, such as the standardization of rituals, charity activities, public lectures, national examinations of Chinese literature, and political support for candidates (*Daxiangshandaokan* 2000: no. 2, 26). The NAYGD claims to represent 90% of all Taiwanese YGD believers, registered or not. The NAYGD bylaws provide for a board of directors as the decision-making center. The allocation of directors, chair director, deputy directors, general secretaries, deputy secretaries, and other important positions reflects an attempt to keep a delicate balance among all YGD branches.[35] Basically, the NAYGD is run by a collective leadership composed of the senior masters and masters of all branches who can be reelected to the board of directors without term limits (*Daxiangshandaokan* 2000: no. 2, 26, no. 7, 22–23; Song 1996: 277). Each branch retains its full autonomy inherited from the 1987 period. In 1996, the world Yiguandao headquarters was established in Los Angeles to coordinate the activities of the one million or so overseas YGD believers.

Within each branch, the religious hierarchy is well established by norms and rituals. The subordinates always seek enlightenment on religious texts and their personal lives from their superiors. They are not supposed to challenge their superiors. At important ceremonies, believers of different ranks need to follow written protocols when sitting, standing, moving, worshiping, and greeting other people. The internalization of seniority norms thus makes YGD very effective mobilization machinery, making itself a target of both love and distrust by political leaders.

The seniority norms work well when a charismatic leader rules. However, once the leader passes away without formally appointing a successor, serious family feuds frequently occur. A potential challenger can always cite from the divine revelation conducted by his or her three persons to claim the right to succession. As discussed before, both the great master and the great mistress were involved in such a dispute. After the great mistress died in 1975, a renegade manager, Ma Yong-chang, claimed that he would be the nineteenth great master by divine revelation. The majority of YGD dismissed his claim (Dong 1986: 445).

At the branch level, similar succession crises may occur as well. Once the largest branch of YGD, the Xingyizu collapsed into independent sects and the managers traded nasty words after the senior master's sudden death in the mid-1980s (Song 1996: 76–77, 149, 277).[36] The whole branch almost collapsed as a result. At another branch, a senior manager was rumored to have established an independent branch and named himself master after the ex-master's sudden death and appointment of another junior manager as successor. Two senior masters from abroad came to visit him and requested a public meeting to calm him down (*Daxiangshandaokan* 2002: no. 8, 42–49).

The ecclesiology of YGD reveals both democratic and undemocratic elements. On the democratic side, YGD does not have the problem of the superiority of clergy over lay believers, because the clergy rarely exists. Except for a few, the overwhelming majority of YGD religious teaching staff are part-time "clergy." They usually own a successful secular business in order to finance the religious activities of the temple or the whole branch.[37] Without giving up his or her marriage and career, every believer has the potential to become a manager, a master, a senior master, or even a great master, as long as she or he works hard for the religion and acquires divine revelation.

Gender equality is also a democratic attribute of YGD in Taiwan. For one thing, the supreme deity of the religion is reincarnated as a female deity named the Venerable Mother. For another, the great mistress was proclaimed the co-great master of the religion (Fu 1999: 17). She was a more successful manager than the great master had been before he assumed the position. She helped the great master build the religious empire. She had more followers than the great master's wife and son after he died in 1947. She led believers through the hardships of the civil war and political suppression by both the communist and KMT regimes. YGD rose as a phoenix in Taiwan. Her example left a legacy of female leadership at every echelon of YGD, as can be witnessed by the great number of female senior masters, masters, and managers. Among the 3,600 managers that Great Master Zhang planned to recruit, 600 were reserved for women (Zhang 1942, 1993: 13).

Another democratic feature of YGD is the autonomy of each branch after the great master and the great mistress die. The National Association of YGD is only a coordination center and not a centralized governing body, as its predecessor in China was under the leadership of the great master.

However, on the undemocratic side, YGD ecclesiology indoctrinates its believers with authoritarian and theocratic values. The great masters, senior masters, masters, and managers command intellectual, spiritual, and supernatural authority over their subordinates. Their writings are studied and memorized, their words followed, and their behaviors eulogized. After their deaths (above the rank of managers), their successors give them a royal title through divine revelation, such as Buddha, Great Emperor (*dadi*), and Authentic King (*zhenjun*), implying they are reincarnations of deities. Although this may be interpreted as a democratic practice because every believer has the potential to become a deity, it is not applicable to those believers below the rank of manager. One senior manager we interviewed in his temple showed me a large mural of him with a radiant light behind his head—a symbol of a deity in religious paintings.

Interaction with the State

The early history of interaction with the state in pre-1949 China had a much more significant impact on the development of YGD in Taiwan than it had on any other major Taiwanese religion. YGD was first regarded as a communist ally by the KMT regime, a Chinese guerrilla force by the invading Japanese troops, a KMT collaborator by the communist regime, and, at the same time, a communist conspirator by the KMT regime.

After he became the Great Master of YGD, Zhang Tian-ran rapidly expanded his religious organization in northern and eastern China. The rapid expansion caught the attention of the KMT regime, which was fighting a civil war with the communists. Since the home base of YGD was in the north where the communists retained some strongholds, the KMT regime suspected YGD was a supporter of the communists. In 1936, Zhang Tian-ran went to the capital of the KMT regime, Nanjing, with the intention of developing his religious organization there. He was arrested by the KMT secret police, the Blue Shirt Society (*lanyishe*), and charged in the name of collaboration with the communists. Although no concrete evidence of any crime was found, Zhang was detained in jail for nine months before he was released.

In 1937, the KMT regime formally declared war on the invading Japanese forces from northeastern China. The Japanese soon occupied the northern and eastern part of China, and established a puppet regime in Shanghai. Some YGD believers joined the anti-Japanese guerrilla forces but to no avail. The Japanese forces were worried about YGD's strong and immense organization and began a massive crackdown on the religion (Song 1983: 126; Jordan and Overmyer 1986: 216). This forced Zhang Tian-ran to change his religion's relationship with the ruling regime, for the sake of organizational survival and expansion. He explained the Japanese invasion as the last tribulation of the third epoch, and that Maitreya Buddha was coming to save all his children. He proposed to his followers a new political attitude toward the Japanese—"treasure harmony, uphold endurance" (*he wei gui, ren wei gao*). One should "reflect on one's misbehaviors, and don't pass judgment on others' rights and wrongs" (*xian zuo si ji guo, mo bian ren shi fei*). Some of Zhang's followers even proposed a new political exegesis that the Japanese were following the heavenly mandate to bring peace and prosperity to the world (Qin and Yan 2000: 253–254).

With the change of political exegesis, YGD actively sought connections with the Japanese forces and the puppet regime by recruiting believers from these two regimes. Many senior believers became employees of these regimes (Song 1996: 90; Qin and Yan 2000: 277–279). The new strategy worked very well. YGD expanded further in the Japanese occupied areas with the approval and protection of high officials in the Japanese regimes, who became YGD believers. In 1945, a few months before the Japanese conceded defeat, Zhang Tian-ran was even appointed advisor to the foreign ministry of the puppet regime, and his only son a special agent of the same ministry (Lu 1998: 32–38).

Because of these political connections, the KMT declared YGD an evil cult and charged many of its leaders for treason in 1946 (Lu 1998: 40). In retrospect, YGD's connections with the Japanese regimes were more individual than institutional. It was a strategy of convenience for the survival and expansion of the religion, rather than a means for YGD to establish itself as a state religion or political regime. The evidence cited for the charges of treason was weak and there was not much of it. One could find believers of other religions working for the Japanese regimes and performing religious functions as YGD did. Therefore, once YGD changed its political strategy again after 1946, most of the charges against YGD were dropped.

After the war, YGD rapidly adjusted its political strategy in order to survive political suppression by the KMT regime. Similar to the Japanese occupation period, YGD successfully recruited KMT high officials to become believers, through whom the treason charges were dropped and confiscated assets returned (Qin and Yan 2000: 292–293). YGD continued to expand its organizational structure throughout China.

But YGD had placed its political chips on the wrong side again. The atheist communists suppressed YGD in the communist-controlled provinces during the anti-Japanese war. After winning the civil war, the communist regime declared that YGD "is a superstitious organization that is antirevolutionary and against the people. Under its leadership, it formed an alliance with the Japanese bandits, the collaborators, and the spies of the Jiang Jie-shi and American regimes." A ban on YGD was issued in the 1950s, and the ban remains in effect today (Qin and Yan 2000: 308).

Did the name "KMT collaborator" help YGD's expansion in Taiwan after 1949? Ironically, it did not. Most of its political patrons either did not come to Taiwan or were on the wrong side of the political struggle within the KMT regime. The memory of YGD's collaboration with the Japanese regime was still in the institutional memory of the KMT secret police. This institutional opposition to YGD is probably the major reason why YGD did not become a legalized religion until after the lifting of martial law in 1987, despite the fact that YGD established a strong political lobby in the early 1980s. From 1951 to 1970, the KMT government actively suppressed YGD activities and arrested its leaders. Many of the alleged crimes were related to "interference in elections," "antiwar propaganda," "criticizing the government," and "supporting China's unification efforts" (He 1996: 68, 73, 184, 209, 212, 235; Song 1996: chap. 6). In 1963, several senior managers were under pressure from the KMT to call press conferences and declare the dismissal of YGD (Song 1983: 9–12; Song 1996: 182–184; He 1996: 134, 148).

From 1970 through the late 1970s, police harassment of YGD continued (Song 1996: 186–187; Jordan and Overmyer 1986: 242). Despite the harassment, YGD expanded even further by joining the newly established National Association of Daoism and other Buddhist associations. One senior master, Zhang Pei-cheng, helped to establish the Taiwan Provincial Association of Daoism (TPAD) in 1964 and encouraged many YGD branches to join the TPAD to avoid harassment by the KMT police (Song 1983: 9–10, 36; Song 1996: 190–191). Senior Master Zhang even became the acting president of the National Association of Daoism in the early 1980s until 1987, probably due to the organizational power of YGD members within the association.

YGD often cited inter-religious competition as the major reason why it remained illegal from 1953 to 1987 (Song 1983: 23–37).[38] The major competitor and prosecutor of YGD was Buddhism. Before 1949, a popular form of Buddhist organization was a nonclerical sect called the Vegetarian Religion (*zhaijiao*). Senior lay believers allocated a portion of their house as Buddhist temples for other believers to worship Buddha and learn scriptures taught by these senior believers. After 1949, Chinese monks came to Taiwan to develop traditional Buddhist organizations led by clergy. Buddhist scholars claimed that the Vegetarian Religion declined as a result. It didn't, according to YGD; it was transformed and taken over by YGD. YGD called its basic unit of religious organization Buddhist House (*fotang*), and its part-time managers were well versed in Buddhist scriptures. Because YGD had a stronger social network and a greater variety of deities than traditional Buddhism to satisfy the religious appetite of the Taiwanese, many believers of the Vegetarian Religion became YGD believers and did not join traditional Buddhist organizations (Clart 1997: 12; Lin 1985: I-269). The rapid expansion of YGD was in sharp contrast with the slow development of traditional Buddhism from the 1950s to the early 1980s.

YGD also threatened the religious market share of other major religions, such as Daoism, Confucianism, and Christianity, because of its claim that it integrated all these religions under the ultimate leadership of the Venerable Mother. YGD believers have provided evidence that the Zhongguo Fojiaohui, Zhongguo Kongxuehui, Zhonguo Daojiaohui, and many Buddhist clergy had publicly denounced YGD as an evil cult and asked the KMT government to retain its ban on it (Song 1996: 192–193).[39] But all these anti-YGD documents were published in the mid-1970s and 1980s, and, therefore, cannot account for the political prosecution of YGD from the 1950s to 1960s.

A balanced explanation of YGD-state relationships from the 1950's to the early 1980s should combine both the secret police's institutional inertia and bias against YGD and the religious competition thesis, with the former reason more important than the latter.[40] Like their Chinese counterparts, Taiwan's secret police were worried that the well-organized YGD would be controlled by competing political forces (Song 1996: 158). YGD's memory of religious competition is probably due to the fierce conflicts between YGD and other religions in the late 1970s and early 1980s. After all, once the lifting of martial law dramatically cut back on the political legitimacy of the secret police, YGD immediately became a legalized religion despite continued complaints from Buddhists and other religious leaders.

YGD developed yet another political exegesis in order to win approval from the KMT regime. It claimed that presidents Jiang Jie-shi and Jiang Jing-guo were legitimate successors to the Chinese apostolic line of great emperors, and that YGD promoted national spirit to fight Chinese communism (Song 1983: 41).

Putting this political exegesis into practice, YGD actively supported KMT candidates at various elections and recruited KMT high officials (and their relatives) as believers. In 1971, YGD helped elect the KMT candidate for the Taipei County Magistrate. After the election, the candidate kept his promise not to ban YGD activities in the county (Song 1996: 222). In the 1983 legislative election, YGD helped elect all seven KMT candidates in Taipei. The city's party secretary commented: "one YGD is worth three precinct party organizations" (Song 1996: 245). Other county magistrates, such as Lin Feng-zheng and Wu Bo-xiong, all received organized support from YGD and became advocates for its legalization in the late 1980s. In the 1986 legislative election, YGD flexed its muscles again and helped elect thirteen candidates assigned by the KMT. In 1987, forty legislators requested that the government legalize YGD and received approval by the end of the year—thus, the National Association of YGD was established (Song 1983: 41; Song 1996: 262–268). Because of YGD's impressive record in election campaigns, it became fashionable for candidates to join YGD or cite one of their close relatives as YGD believers when they addressed YGD audiences (Song 1996: 297).

We might attribute YGD's political support of the KMT to the fact that most of the senior masters and masters came from China and had a natural inclination toward the mainlander-dominant KMT, as had the Mandarin-speaking Christians and the Mandarin-led three largest Buddhist organizations. However, the story of YGD is more complicated than it appears. While other religions' leaders continued using Mandarin for religious studies, YGD's Chinese leaders blended very well with the Taiwanese by earnestly studying the Taiwanese dialect and using the dialect in formal religious indoctrination (Song 1983: 129–132). Therefore, YGD's support for the KMT was based more on practical than ideological reasons; and the same can be said about its later support for the DPP as well.

After the lifting of martial law, the relationship between YGD and the KMT took another turn. Tensions arose in 1990 when the KMT experienced an internal power struggle between the "mainstream faction" led by the first Taiwanese president, Li Deng-hui, and the "non-mainstream faction" consisting of mainlanders who moved to Taiwan after 1949. Both sides sought political support from YGD, and the senior masters and masters decided to leave it to the discretion of each believer. The first conflict between YGD and the KMT occurred in the 1991 election of the National Assembly representatives. The KMT had promised YGD to put a YGD representative on the KMT slate of representatives at large, who were to be elected according to the party's share in total votes. After the votes were counted, the KMT skipped the YGD representative and chose two female candidates, who were ranked far behind him on the slate, for the slots. The KMT later apologized to YGD, saying that it had not mentioned this female quota rule before the election. Distrust between YGD and the KMT emerged. The second formal conflict between YGD and the KMT occurred in the 1992 legislative election, in which the son of an influential master ran as an independent against a KMT candidate in Tainan City. The KMT candidate won the election by a small margin. In the 1994 Taipei mayoral election, a more significant conflict between YGD and the KMT broke out that would have a more dramatic impact on Taiwan's regime change. The DPP candidate Chen Shui-bian had just joined the Chongde division of the Fayi branch as a relative of the Way a few months before the election. YGD believers in Taipei used to be strong supporters of the KMT. But this time, under the coordination of YGD manager Zhang

Rong-fa, who happened to be the president of the Evergreen Conglomerate, many YGD believers supported Chen and got him elected (Qin and Yan 2000: 339–340; Song 1996: 286–300).[41] In the 2000 presidential election, the Republic of China I-Kuan Tao Association still openly endorsed the KMT candidate, but a substantial portion of YGD believers in southern Taiwan supported Chen Shui-bian and got him elected.[42] In the 2004 presidential election, the Republic of China I-Kuan Tao Association did not throw its weight behind the KMT; the majority of YGD members were allegedly voting for Chen's reelection. Before this election, YGD leaders circulated the heavenly mandate that Chen would be the chosen one.[43]

Although YGD is probably a more influential political force than any other religion in Taiwan, its political influence should be not exaggerated. For one thing, their pre-1987 political influence was based on a common goal of all believers—to become a legalized religion. This certainly generated strong political support for the KMT government for this common religious goal. However, in 1987 this religious goal was accomplished, and no other goal has attracted as much cohesion. For another, YGD is highly centralized within each branch but highly decentralized among branches. Once the leader of a particular branch passes away, this branch is likely to become decentralized again. Therefore, the political preference of each senior master, master, and, particularly, manager who has frequent contact with his or her believers becomes decisive at elections. In general, a geographical line divides YGD's political preference: northern YGD believers tend to support pan-blue (KMT, PFP, NP) candidates, while southern YGD believers tend to support pan-green (DPP, TSU) candidates.[44] But the majority of YGD managers prefer to stay neutral, unless the election has vital implications for their religious life.[45]

Two cases exemplify the constraints on YGD's political influence. The first is the 1992 legislative election in which the son of Senior Master Wang Shou was running as an independent against a KMT candidate. Several YGD branches came to help his campaign without success. The second case is the 2003 legislative election in Nantou County, in which YGD senior believer Xü Jun-xi ran as an independent with help from his YGD branch. The local newspaper labeled him a strong candidate.[46] But he got only 233 votes, less than 0.2% of the total votes in his constituency. It seems that YGD plays the role of kingmaker better than the king himself.

The role of kingmaker is what is needed to explain YGD's political influence in the 2000 and 2004 presidential elections, both of which were characterized by very close competition. In 2000, KMT candidate Lian Zhan competed with the KMT renegade James Song for pan-blue votes. So, YGD pan-blue votes, as represented by the Republic of China I-Kuan Tao Association, were split between the two. YGD pan-green votes, as represented by the open support of the owner/manager of the Evergreen Conglomerate, could concentrate on the DPP candidate who was a relative of the Way. YGD played the role of balancer in this competitive election. A similar thing happened in the 2004 election. President Chen won the election by a razor-sharp margin of less than thirty thousand votes. With a proclaimed registered membership of over one million, YGD could be called the kingmaker this time. The DPP had developed a good rapport with YGD through the frequent visits by the general secretary of the Examination Yuan, Zhu Wu-xian, who was the college classmate of President Chen and also a Way relative.[47] On numerous occasions, he and President Chen promised to resolve two religious-legal problems many of YGD branches face: illegal appropriation of public land for the use of temple construction and illegal construction of towers for the storage of cremated human remains (*naguta*). These religious and practical factors drew YGD away from the KMT and toward the DPP.[48] By contrast, the KMT did not visit YGD temples as often as they had at previous elections. In a couple of incidences, the KMT candidate irritated many YGD believers by canceling meetings with several masters accompanied by hundreds of managers and thousands of relatives of the Way at the last minute—an irrevocable mistake the KMT had never made before 2000.[49]

THE MAZU BELIEF

Mazu was the honorary name of a young woman, Lin Mo-niang, born in the year 960 CE in a coastal village in Fujian Province. She had knowledge of medicine and Daoist rituals to treat the physical and spiritual problems of villagers. She was about thirty years old when she died. After her death, legends reported many miracles associated with her spirit. The most reported cases were linked to her providence in various natural disasters, particularly to fishermen in storming seas (L. Li 1995: chap. 1–8; Cai 1994). Villagers would bring an image of Mazu with them when traveling or migrating to other provinces or overseas. Once arriving at their destination, they would build a temple for the Mazu image in appreciation of her providence. This is how the Mazu belief started in Taiwan during the late Ming dynasty, when Fujian immigrants sailed across the sometimes turbulent Taiwan Strait to Taiwan.

The Mazu belief is the largest belief "system" in Taiwan, claiming a "worship population" of over six million.[50] I use the words "system" and "worship population," instead of "organization" and "membership," because the Mazu belief is a highly disorganized religion and does not provide for any membership admission ritual as Buddhism, Christianity, and Daoism do. Its organizational traits will be elaborated upon further on.

Although scholars disagree on their religious categorization, most Mazu temples and religious behaviors in Taiwan can be categorized as synthetic Daoist, mixing Daoism, Buddhism, Confucianism, and folk religion.[51] The legends about Mazu claim that she was born to a Guanyin believer. She learned Daoist rituals and magic powers from a Daoist priest. After she died, she was worshiped in both Daoist and Buddhist temples in China.

Most Taiwanese Mazu temples hire Daoist priests and adopt Daoist rituals on Mazu holidays (e.g., Songshan Ciyougong), while some Mazu temples do so in a Buddhist manner (e.g., Taipei Guandugong and Beigang Chaotiangong), and still others combine Daoist and Buddhist ways (e.g., Dajia Zhenlangong). More importantly, most Mazu temples in Taiwan, as well as in China, worship both Daoist and Buddhist deities together with Mazu (Y. Zhang and S. J. Zhang 1989: 21; Liao and L. Huang 2003: 14–21; Ye 2003: 86). As both Lee Fong-mao and Zheng Zhi-ming have correctly commented, the Mazu belief was born as a folk religion, but decorated with Daoist and Buddhist coats by temple leaders who were Daoists, Buddhists, or both (Lee 1993: 40; Zheng 1997: 158).

Democratic Theology

Mazu never wrote any religious texts. Neither did her followers establish an interpretive system to explain Mazu theology or write any articles on political issues (Zheng 1997: 155). However, as in other Daoist beliefs, there were legends about Mazu that had political implications. In the early Qing dynasty, the government suppressed Taiwan's rebellion movements by soliciting Mazu's blessings. After each successful suppression, the government would provide honorary titles and finances to glorify Mazu (L. Li 1995: 194–199). Therefore, like other Daoist deities, Mazu was regarded as a progovernment deity.

This might be inconsistent with the allegedly nationalist character of Daoism and the Mazu belief in the late Ming dynasty. As discussed before, the decline of Daoism in the Qing dynasty is often attributed to its nationalism, as the foreigner-controlled government distrusted nationalist Daoism. When Zheng Cheng-gong established a rebellion force in Taiwan while the Qing dynasty controlled China, he promoted Daoism, and particularly the Mazu belief, to give religious legitimacy to his rebel government.

But the Quig dynasty successfully undermined Zheng's religious legitimacy by appealing to the same deity and claiming that Mazu was on the new government's side, as evidenced by successful military campaigns. After the abolishment of Zheng's government and the suppression of various rebellions, Mazu became an ardent supporter of the foreign government. Those Mazu temples that harbored antagonism toward the new government gradually lost their legitimacy and worshipers (M. Huang 1994: 61–67). Hence, the Mazu belief can be both nationalist and antinationalist at times of political uncertainty, just as Chinese Daoism in general had been during political tribulations.

In the past decade, some scholars have raised the issue of a pro-Taiwanese theology of the Mazu belief. It is claimed that the Mazu belief provided a religious foundation for the rising Taiwanese nationalism. But this claim has never been seriously elaborated by other Mazu scholars nor attended to by most Mazu believers.

The controversy over a pro-Taiwanese Mazu theology emerged on the 1987 pilgrimage of Djia Zhenlangong to the home temple of Mazu on Meizhou Island in Fujian Province and during the island-wide tour of the Meizhou Mazu image across Taiwan in 1997. Taiwanese independence activists worried that the pilgrimage and the tour would strengthen the cause for national unification under the Chinese government, which was probably a correct assessment of China's "patriotic united front strategy" toward religions (X. Gong 2000). Therefore, they proclaimed that "the communist Mazu is not the same as the Taiwanese Mazu," "the Taiwanese Mazu has been independent," "the Chinese Mazu is a local deity," and "the Chinese Mazu is not authentic" (Mio 2003: 202; Taiwan Association of University Professors 1997: 1–11).[52] This pro-independence theology was probably a minority view at best and espoused by non-Mazu specialists. Among the more than dozen interviews we conducted with Mazu scholars and senior leaders at various Mazu temples, few have heard of such an independence theology and none take it seriously. Most believers simply ignore the political controversy the pilgrimage and the tour created. Those who suggested a Mazu independence theology probably confused national identity with local identity, which most Mazu scholars agree is an important function of Mazu temples or of any large local temple (Bosco 2003: 112; M. Huang 1994: 194; M. Lin 1991: 352–354, M. Lin 1997: 107; X. Zhang 1995; Sangren, 1993: 576; B. Lin 1997: 14–15; Fong 1996: 124).[53]

Democratic Ecclesiology

The relationship between Mazu temples and most of their believers can be characterized as individualistic and noninstitutional. Most worshipers do not know one another and do not interact with one another. They come to the temple to do just one thing: worship. Most of these temples do not offer regular lessons of scripture readings, nor do they conduct frequent collective worship services, except on religious holidays.[54] Most worshipers remain anonymous to the temples unless they request otherwise in the donation books.

While small-scale Mazu temples may be owned by individuals, most of the medium and large-scale Mazu temples in Taiwan establish governing committees (guanliweiyuanhui) or boards of trustees (dongshihui) to govern temple affairs. Usually, the believers residing in the local villages surrounding a Mazu temple are eligible to elect their representatives, who in turn elect members of the governing committee or of the board of trustees. These members are usually the economic, social, or political elites in the villages, who then elect a chairperson from among themselves.[55] Some chairpersons serve fixed terms of three to five years, while some serve without term limits. In many Mazu temples, politicians such as precinct heads (lizhang), mayors, and village councilmen are statute members of the governing committees and boards of trustees. These governing committees and boards of trustees are the real decision-making centers of Mazu temples, not the assemblies of local believers. Worshipers from outside the temple villages have no voting rights (Y. Yang and S. J. Zhang 1989: 19; M. Lin and G. Xü 2003: 119–120; Ye 2003: 120; M. Huang 1994: 152–155; G. Yü 1994).

Although democratic formality is adopted, many Mazu temples are not necessarily democratic in practice. Family elders, local elites, and local factions often prevail in the election process. In the larger Mazu temples, gangsters frequently are involved in the elections of temple trustees and chairpersons in order to take part in the distribution of donation money (Chin 2003).

Clergy in Mazu temples have little influence on temple affairs. Very few Mazu temples hire Buddhist or Daoist priests to live in residence. They hire these professionals on a case-by-case basis and may recruit different priests in different years or on different occasions. Those who are hired as resident priests are not treated very well either in terms of salary or respect. In the early history of one Mazu temple we interviewed, an old Buddhist monk was fed canned vegetarian food and received only a meager salary that was just enough to buy a new religious outfit every year. Except for conducting religious rituals, these resident priests have no right to interfere with temple affairs, such as personnel and spending. Even on matters of religious rituals, priests, residents or not, need to obey the instructions given by lay leaders. For instance, Beigang Chaotiangong's worship rituals are famous for their creativity and complexity. The architect of all these rituals, however, is a lay employee who used to be a journalist and has no background in religious training. He designs the rituals and writes prayers as he sees fit. The priests simply follow his instructions. In the other major Mazu temple, Dajia Zhenglangong, the board of trustees makes decisions on rituals and need not consult the priests.[56]

Each Mazu temple is totally independent from other Mazu temples in terms of financial and personnel matters, but the coordination between Mazu temples is very impressive, as evidenced by the number of participants and the variety of activities during Mazu holidays (X. Zhang 1995). However, this strong coordination ability does not necessarily imply organizational cohesion. Most coordination committees are organized temporarily, and disband after each holiday. In only a few Mazu temples do coordination committees maintain simple social functions after the holiday (M. Lin and G. Xü 2003: 150, 153).[57]

Occasionally, cooperation is also mixed with competition among major Mazu temples. In order to attract worshipers, large Mazu temples often claim the titles such as being the oldest, the first in Taiwan, the officially endorsed, or the direct copy from the Mazu image of the Meizhou temple (M. Huang 1994: 57–67). After 1987, many large temples organized pilgrimages to the home temple of Mazu in Meizhou, Fujian, to establish a direct relationship (Y. Yang and S. J. Zhang 1989: 350–351). Most worshipers pay little attention to this symbolic competition and continue to visit as many Mazu temples as possible (Sangren 1993: 576; M. Huang 1994: 199).

A large Mazu temple often releases copies of the hosting Mazu image to other temples, thus establishing an ancestor-descendant relationship. However, this ancestor-descendant relationship entails little obligation and cohesion. The descendant temple pays a nominal fee to request an image copy from the ancestor temple. On Mazu holidays, the descendant temple will often bring back the image copy and a voluntary donation to the ancestor temple to honor the relationship. Other than these coordination activities, there is little interaction between the ancestor temple and its descendants.

Interaction with the State

Before 2000, most of the major Mazu temples had a political preference for KMT candidates from the local to national governments. This was not caused by the mainland Chinese leadership as was the case with several of the largest Buddhist organizations, Catholics, and Mandarin-speaking Protestants. Almost all the leaders in Mazu temples were Taiwanese. The conservative Daoist theology, which favored the peaceful status quo, might partly explain the political preference. But the major reason was related to the organizational structures of these Mazu temples, as discussed in the previous section. The KMT held an overwhelming advantage over its opponents in local elections and administrative systems, such as precinct heads, mayors, village council men, and agricultural cooperatives, who constituted the majority of the boards of trustees of these temples. Therefore, KMT politicians often took advantage of the temple's social and political networks to garner votes.

Although the KMT held the upper hand in Mazu temples, the political influence of these Mazu temples was constrained by three structural factors: local faction competition, weak temple-worshiper connection, and types of elections. When more than two local factions existed in a temple's religious constituency, power struggles between local factions could undermine the effectiveness of KMT campaign strategies. The weak connection between the temple and its worshipers reflects the individualistic and noninstitutional characteristics of Mazu worshipers as discussed in the previous section. Politicians could hardly extend their influence beyond the boards of trustees or governing committees to the regular worshipers. Finally, Mazu temples might have more influence at local elections through their local factional networks but less influence in large district elections.

During the democratization process, the political influence of Mazu temples on elections declined further. Some DPP politicians joined the boards of trustees and governing committees of these temples. In order to maintain a harmonious image of governance and to avoid losing politically sensitive donors, most Mazu temples decided to maintain political neutrality during elections. They avoid formally endorsing any candidate and open their space outside the temple to all candidates for political campaigning (Liao and Huang 2003: 49).

One example is the Beigang Chaotiangong. It was once associated with prominent opposition leaders such as Li Wan-jü and Su Dong-qi in the 1940s and 1950s. However, a KMT local faction, the family of Zengcai Mei-zuo, later took over the board of trustees. After 2000, DPP politicians were elected to the board. Although still a minority, DPP members have been able to keep the temple politically neutral. Recollecting the temple's political history, the chief of the temple's cultural division, Ji Renzhi, summarized:

> Because of its public nature, the temple had been open to politicians to hold campaign activities inside. However, in the past two decades, it was no longer open for campaign use. Even the chairperson of the temple's governing committee, Zengcai Mei-zuo, had to move her campaign headquarters outside the temple wall.[58]

Similar change of political climate occurred in Zhenglangong as well. In fact, a senior staff welcomes this change. He said:

> The reason why the temple is politicized is because the heads of the villages and precincts are the members apparent of the governing committee. Since these heads are also factional members, factional politics thus interferes with temple affairs. But this is good for the temple, because we have the Black faction in power, while the Red faction behaves like the loyal opposition party to monitor temple affairs.[59]

The decline of the Mazu temple's political influence is most conspicuous in national elections. In both the 2000 and 2004 presidential elections, the chairperson of Dajia Zhenglangong, Yan Qing-biao, a notorious underworld boss in central Taiwan (Chin 2003: 88–91),[60] personally endorsed the PFP candidate and then the KMT-PFP ticket, claiming that Mazu instructed him to do so.[61] However, Chen Shui-bian received more votes than the other candidates in the four villages that made up the temple's religious constituency.[62] Nine months after the 2000 presidential election, Yan was prosecuted and imprisoned on felony charges. He was bailed out ten months later and continued his appeals. Four months after the 2004 presidential election and three months before his legislative reelection, Yan lost several of his appeals in court.[63] He was reelected again with strong local factional support, but his legal problems are still haunting him.

The other major pro-KMT Mazu temple, Beigang Chaotiangong, went through a similar political decline. In the 2000 presidential election, 53% of the Beigang Township voters voted for the DPP candidate, while only 25% and 22% voted for the KMT and PFP candidates respectively. The temple's political influence declined even further in the 2004 election, in which 65% of the town voters voted for the DPP candidate, and only 35% voted for the combined KMT and PFP ticket.[64] Four months after the 2004 presidential election, the DPP government prosecuted and requested a jail term of twelve years for Zengcai Mei-zuo for her involvement in a scandal in which she exercised political clout in order to facilitate the illegal harvesting of riverbed sand.[65]

Another sign of the increasing political neutrality of Mazu temples is the display of templates and calligraphies donated by politicians. Most Mazu temples now display templates and calligraphy donated by politicians of both parties in relatively equal positions. One of the few exceptions is Dajia Zhenglangong, which still favors pan-blue over pan-green donations in terms of both number and location. While many pan-blue templates and calligraphy examples are displayed in the hall hosting the Mazu image, only two DPP templates are displayed in a small side-wing room hosting the images of Mazu's parents. A high-ranking official of the temple we interviewed offered a succinct explanation: there is no pro-DPP member on the temple's board of trustees at the moment.[66]

CHAPTER 5

Statistical Analysis

by Kuo Cheng-tian and Kuan Ping-yin

His facial expression was vivid but very difficult to describe. It was like a drowning person who suddenly found a piece of log floating by, a tourist lost in the desert and seeing a mirage, or a religious martyr visioning her savior; I was not sure. He was a department head of the KMT national headquarters. One year after the KMT lost the 2004 presidential election by about thirty thousand votes, the KMT headquarters was still immersed in pointing fingers at every possible wrongdoer. He had heard enough bad news and nasty verbal exchanges. But when I told him about my recent statistical finding showing that the largest religious group in Taiwan, Ciji, which proclaimed a membership of four million, was a staunch supporter of the pan-blue parties, his theatrical facial expression surfaced. It was a mixture of surprise, relief, excitement, comfort, elation, and hope. He was so jubilant to hear the news that he earnestly asked me to consider the possibility of delivering a speech at the KMT central committee meeting to cheer everybody up, which I politely declined.

The statistical finding, which will be presented later in this chapter, was equally a shocking surprise to everyone, including myself, who had prior knowledge about Taiwanese politics and religion. There had been voluminous evidence proving that the abbot of Ciji, Ven. Zhengyan, had done much more than any other religious leader did to maintain the political neutrality of her vast organization. Therefore, most observers would predict that Ciji members have no salient party preference. If anything, they should tilt slightly toward the pan-green parties because Ven. Zhengyan was the only Taiwanese among the four major Buddhist leaders in Taiwan, and the Taiwanese dialect, which the DPP government promoted, was commonly used in the organization. Why was there such a huge gap between qualitative evidence and quantitative finding? This chapter will provide some possible answers to this question and other related questions.

To our knowledge, until now there has never been a full-scale statistical study of the relationship between religion and the state in Taiwan, either in English or Chinese. Most of the current qualitative research finds that interactions between religion and the state exist to some degree. However, convincing as they are, at least three doubts can be raised about the arguments of these qualitative research studies. First, in the past, statistical analyses on democracy in Taiwan never reported that such a relationship existed. In fact, after one or two trials, the major survey teams in Taiwan simply dropped either the political questions in their religious studies or the religious questions in their political studies, until Kuo and Kuan (2005) put religious questions back into democracy surveys. In the 1995 World Value Survey, there were both religious and political questions, but no scholar conducted research on the relationship between the two in Taiwan.

Second, as scholars and news reporters have observed, many Taiwanese religions adhere to separation between religion and the state or maintain political neutrality. How do these cases reconcile with those cases that show direct connections? Are the cases reporting connection between religion and the state part of a minority or majority?

Third, building on recent literature on the differences between the pulpit (clergy) and the pews (lay believers) (Jelen and Wilcox 2002), the clergy might be experiencing increased difficulty in dictating the political attitude and behavior of believers, particularly in Taiwan's open society.

Furthermore, using the Taiwan Election and Democracy Study (TEDS) 2003 data set, Kuo and Kuan (2005) found that Taiwanese believers are not as institutionalized and theological as their Western counterparts, and that Taiwan's religious demarcations are not as clear as in Christian or Islamic monotheist countries. These factors tend to limit the political influence of religious leaders on their believers as well as blur the differences in political attitude and behavior across religions. Since the TEDS 2003 data set did not include good data on Taiwan's important religious groups, Kuo and Kuan were not able to directly verify the arguments about these religious groups' democratic theology, ecclesiology, and interaction with the state.

Finally, even if we collect good qualitative data revealing the party preferences and democratic aptitudes of certain religions and religious groups, it will be difficult to rank them by qualitative data alone, as has been shown in the previous case-study chapters. All Taiwanese religions and religious groups consist of believers with opposite party preferences and with disparate elements of democratic theology, democratic behavior, and interaction with the state. A statistical analysis will help us verify the arguments derived from the qualitative data and rank these religions and religious groups by quantitative criteria.

In 2004 we joined the survey team of the Taiwan Social Change Survey 2004 (Questionnaire II), sponsored by Academia Sinica in Taiwan. Slightly revising the standard 3-Bs questions (belief, behavior, and belonging) commonly included in large surveys such as the World Values surveys, the Gallup

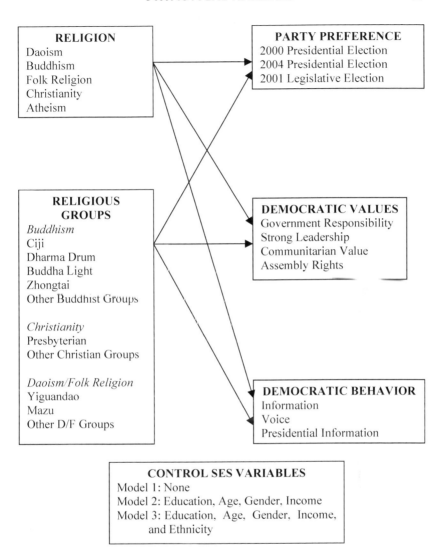

FIGURE 5.1 Statistical Research Design

surveys, and ICPSR election surveys, we introduced ten religious questions into the questionnaire. The data set collected a random sample set of 1,781 valid cases during the summer of 2004.

Matching the analytical framework of the previous case study chapters, our statistical research design (see figure 5.1) contains two sets of independent variables (religion and religious groups), three sets of dependent variables (party preference, democratic values, and democratic behavior), and controls for the influence of five socioeconomic status variables (education, age, gender, income, and ethnicity). Party preference variables use the respondent's votes in the 2000 and 2004 presidential elections and 2001 legislative election. Binary logistic models are applied to these party preference variables. For variables of democratic value and behavior, we use the factor analysis method (principal component extraction and varimax rotation) to construct composite indicators (adding the statistically and logically relevant variables together). OLS regression models are then applied to these variables.

Each statistical test is conducted three times, using models 1, 2, and 3. Model 1 examines the impact of religion or religious groups on party preference, democratic value and behavior without controlling for socioeconomic status (SES) variables. This model gives us a preliminary answer to the common questions: "which religion (or religious group) tends to support pan-blue (or pan-green) candidates?" or "which religion (or religious group) ranks higher on the scales of democratic values and democratic behavior?"

Model 2 examines the data with the control variables of education, age, gender, and income.[1] Model 3 adds ethnicity to the control variables. With the control of these variables, the relatively true effect of the religion (or religious group) is observed. A comparison among Models 1, 2, and 3 provides us with more interesting and accurate conclusions than each of the models could individually.

TAIWAN'S RELIGIOUS PROFILE

Before introducing the regression results, some descriptive statistics about the 3 Bs (belief, behavior, and belonging) of Taiwanese believers is helpful to provide a general background on the Taiwanese religious profile. Furthermore, the descriptive statistics will offer important explanations for why religion matters or doesn't matter in certain cases.

The first religious question we asked respondents was "What is your religious belief?" A list of Taiwan's most popular religions was provided for them to choose from. Table 5.1 reports the statistics.[2]

Compared to other data sets collected in Taiwan, the Taiwan Social Change Survey 2004 shares some similarities as well as some differences, particularly in the categories of Buddhism, Daoism, and folk religions. Table 5.1 includes those percentages reported by the Taiwan Election and Democracy Study (TEDS) 2003 and two surveys conducted by the Taiwan Social Change Survey (TSCS) team from Academia Sinica in 1994 and 1999. It is well known that most Chinese folk religions are synthetic religions combining Confucianism, Daoism, and Buddhism (Ching 1993; Lopez 1996; Thompson 1996; Yang 1961). One explanation for these statistical differences is that respondents neither exactly know which religion they belong to, nor do they care much about these academic categories. Another explanation is the high mobility across Taiwanese religions. Based on a comparison of 1994 and 1999

TABLE 5.1 Religious Beliefs in Taiwan (%)

BELIEF	TSCS 2004	TEDS 2003	TSCS 1999	TSCS 1994
Buddhism	28.2	36.4	26.3	38.5
Daoism	17.5	19.0	12.7	9.1
Folk Religion	25.5	14.6	33.6	31.0
Yiguandao	2.7	1.2	2.7*	2.6*
Xuanyuanjiao	0.1			
Catholicism	0.6	0.8	2.4	1.1
Protestantism	3.4	4.2	4.8	4.2
Luantang	0.1			
None	21.4 (8.4)**	23.3 (6.9)**	13.6	13.0
Others	0.5			
Don't Know	0.1			

Sources: TEDS 2003, Zhang Ying-hua (2000: 240).

* Includes other small Daoist sects.

** Percentages in parentheses are nonbelievers who do not worship any deity

TSCS data sets, Ben-xuan Lin (2004) found that the percentage of religious conversions increased from 19.3% to 26.6%. Atheists, folk religions, Buddhism, and Daoism had the largest exodus (B. Lin 2004). The other explanation for the differences might be related to differences in the training of interviewers and the syntax of the belief questions in these surveys. Despite these ambiguities and inconsistencies in the data set, we assume that the subjective feeling and cognition of the respondents regarding their religious identification not only deserve respect but could also be consistent with their democratic values and behavior. Recategorizing their beliefs according to archaic academic standards might create more analytical problems than it resolves.

The general impression that the Taiwanese are a very religious people does not seem to be supported by the high percentages of nonbelievers (atheists) in both the TSCS 2004 and TEDS 2004 data sets. However, in both questionnaires another belief question was asked: "Do you worship Tudi-gong, Guanggong, Mazu, or other deities?"[3] It turns out that only 8.4% and 6.9%, respectively, of Taiwanese are true atheists. This is consistent with the findings of Zhang and Lin (1992) that most of the Taiwanese who claim no religious belief are actually less committed believers of folk religions (Zhang and Lin 1992: 92–124).

But the question about the religious sincerity of Taiwanese believers takes another twist when we asked, "How important is religion in your daily life?" in the TSCS 2004. While 9.1% and 32.1% responded "very important" and "important" respectively, 51.6% and 6.9% answered "not very important" and "not important at all." For the purpose of comparison, in the American National Election Survey 2000, 76.3% of American respondents regard religion as important to them, while 23.7% replied "not important."[4] Therefore, most of the Taiwanese are believers, but they do not consider religion important in their daily life. This observation is consistent with the findings of the next set of religious questions.

After the religious belief questions, we asked three questions about religious behavior. On the first question, "How often did you participate in religious activities?" A total of 10.1% answered either "a few times every week," "once every week," "a few times every month," or "once every month." A total of 27.4% answered "a few times every year," and "about once every year" while 62.4% responded "almost none" or "never." In the American National Election Survey 2000, 38.5% attend religious services every week, 16.5% do so almost every week, 21.7% once or twice a month, 22.7% a few times a year, and only 0.6% never do so.

The second question about religious behavior was: "In the past year, how often did you worship, pray, meditate, cite sutra, or engage in other kinds of religious ceremonies?" A noticeable 26% of the respondents answered "very often," and 31.9% said "sometimes," while 22.7% answered "few," and 19.4% said "never." The third behavioral question was: "In the past year, how often did you read religious texts, books, exegeses, or listen to religious programs?" Only 8.3% answered "often," and 13.2% responded "sometimes," while 25.4% said "few," and 53.1% replied "never."

According to the American National Election Survey 2000, 31.8% pray several times a day, 22.5% pray once a day, while 17.5% and 15.9% pray a few times a week or once a week or less. Only 10.8% never pray. About 3.6% of Americans read the Bible several times a day, 10.4% once a day, 13.7% a few times a week, 31.1% once a week or less, and 38.5% replied "never."

These three attributes of Taiwanese religious behavior, along with the following low-membership attribute, are consistent with Kuo and Kuan's (2005) findings that Taiwanese believers in general are deinstitutionalized and nontheological, similar to their European counterparts (Davie 1999). They are deinstitutionalized in the sense that most of them do not actively participate in collective religious activities, nor do they become members of religious groups. But they are quite interested in conducting religious ceremonies in private. Therefore the phenomena of large-scale religious activities, such as the parade of Mazu, should not be equated with the sincerity of Taiwanese believers in general. These are probably attended by their believers once a year, and only a small percentage of their believers attend. Nevertheless, Taiwanese believers are quite sincere in their private religious activities, as evidenced by the proliferation of home altars and small shrines of various deities on almost every street in Taiwan. Lastly, although Taiwanese believers are sincere in holding private religious ceremonies, they are not very interested in theology. This is probably due to the fact that most temples of Daoism and folk religions do not offer theological lessons, and few believers take advantage of the free virtue books (*shanshu*) piled up at these temples.

Finally, we asked two questions about religious belonging. First, we asked the respondents whether they are members of a religious group or a group supported by a religion. About 24.1% of the respondents replied that they have such a group membership. By contrast, about 53.9% of American believers belong to a church or denomination. This difference can be explained by the fact that many of the Taiwanese folk religions and Daoist temples do not strongly encourage formal membership as their Christian, Catholic, or Islamic counterparts do. In Taiwan, the religious group that has the highest enrollment rate is Christianity (69%), followed by Daoism (36.4%), Buddhism (28.3%), folk religions (18.1%), and nonbelievers (5.8%).

Once religious membership is confirmed, we asked the respondents to choose among the major religious groups listed in the questionnaire.[5] Among the 1,781 respondents, 429 identified their religious group affiliation, an enrollment rate of about 24.1%. Among the Buddhist groups, Ciji is the largest (109 cases), constituting 6.1% of the whole sample, or 25.4% of those believers who hold a religious group membership. Its membership outnumbers those of Buddha Light (9 cases), Dharma Drum (8 cases), and Zhongtai (6 cases) combined (0.5%, 0.4%, and 0.3%, respectively). Among Daoism and folk religions, the Wangye belief (44 cases) and the Mazu belief (45 cases) are the largest religious groups, claiming a membership rate of 2.5% each, and followed by Yiguandao's 2.3% (41 cases). The largest Christian group is the Presbyterians (17 cases, 1%), followed by the Local Church (10 cases, 0.6%), the Holy Bread (6 cases, 0.3%), the True Jesus (5 cases, 0.3%), and the Baptist (3 cases, 0.2%). Among the ten Catholics in the sample, only one claimed to belong to a church, constituting only 0.1% of the total sample size.

If we use these percentages as a basis to estimate the real numbers of membership, the relative political influence of religious groups based on membership may tell us a different story than the often-exaggerated memberships do. According to these percentages and using the 2004 Taiwan census data of an adult population around 22,615,000,[6] Ciji's membership is about 1,020,000, Buddha Light's is 110,000, Dharma Drum's is 90,000, Zhongtai's is 70,000, the Presbyterian Church's is 230,000, the Baptist Church's is 50,000, the Bread of Life Church's is 70,000, the Catholic Church's is 20,000, the Mazu belief's is 570,000, and Yiguandao's is 520,000. These membership numbers are very different from what the major religious groups often claim to be in the millions. However, because of the possibility of sampling error, especially for smaller religious groups such as Dharma Drum, Zhongtai, and other non-Presbyterian churches, these numbers are for reference use only.

In the following section, we report the results of regression models and provide preliminary analyses of the religious impact on party preference, democratic values, and democratic behavior, at both religion and religious group levels.

RELIGION AND PARTY PREFERENCE

For party preference variables, we selected three variables for testing: the 2000 presidential election, the 2004 presidential election, and the 2001 legislative election. Voting outcomes are recoded as binary variables of "pro-pan-blue" (value = 0) and "pro-pan-green" (value = 1). Three binary logistic models are applied to each of these dependent variables. The first model does not include control variables. The second model controls for the variables of education, age, gender, and income. The third model adds ethnicity to the control variables.[7]

An important caveat needs to be made before these party preference numbers are interpreted. The survey results of these elections deviate significantly from actual outcomes. For instance, in the 2000 presidential election, about 39% actually voted for Chen Shui-bian, 39% voted for James Song, and 23% voted for Lian Zhan, but the survey reports 56% voted for Chen, and a combined 43% for the other two pan-blue candidates. In the 2004 presidential election, 50.11% actually voted for Chen, and 49.89% voted for the joint ticket of KMT and PFP, while the survey reports 60% for Chen and 40% for the pan-blue ticket. We tried a weighted data set adjusted for gender, age, geography, and education in the government's census data, but failed to make a significant difference in the voting outcomes. In past research, such an underestimation of the loser's votes was not uncommon, probably because the respondent did not want other people to know that their favored candidate lost the election. This large difference between the actual voting outcome and the survey results will not affect the accuracy of the following statistical analyses. We will compare only relative, but not absolute, support for candidates.

The education variable is recoded into four levels of education: elementary or below, junior high, senior high, and college or above. The age variable uses raw scores. The gender variable recodes female as 1 and male as 0. The income variable uses the household income divided into 26 levels. The ethnicity variable uses the respondent's father's ethnicity and is transformed into three dummy variables of mainland Chinese, Taiwanese, and aboriginal. The Hakka ethnic group is treated as the reference group.

Religions and religious groups are recoded as dummies, using atheists and other Daoist/folk religious groups as reference groups respectively. Atheists are treated as the reference group because, theoretically, they are not affected by any religion. A preliminary cross-tabulation also shows that they are relatively equally divided between pro-pan-blue and pro-pan-green. The Daoist/folk religious groups are treated as the reference group for three theoretical and methodological reasons: 1) they consist of a large number of cases;

2) they are strong supporters of pan-green candidates; And 3) they tend to rank low in terms of democratic values and behavior, due to their weaknesses in democratic theology and ecclesiology.

Because of their small number of cases, non-Presbyterian Christians, including Catholics, are merged into the variable of OTChris, while Buddha Light and Zhongtai Cansi members are merged into the BLZT variable, and those Buddhist members who do not belong to any one of the four major Buddhist groups are merged into the OTBud variable. Tables 5.2, 5.3, and 5.4 report the binary regression results for the 2000 and 2004 presidential elections and 2001 legislative election.

As compared to the case studies discussed earlier, these statistical tables reveal a number of interesting results. First, as compared to the atheists, the Daoists and folk religion believers were the strongest supporters of President Chen in both the 2000 and 2004 elections (model 1 in table 5.2). After controlling for the education, age, gender, and income variables, the pattern remains relatively the same, except for the coefficient of folk religion in model 2 of the 2000 election, which dropped a little below the 0.05 significance level. Past studies of Taiwanese elections have found that the core supporters of the DPP tend to be those with lower education. Table 5.2 confirms this argument, but proves further that belief still matters after controlling for education. However, the ethnicity effect takes away all the religious impact on presidential elections.

The pro-pan-green orientation of the Daoists and folk religion believers does not seem to be consistent with previous case studies, which implied a pro-pan-KMT orientation due to their conservative political theology and the KMT-dominated governing boards of these temples. We have not yet found a very good explanation for this inconsistency based on their theology, ecclesiology, or the history of interaction with the state. Do ordinary Daoist and folk religion believers favor DPP candidates because they dislike KMT local elites and factions who dominate the temple committees? Whatever the explanation is, the statistical findings partially confirm the theoretical argument about the gap between the pulpit and the pew in an open, democratic environment. However, it should be reminded that the "pulpits" of the Daoist and folk religion temples are not the same as their counterparts (priests, pastors, ulamas, and abbots) of the much more institutionalized Catholic, Christian, Islamic, or Buddhist organizations. Because of their theological training, the clergy of the institutionalized religions apparently have more influence over their believers than the lay leaders of the much-less institutionalized Daoism and folk religions do.

Secondly, the "incumbent advantage" occurs among the Daoists, Buddhists, and folk religion believers, but the "incumbent disadvantage" seems to emerge among the Christians, although the coefficients are not significant in the latter case (table 5.2). The "incumbent advantage" refers to the advantage of incumbents over the challengers because the incumbents can claim credit

TABLE 5.2 Binary Logistic Models of Beliefs and Presidential Elections in Taiwan

	2000			2004		
	MODEL 1	MODEL 2	MODEL 3	MODEL 1	MODEL 2	MODEL 3
Daoism	**.600	*.399	.083	***.633	*.397	.024
	(.194)	(.201)	(.214)	(.187)	(.194)	(.209)
Buddhism	.078	-.113	-.299	.121	-.106	†-.347
	(.179)	(.187)	(.199)	(.168)	(.177)	(.192)
Folk Religion	***.594	†.347	.151	***.749	**.479	.225
	(.185)	(.193)	(.203)	(.179)	(.186)	(.200)
Christianity	.183	.266	†.656	-.156	-.117	.266
	(.320)	(.326)	(.385)	(.304)	(.312)	(.372)
Education		***-.363	***-.294		***-.404	***-.337
		(.068)	(.072)		(.068)	(.073)
Age		-.001	.007		-.005	.003
		(.005)	(.006)		(.005)	(.005)
Gender		†-.253	*-.317		-.192	†-.247
		(.127)	(.133)		(.125)	(.133)
Income		-.010	-.013		-.016	†-.024
		(.014)	(.015)		(.014)	(.014)
Mainlander			***-1.990			***-2.278
			(.355)			(.362)
Taiwanese			***.605			***.675
			(.178)			(.175)
Aboriginal			†-1.437			*-2.000
			(.749)			(.839)
Constant	-.061	**1.246	.588	.042	***1.737	*1.144
	(.142)	(.417)	(.473)	(.130)	(.399)	(.457)
N	1134	1134	1134	1204	1204	1204

*** p ≤ .001, **p ≤ .01, * p ≤ .05, † p ≤ .1

for the benefits they have brought to their constituents. The "incumbent disadvantage" occurs when the incumbents did something wrong during their tenure. It seems that the Daoists, Buddhists, and folk religion believers tend to look favorably on the achievements of President Chen during his first term; while the Christian voters, particularly the Mandarin-speaking Christians

TABLE 5.3 Binary Logistic Models of Religious Groups and Presidential Elections in Taiwan

	2000			2004		
	MODEL 1	MODEL 2	MODEL 3	MODEL 1	MODEL 2	MODEL 3
Ciji	*-.754	-.362	-.165	***-1.535	***-1.191	**-1.052
	(.332)	(.363)	(.376)	(.352)	(.372)	(.386)
DD	-.143	.461	.583	-.679	-.171	-.038
	(.897)	(.920)	(.939)	(.905)	(.927)	(.955)
Presb	.550	1.035	†1.491	-.679 (	-.233	.451
	(.687)	(.721)	(.795)	.068)	(.650)	(.787)
Mazu	-.094	-.223	-.245	-.679	†-.877	*-1.000
	(.450)	(.464)	(.466)	(.454)	(.470)	(.479)
YGD	-.143	.286	.530	*-1.036	-.740	-.564
	(.471)	(.502)	(.526)	(.491)	(.518)	(.538)
OTChris	*-1.037	-.527	.087	***-1.858	**-1.441	-.913
	(.507)	(.541)	(.614)	(.521)	(.549)	(.612)
OTBud	*-1.003	-.634	-.321	***-1.526	*-1.113	†-.999
	(.472)	(.494)	(.521)	(.474)	(.498)	(.521)
BLZT	-.325	.104	.752	*-1.372	-.975	-.343
	(.767)	(.795)	(.969)	(.685)	(.702)	(.817)
Education		*-.312	-.241		*-.310	†-.299
		(.140)	(.147)		(.147)	(.157)
Age		.008	.013		-.004	-.002
		(.011)	(.012)		(.011)	(.012)
Gender		†-.485	†-.470		***-.915	***-.971
		(.268)	(.279)		(.274)	(.289)
Income		.003	-.009		-.008	-.017
		(.030)	(.031)		(.030)	(.032)
Mainlander			**-2.308			*-2.115
			(.871)			(.886)
Taiwanese			.551			†.772
			(.422)			(.441)
Aboriginal			-1.814			-21.815
			(1.438)			(18327.372)
Constant	***.836	1.209	.410	***1.37	***2.771	*2.013
	(.235)	(.809)	(.984)	(.264)	(.864)	(1.021)
N	290	290	290	298	298	298

*** $p \le .001$, **$p \le .01$, *$p \le .05$, † $p \le .1$

TABLE 5.4 Binary Logistic Models of Beliefs, Religious Groups, and Legislative Election in Taiwan

	2001					
	MODEL 1	MODEL 2	MODEL 3	MODEL 1	MODEL 2	MODEL 3
Daoism	**.561 (.206)	.347 (.213)	-.017 (.229)			
Buddhism	-.004 (.192)	-.129 (.199)	-.334 (.214)			
Folk Religion	**.570 (.199)	†.391 (.205)	.191 (.218)			
Christianity	.047 (.342)	.113 (.348)	.406 (.403)			
Ciji				***-1.325 (.358)	**-1.075 (.381)	**-1.043 (.393)
DD				-.676 (.949)	-.278 (.971)	-.330 (.991)
Presb				-.571 (.578)	-.305 (.608)	.139 (.686)
Mazu				-.440 (.469)	-.519 (.478)	-.585 (.482)
YGD				-.859 (.540)	-.673 (.553)	-.519 (.576)
OTChris				**-1.593 (.578)	*-1.324 (.598)	-.704 (.661)
OTBud				*-1.282 (.519)	*-1.074 (.535)	†-.986 (.548)
BLZT				-.859 (.719)	-.635 (.743)	.044 (.862)
Education	***-.270 (.070)	**-.194 (.075)			-.122 (.142)	-.059 (.151)
Age	†-.010 (.005)	-.003 (.006)			.008 (.012)	.012 (.013)
Gender	**-.366 (.135)	**-.433 (.142)			-.399 (.285)	-.408 (.296)
Income	*-.028 (.014)	*-.035 (.015)			-.023 (.029)	-.033 (.030)

(continued)

TABLE 5.4 *(continued)*

	2001					
	MODEL 1	MODEL 2	MODEL 3	MODEL 1	MODEL 2	MODEL 3
Mainlander			***-1.733			*-2.241
			(.359)			(.807)
Taiwanese			***.762			.079
			(.195)			(.477)
Aboriginal			-1.820			-22.139
			(1.150)			(27381.812)
Constant	-.187	***1.487	.792	***1.082	1.249	.977
	(.153)	(.448)	(.515)	(.259)	(.840)	(1.039)
N	995	995	995	258	258	258

*** p ≤ .001, **p ≤ .01, * p ≤ .05, † p ≤ .1

who were mobilized in the 2004 election, may have focused on the negative aspects of President Chen's tenure.

Thirdly, as compared to other Daoist/folk religion groups, the Presbyterians, Dharma Drum members, YGD members, and Mazu believers tend to side with President Chen, although none of their coefficients reaches a significance level (table 5.3). This means that the political orientation of these religious groups is not significantly different from the reference group of Other Daoist and folk religion believers who are strongly pro-pan-green. The Presbyterian case is consistent with the previous case study that demonstrates the pro-pan-green orientation of the Presbyterian Church. For the case of YGD, the statistical result is also consistent with the previous case study in that YGD members began to shift from a strongly pro-KMT position toward pro-pan-green. The fact that the YGD coefficient becomes larger and more significant in model 1 of the 2004 election than model 1 of the 2000 election is consistent with the report in the case study that the YGD headquarters first announced its support for the KMT candidate in 2000 yet allowed its members to make other choices, but in 2004, the headquarters did not endorse any candidate. After all, President Chen is a relative of the Way (initiated member) of the YGD.

The case of Dharma Drum is somewhat confusing because this Buddhist organization always gives the impression of being attractive to urban professionals, who are usually pro-pan-blue, and the previous case study tells us that the mainland Chinese leader of Dharma Drum has tenuously kept political neutrality during elections. Therefore, the coefficients should have pointed to pro-pan-blue or at least neutrality. But they are either as pro-Chen as the YGD members in 2000 or even more pro-Chen than YGD members in the 2004 election. So far, we do not have other data to explain this anomaly, except that a sampling error might have occurred due to the small number of cases for Dharma Drum members.

The case of Mazu believers is also interesting. The previous case study and other current research have indicated that the major Mazu temples are dominated by pan-blue local factions. But the statistical results reveal that ordinary Mazu members tend to support President Chen. This is also consistent with the election outcomes reported in the case study that there are more supporters for pan-green candidates than those for pan-blue candidates in villages near where the major Mazu temples are located. The dominance of pan-blue factional leaders in Mazu temples seems to have alienated most of the villagers. However, pan-blue factional leaders may have continued to provide solid support to pan-blue candidates, as shown in model 3 of the 2004 election as well as in the previous case study.

Fourthly, at the other end of the political spectrum, Other Buddhists, Other Christians, and Ciji members are less likely to support President Chen, and their coefficients are significant in model 1 of the 2000 election, model 1 of the 2004 election, and model 2 of the 2004 election. The historically close connection between Taiwanese Buddhists and the KMT might have explained the political attitude of Other Buddhists and the Other Christians (mainly Mandarin-speaking Christians) who became politically active in response to the Taiwanese-speaking Presbyterian Church's support for President Chen in the 2004 election.

The statistics of the Buddha Light and Zhongtai group deviates somewhat from the previous case study, which provides solid qualitative evidence for their pro-pan-blue position. This group's political position stands in the middle of all religious groups, as demonstrated by its coefficients, which are not larger than those of Other Christians, Other Buddhists, or even the "politically neutral" Ciji. Besides, except for model 1 in the 2004 election, the groups' coefficients are insignificant, as compared to the strongly pro-pan-green reference group of other Daoists and folk religion believers. The inconsistency between the case study and the survey data in this Buddhist group seems to provide a good example of the theoretical gap between the pulpit and the pew discussed in the theoretical chapter of this book (chapter 1). The party preference of these religious leaders does not necessarily dictate those of their followers.

The most amazing finding is regarding Ciji, the single largest religious group in Taiwan. Despite the consistent effort of its paramount leader Ven. Zhengyan to claim political neutrality, its members reveal strong and consistent support for pan-blue candidates, and even more so in 2004 than in 2000. Some might attribute this to the overwhelming female membership in the group. However, even after controlling for the gender effect in the 2004 election, the group's political attitude is still in favor of the pan-blue.

Others might have predicted Ciji's pro-pan-green position, because Ven. Zhengyan is the only Taiwanese leader among the four major Buddhist organizations, and she frequently uses Taiwanese dialect to speak to her believers. Again, the statistical results contradict the prediction. After controlling for ethnicity, Ciji members still reveal their pro-pan-blue orientation in model 3 of the 2004 election.

Three possible explanations are in order. First, this is probably related to the fact that the fast growth of Ciji during the 1980s and 1990s recruited many housewives of pro-KMT politicians and businessmen. These women later on assumed middle to upper-level leadership positions in the group. A second explanation can be attributed to the fact that Ciji's rapid expansion of religious buildings and activities required the cooperation of the KMT government and politicians, which left a good impression on the Ciji members (C. Huang 2005: 5–9). Lastly, as explained in the previous case study, Ven. Zhengyan frequently espouses the virtues of obedience, meekness, peace, and harmony, which might be more consistent with the political styles of KMT candidates than that of DPP candidates (Huang 2005).

In the 2001 legislative election (table 5.4), as compared to the atheists, the pan-green political support of the Daoists and folk religion believers is significant in model 1 but not in models 2 and 3, after controlling for SES variables. This is probably due to the differences between national elections and local elections, which use the single-non-transferable-voting system that stresses local factional demarcation over political parties. Among the religious groups, again, we find that Ciji members, Other Christians, and Other Buddhists are the strongest supporters of pan-blue candidates, and their coefficients are the only significant ones in both model 1 and model 2. The coefficients of the Buddha Light/Zhongtai group continue to reveal the gap between the pulpit (religious leaders' pro-pan-blue position) and the pew (the laity's pro-pan-green position).

RELIGION AND DEMOCRATIC VALUES

For the variables of democratic values, we constructed four composite indicators: government responsibility, strong leadership, communitarian value, and assembly rights. The government responsibility indicator consisted of five questions that asked the respondent to rank the importance of the values "That all citizens have an adequate standard of living," "That government authorities respect and protect the rights of minorities," "That government authorities treat everybody equally regardless of their position in society," "That politicians take into account the view of citizens before making decisions," and "That people be given more opportunities to participate in public decision-making." The higher the score of government responsibility, the higher is the respondent's acceptance of democratic value. The reference groups are still the atheists for all beliefs, and the Other Daoist/folk religion groups for all religious groups.

Model 1 does not control for any SES variable; model 2 controls for education, age, gender, and income variables as did the previous binary logistic regression models for various elections; and model 3 adds ethnicity to the control list. Although these control variables are included in the calculation, their coefficients and variances are not reported here for the sake of simplicity: these control variables are not the focus of this book.

Table 5.5 reveals that, using the atheists as a reference group, Christians have a higher expectation of government responsibility than Buddhists do, followed by Daoists. Believers in folk religion rank the lowest. When comparing these religions, it is interesting to note that the coefficients of Daoism and folk religion become significant *after* controlling for SES variables.

With regard to religious groups, the Presbyterians (p ≤ 0.05) rank the first among all religious groups, followed by Yiguandao (p ≤ 0.05), Dharma Drum, Ciji (p ≤ 0.01), Other Christians, Buddha Light and Zhongtai, Other Buddhists, and Mazu members. After controlling for SES variables, none of the coefficients is significant, except for Ciji's. But the rank orders of these groups remain roughly the same. A common factor may explain the high scores of the Presbyterians, YGD members, and Ciji members: all of these three religious groups have intense interaction with the state to take care of socially, economically, or politically disadvantaged groups.

The strong leadership indicator includes four questions: "To a political leader, accomplishing his/her goals matters the most, regardless of the means," "A political leader will not concede if he/she believes they are in the right position, even though most people are against it," "A political leader need not tolerate the people challenging their political belief," and "A political leader will persist with his/her belief supported by the majority, regardless of the minority." The higher the score of Strong Leadership, the higher the respondent's acceptance of democratic values, that is, he/she opposes unrestrained strong leaders.

In model 1, the Daoists and folk religion believers are the least democratic among the religions, while the Buddhists and the Christians are more democratic, although only the coefficients of Daoism and folk religion are significant. In model 2 only the coefficient of Buddhism is significant, the rank orders of all the coefficients remain the same.

With regard to religious groups, the Buddha Light and Zhongtai (p ≤ 0.05) rank the highest, followed by the Presbyterians (p ≤ 0.01), Ciji (p ≤ 0.001), Yiguandao (p ≤ 0.01), Other Christians (p ≤ 0.05), Other Buddhists (p ≤ 0.05), Dharma Drum, and Mazu members. After controlling for SES variables, the rank order remains roughly the same, but only the coefficients of Ciji and the Buddha Light and Zhongtai groups are significant in both models 2 and 3.

The relatively high score of Presbyterians is consistent with the previous case study, while those of Buddha Light, Zhongtai, and Ciji are not. The previous case studies suggest that these major Buddhist organizations con-

TABLE 5.5 Beliefs, Religious Groups, and the Democratic Values of Government Responsibility and Strong Leadership in Taiwan

		GOVERNMENT RESPONSIBILITY			STRONG LEADERSHIP		
RELIGION		MODEL 1	MODEL 2	MODEL 3	MODEL 1	MODEL 2	MODEL 3
Beliefs	Daoism	.436 (.279)	**.748 (.280)	**.823 (.284)	**-.569 (.216)	-.308 (.214)	-.212 (.216)
	Buddhism	**.680 (.260)	***1.032 (.263)	***1.058 (.264)	.262 (.202)	**.540 (.202)	**.593 (.201)
	Folk Religion	.201 (.266)	*.618 (.270)	*.643 (.272)	*-.491 (.208)	-.127 (.208)	-.047 (.208)
	Christianity	*1.116 (.493)	*1.135 (.489)	*1.153 (.513)	.150 (.383)	.116 (.375)	-.158 (.393)
	Constant	***31.462 (.196)	***30.769 (.565)	***31.200 (.612)	***-14.342 (.151)	***13.656 (.434)	***13.782 (.468)
	N	1589	1585	1582	1545	1541	1538
Religious Groups	Ciji	**1.436 (.484)	*1.044 (.498)	*.946 (.501)	***1.441 (.413)	.949 (.428)	.853 (.430)
	DD	1.580 (1.371)	.700 (1.364)	.464 (.377)	.879 (1.145)	.067 (1.150)	.036 (1.149)
	Presb	*1.984 (.916)	1.217 (.926)	1.037 (.936)	*1.937 (.767)	1.258 (.783)	1.000 (.788)
	Mazu	-.890 (.642)	-.691 (.630)	-.667 (.630)	.184 (.566)	.291 (.561)	.332 (.558)
	YGD	*1.644 (.674)	.957 (.684)	.899 (.685)	**1.365 (.560)	.770 (.571)	.687 (.569)
	OTChris	.833 (.724)	.053 (.746)	-.062 (.779)	*1.245 (.607)	.500 (.629)	.006 (.653)
	OTBud	.251 (.654)	-.140 (.654)	-.183 (.656)	*1.240 (.566)	.776 (.571)	.671 (.569)
	BLZT	.509 (.998)	.393 (.994)	.336 (1.003)	**2.450 (.834)	*2.031 (.838)	*1.776 (.842)
	Constant	***31.134 (.333)	***31.169 (1.058)	***31.950 (1.255)	***13.121 (.284)	***12.335 (.899)	***12.733 (1.057)
	N	386	382	379	370	366	363

Note: Model 2 controls for SES variables; model 3 controls for ethnicity variables; model 1 coes not control for either set of variables. Numbers without parentheses are coefficients; variances are in parentheses. Reference group for belief is atheism; reference group for religious groups is the other Daoist and folk religion group.

*** p ≤ .001, ** p ≤ .01, * p ≤ .05, † p ≤ .1

tain supreme masters who might have cultivated an authoritarian culture in these organizations. One plausible explanation may point to the difference between religious and political leaders in the mind of believers. Therefore, even though religious members fully trust their religious leaders, they abhor political leaders. A more plausible explanation lies in the fact that these Buddhist organizations all provide large nonclerical charity organizations for their members to practice democratic value and behavior. They need not respect their lay superiors as they do their religious leaders.

In table 5.6, the communitarian value indicator is composed of five questions: "To be active in social or political association," "To try to understand the reasoning of people with other opinions," "To choose products for political, ethical, or environmental reasons, even if they cost a bit more," "To help people in Taiwan who are worse off than yourself," and "To help people in the rest of the world who are worse off than yourself." The higher the score of communitarian value, the higher is the respondent's level of democratic values.

Christians rank the highest among the religions in communitarian value in model 1, followed by Buddhists, Daoists, and believers in folk religions, although only the coefficients of Buddhism are significant in models 2 and 3. After controlling for the SES effects, the rank order of these religions remains the same.

Among the religious groups in Model 1, the Presbyterians (p ≤ 0.001) rank the first, followed by Yiguandao (p ≤ 0.001), Dharma Drum, Ciji (p ≤ 0.001), Buddha Light/Zhongtai, Other Buddhists, Other Christians, and Mazu believers. After controlling for SES effects, the coefficients of Presbyterians, YGD, and Ciji remain significant, and the rank order remains relatively the same. There are two sets of interesting comparisons here. The first comparison is between the Presbyterians and Other Christians. The Taiwanese Presbyterians are known for their commitment to social and political issues, which probably explains their high level of communitarian value. In contrast, most other Christians emphasize spiritual salvation and personal relations with God, which probably explains their low level of communitarian value. The second comparison is between Yiguandao and Ciji. Ciji members are well known for their devotion to community charity and disaster relief efforts. However, their community value score ranks not only behind the Presbyterians but also behind Yiguandao members. The diversity of Ciji members and the media effect probably explain this discrepancy between perception and reality.

The assembly rights is a composite indicator of three questions: "Should religious extremists be allowed to hold public meetings?" "Should people who want to overthrow the government by force be allowed to hold public meetings?" and "Should people prejudiced against any racial or ethnic group be allowed to hold public meetings?" Because of the negative implications of these questions, the composite scores are transformed into negative values

TABLE 5.6 Beliefs, Religious Groups and the Democratic Values of Communitarianism and Assembly Rights in Taiwan

		COMMUNITARIAN VALUE			ASSEMBLY RIGHTS		
RELIGION		MODEL 1	MODEL 2	MODEL 3	MODEL 1	MODEL 2	MODEL 3
Beliefs	Daoism	-.036 (.446)	.196 (.451)	.239 (.456)	-.168 (.139)	-.094 (.141)	-.108 (.143)
	Buddhism	†.803 (.415)	*.884 (.423)	*.884 (.423)	-.134 (.130)	-.044 (.132)	-.051 (.133)
	Folk Religion	-.347 (.426)	-.108 (.436)	-.159 (.437)	**-.355 (.134)	†-.252 (.137)	†-.259 (.138)
	Christianity	†1.308 (.788)	1.111 (.788)	1.262 (.854)	.278 (.248)	.294 (.248)	.301 (.261)
	Constant	***24.332 (.313)	***21.838 (.913)	***22.592 (.984)	***-9.662 (.097)	***-9.681 (.285)	***-9.742 (.309)
	N	1584	1580	1577	1498	1494	1491
Religious Groups	Ciji	***2.622 (.742)	**2.006 (.775)	*1.833 (.773)	.087 (.235)	.027 (.247)	.089 (.250)
	DD	†3.638 (2.068)	2.409 (2.079)	1.961 (2.085)	*1.607 (.663)	*1.386 (.671)	*1.522 (.675)
	Presb	***6.378 (1.382)	***5.100 (1.413)	***4.680 (1.429)	.305 (.443)	.165 (.456)	.242 (.462)
	Mazu	-.636 (.998)	-.391 (.988)	-.353 (.935)	.406 (.316)	.358 (.316)	.344 (.315)
	YGD	***3.801 (1.018)	**3.207 (1.043)	**3.078 (1.043)	.121 (.330)	.041 (.338)	.076 (.339)
	OTChris	.625 (1.078)	-.427 (1.121)	-.892 (1.193)	†.708 (.365)	.593 (.382)	.649 (.396)
	OTBud	†1.712 (1.008)	1.127 (1.020)	1.057 (1.020)	.032 (.326)	-.040 (.333)	.006 (.334)
	BLZT	†2.567 (1.505)	2.193 (1.517)	2.061 (1.527)	.726 (.517)	.812 (.523)	†.893 (.525)
	Constant	***23.505 (.504)	***20.214 (1.628)	***21.429 (1.921)	***-9.893 (.161)	***-9.829 (.524)	***-10.397 (.626)
	N	376	372	369	373	369	366

Note: Model 2 controls for SES variables; model 3 adds ethnicity to the control list; model 1 does not control for either set of variables. Numbers without parentheses are coefficients; variances are in parentheses. Reference group for belief is atheism; reference group for religious groups is the other Daoist and folk Religion group.
*** p ≤ .001, ** p ≤ .01, * p ≤ .05, † p ≤ .1

so that the higher the score of assembly rights, the higher the respondent's democratic values.

In model 1, again, Christians rank the highest among all religious groups in supporting assembly rights, followed by Buddhists and Daoists; folk religion believers rank the lowest, and only their coefficient is significant. In models 2 and 3, none of the coefficients is significant, but the rank order remains the same.

Among the religious groups, Dharma Drum ranks the first in assembly rights, followed by Buddha Light/Zhongtai, Other Christians, Mazu believers, Presbyterians, Yiguandao, Ciji, and Other Buddhists, although only the coefficient of Dharma Drum is significant in all three models. After controlling for SES effects, the rank order remains relatively the same. The high score of Dharma Drum believers can be attributed to the relative equality between clergy and laity in the religious group's vast non-clerical organizations.

RELIGION AND DEMOCRATIC BEHAVIOR

For the variables of Democratic Behavior, we constructed three composite indicators of information, voice, and presidential information. The information indicator consists of four questions: "On average, how often do you read the political content of a newspaper?" "On average, how often do you watch political news on television?" "On average, how often do you listen to political news on the radio?" and "On average, how often do you watch or listen to political call-in programs?" The respondent could answer "everyday," "three or four times a week," "once or twice a week," "fewer than once or twice a week," or "never." Other answers are coded as missing. Because of the negative implications of these questions, the information scores are transformed into negative values so that the higher the score of information, the higher the level of democratic behavior is (table 5.7). We still used the atheists as a reference group for all beliefs, and the other Daoist/folk religion for all religious groups.

Among the religions, as compared to the atheists, Christianity ranks the highest in information, followed by Buddhism, Daoism, and folk religion, although only the coefficient of Christianity is significant. After controlling for SES effects, however, the rank order remains the same but the coefficients of Christianity, Buddhism, and Daoism (in model 3) become significant.

Among the religious groups in model 1, Presbyterians ($p \leq 0.01$) rank the highest, followed by Buddha Light/Zhongtai ($p \leq 0.05$), Dharma Drum, Ciji ($p \leq 0.001$), other Christians, Yiguandao, other Buddhists, and Mazu believers. After controlling for SES variables, the rank order remains roughly the same. But it is somewhat surprising to note that in models 2 and 3, the coefficients of Presbyterians are no longer significant and become smaller than that of Buddha Light/Zhongtai. It seems that the relatively strong political activism (pro-pan-blue) of the two Buddhist groups' charismatic leaders has

TABLE 5.7 Beliefs, Religious Groups and Democratic Behavior Regarding Information and Voice

RELIGION		INFORMATION			VOICE		
		MODEL 1	MODEL 2	MODEL 3	MODEL 1	MODEL 2	MODEL 3
Beliefs	Daoism	-.149 (.300)	†.539 (.280)	*.685 (.284)	-.216 (.227)	.217 (.217)	.283 (.220)
	Buddhism	.140 (.279)	**.759 (.262)	**.824 (.262)	-.054 (.212)	.326 (.204)	†.360 (.204)
	Folk Religion	-.373 (.285)	.364 (.269)	†.451 (.270)	-.518 (.216)	-.035 (.210)	.035 (.210)
	Christianity	**1.504 (.532)	**1.325 (.491)	*1.101 (.518)	**1.240 (.400)	**1.171 (.379)	**1.218 (.398)
	Constant	***-13.352 (.211)	***-17.998 (.566)	***-17.503 (.611)	***-7.255 (.159)	***-19.887 (.440)	***-19.807 (.474)
	N	1660	1656	1653	1618	1614	1611
Religious Groups	Ciji	***1.838 (.539)	**1.374 (.530)	**1.293 (.534)	*1.247 (.435)	†.776 (.441)	†.750 (.441)
	DD	2.182 (1.547)	.577 (1.471)	.403 (1.486)	**3.328 (1.230)	†2.149 (1.207)	†2.240 (1.205)
	Presb	**3.249 (1.032)	†1.716 (.997)	1.687 (1.010)	**2.261 (.822)	1.281 (.819)	1.265 (.823)
	Mazu	-.627 (.716)	-.504 (.672)	-.468 (.673)	.736 (.575)	.719 (.556)	.756 (.552)
	YGD	.680 (.750)	.248 (.727)	.172 (.729)	.781 (.604)	.330 (.603)	.253 (.601)
	OTChris	†1.397 (.794)	.408 (.781)	.347 (.825)	***2.239 (.632)	*1.563 (.640)	*1.336 (.667)
	OTBud	.221 (.750)	.083 (.717)	-.144 (.719)	.328 (.611)	-.059 (.601)	-.180 (.600)
	BLZT	*2.397 (1.124)	**2.655 (1.071)	*2.463 (1.082)	**2.543 (.895)	**2.523 (.879)	*2.211 (.882)
	Constant	***-13.897 (.369)	***-17.806 (1.118)	***-16.642 (1.317)	***-17.614 (.296)	***-19.474 (.936)	***-18.938 (1.098)
	N	394	390	387	384	380	377

Note: Model 2 controls for SES variables; model 3 controls for ethnicity variables; model 1 does not control for either set of variables. Numbers without parentheses are coefficients; variances are in parentheses. Reference group for belief is atheism; reference group for religious groups is the other Daoist and folk religion group.

*** $p \leq .001$, ** $p \leq .01$, * $p \leq .05$, † $p \leq .1$

encouraged their members to stay informed about political news. The statistics seems to suggest that they are more motivated than the Presbyterians to obtain political news.

The voice indicator is composed of five questions, asking the respondent how often they conduct the following actions: "Signed a petition," "Took part in a demonstration," "Attended a political meeting or rally," "Contacted, or attempted to contact, a politician or a civil servant to express your view," and "Contacted or appeared in the media to express your views." The respondent chooses among the answers of "Did the action in the past year," "Did the action before the past year," "Will do the action, even if I never have before," and "Will not do the action, even if I never have before." Because of the negative implications of these questions, the voice scores are transformed into negative values so that the higher the score of voice, the higher the level of democratic behavior is.

In Model 1, Christianity ($p \leq 0.01$) ranks the highest among all religions, followed by Buddhism, Daoism, and folk religion ($p \leq 0.05$). In models 2 and 3, the rank orders remain the same, but only the coefficient of Christianity is significant.

Among the religious groups in model 1, Dharma Drum ($p \leq 0.01$) ranks the highest, followed by Buddha Light/Zhongtai ($p \leq 0.01$), Presbyterians ($p \leq 0.01$), other Christians ($p \leq 0.001$), Ciji ($p \leq 0.01$), Yiguandao, Mazu, and other Buddhists. After controlling for SES variables, the rank orders remain largely the same, but only the coefficients of other Christians and Buddha Light/Zhongtai remain significant. Members of Buddha Light/Zhongtai demonstrate again their relatively high level of democratic behavior, even surpassing that of the Presbyterians and Other Christians. We attribute it again to these religious groups' political activism from which believers learn democratic values and behavior.

In table 5.8, the presidential information indicator includes three questions: "During the presidential election, did you read election bulletins?" "During the presidential election, did you read candidates' flyers or newspaper advertising?" and "During the presidential election, did you watch the televised presidential debates?" The respondent could answer yes or no. The higher the score of presidential information, the higher the level of democratic behavior is.

In model 1, Christianity ($p \leq 0.01$) ranks first among all religions, followed by Daoism ($p \leq 0.05$), Buddhism, and folk religion. After controlling for SES effects in models 2 and 3, the rank orders remain the same and all the coefficients become significant. The impact of religion on presidential information seems to be the strongest among all indicators of democratic values and behavior.

However, at the level of religious groups, none of the coefficients is significant in all models. The rank orders of all models also vary wider than those in the previous tests. Therefore, it is improper to make any tentative conclusions here.

TABLE 5.8 Beliefs, Religious Groups, and Democratic Behavior Regarding Presidential Information in Taiwan

RELIGION		PRESIDENTIAL INFORMATION		
		MODEL 1	MODEL 2	MODEL 3
Beliefs	Daoism	*.203 (.086)	***.346(.084)	***.373(.085)
	Buddhism	.105 (.080)	**.235 (.078)	**.246 (.079)
	Folk Religion	.021 (.082)	*.181 (.080)	*.196 (.081)
	Christianity	**.423 (.152)	**.389 (.146)	**.397 (.154)
	Constant	***1.472 (.060)	**.515 (.169)	***.635 (.183)
	N	1676	1672	1669
Religious Groups	Ciji	.169 (.145)	.036 (.148)	.001 (.149)
	DD	.133 (.417)	-.230 (.411)	-.296 (.413)
	Presb	.335 (.278)	.026 (.279)	.031 (.282)
	Mazu	-.282 (.191)	-.269 (.186)	-.258 (.186)
	YGD	.330 (.202)	.172 (.203)	.145 (.204)
	OTChris	.185 (.212)	-.035 (.215)	-.113 (.227)
	OTBud	-.211 (.198)	†-.330 (.197)	†-.357 (.197)
	BLZT	.276 (.303)	.284 (.299)	.226 (.302)
	Constant	***1.724 (.100)	***1.239 (.312)	***1.530 (.367)
	N	399	395	392

Note: Model 2 controls for SES variables; model 3 controls for ethnicity variables; model 1 does not control for either set of variables. Numbers without parentheses are coefficients; variances are in parentheses. Reference group for belief is atheism; reference group for religious groups is the other Daoist and folk religion group.
*** $p \le .001$, ** $p \le .01$, * $p \le .05$, † $p \le .1$

Finally, the implications of the aforementioned statistical findings need to be balanced against what is not shown in these statistical tables. Two additional sets of tests were conducted. Using the same statistical procedure of factor analysis as in the previous section, a citizen duty variable is composed of three value-related questions asking the respondents to rate the importance of 1) always voting in elections, 2) never trying to evade taxes, and 3) always obeying laws and regulations. A democratic behavior variable, Presidential Campaign, is composed of three questions asking the respondents: during the presidential election, 1) did you participate in any assembly or party held for candidates? 2) did you join any candidate's campaign organization? and

3) did you remind your friends and relatives to vote for a specific candidate? Because these two important variables of democratic values and behavior fail to find significant differences among beliefs and religious groups, we can only conclude that religion makes a difference in many, but not all, dimensions of democratic values and behavior.

COMPARISON OF TAIWANESE BELIEVERS

At both the belief and belonging levels of analysis, religion seems to have a significant impact on believers' party preference. In terms of both the 2000 and 2004 presidential elections, Daoists and folk religion believers tended to favor pan-green candidates, while Christians and Buddhists were divided between pan-green and pan-blue candidates. In terms of the 2001 legislative election, Daoists and folk religion believers still tended to favor pan-green candidates, although the significance levels of their coefficients dropped to insignificance when SES variables are controlled.

Among the religious groups, other Christians, Ciji, and other Buddhists tended to favor pan-blue candidates in the 2000 and 2004 presidential elections, with varying degrees of significance levels for their coefficients. The coefficients of the Presbyterians, Mazu believers, Dharma Drum believers, and YGD believers reveal their pro-pan-green orientation and are not significantly different from the reference group of other Daoists and folk religion believers who strongly favor pan-green candidates. The coefficients of Buddha Light/Zhongtai do not support the general impression that their members are pro-pan-blue. The party preference of their religious leaders does not necessarily dictate those of their believers.

Table 5.9 summarizes the rank orders of all beliefs and religious groups by their scores of four democratic value indicators and three democratic behavior indicators. We use the model 2 scores of indicators, because they are the more accurate presentation of the relationships between religion and democracy than the other two models. Model 2 controls for the effects of education, age, gender, and income, but not ethnicity.

Based on this table, we reach the following conclusions.[8] As compared to atheists, Christians acquire the highest scores of democratic values and democratic behavior among all religions; Buddhists rank second; Daoists, third, and folk religion believers, last. These findings are consistent with previous case studies that revealed relatively high levels of democratic theology and democratic ecclesiology for Taiwanese Christianity and low levels for Daoism and folk religion.

The relative high levels of Buddhist democratic values and behavior are somewhat inconsistent with the previous case study. We attribute them to the dominance of humanistic Buddhism in Taiwanese Buddhism, which provides a large space for democratic learning in nonclerical organizations.

TABLE 5.9 Beliefs, Religious Groups, Democratic Values, and Democratic Behavior

RELIGION		DEMOCRATIC VALUES				DEMOCRATIC BEHAVIOR		
		GR	SL	CV	AR	IN	VO	PI
Beliefs	Daoism	3**	4	3	3	3	3	2***
	Buddhism	2***	1**	2	2	2**	2	3**
	Folk Rel	4*	3	4	4†	4	4	4*
	Chris	1*	2	1	1	1**	1**	1**
Religious Groups	Ciji	2*	3*	5**	7	3**	5†	
	DD	4	8	3	1*	4	2†	
	Presb	1	2	1***	5	2†	4	
	Mazu	8	7	7	4	8	6	
	YGD	3	5	2	6	6	7	
	OTChris	6	6	8	3	5	3*	
	OTBud	7	4	6	8	7	8	
	BLZT	5	1*	4	2	1**	1**	

Note:Numbers are ranks. Blanks are inconclusive ranks due to non-significant coefficients. GR: government responsibility, SL: strong leadership, CV: communitarian value, AR: assembly rights, IN: information, VO: voice, PI: presidential information. *** $p \le .001$, ** $p \le .01$, * $p \le .05$, † $p \le .1$

Among the religious groups, as compared to other Daoists and folk religion believers, Presbyterians have the highest level of democratic values, followed by Buddha Light/Zhongtai members, while Mazu believers and other Buddhists have the lowest level of democratic values. For simplicity's sake, it is not necessary to make a comparison among other religious groups whose scores rank in the middle. The high scores of the Presbyterians are consistent with previous case study revealing their strong development of democratic theology and ecclesiology. The scores of the Mazu believers and Other Buddhists are consistent with previous case studies as well, due to their low development of democratic theology and ecclesiology. Somewhat surprising is the case of Buddha Light and Zhongtai members. We may attribute it to the political activism of these two religious groups, which provides opportunities to learn democratic values. Furthermore, the internal democratic reforms Ven. Xingyun has introduced in the past two decades may have helped to cultivate democratic values among his members.

In terms of democratic behavior, members of Buddha Light and Zhong-tai rank the first, trailed by Dharma Drum members and Presbyterians, while Mazu believers and other Buddhists remain at the lowest level of democratic behavior. The cases of the Buddha Light and Zhongtai, the Presbyterians, Mazu believers, and other Buddhists are consistent with the discussion in the previous paragraph. The relatively high scores of Dharma Drum members can be attributed to its large nonclerical organizations, which provide plenty of opportunity to learn democratic values and behavior.

Somewhat surprising is the relatively low scores of other Christians, given the fact that Christians score higher than other religious believers in the upper half of table 5.9. As explained in the case study, most of the non-Presbyterian Christians started their democratization after 1987. Old values and behavior learned during the authoritarian rule might be hard to forget.

COMPARING TAIWANESE AND KOREAN BELIEVERS

The above findings about the democratic value and behavior of Taiwan-ese Christians, the Presbyterians especially, bear strong similarities to their Korean counterparts. According to the Asian Barometer data set,[9] the major religions in Taiwan are folk religions (39.9%), Buddhism (24.5%), Daoism (11.1%), Protestantism (5.7%), and Catholicism (2.5%); another 15.6% of the respondents do not identify with any religion. In South Korea, the major religions are Buddhism (24.4%), Protestantism (18.5%), Catholicism (8.1%), and folk religions (0.5%), while 48.5% do not identify with any religion.

Using a somewhat different research design than this chapter's, Kuo (2006) conducts statistical tests on the Asian Barometer data set combining Korean and Taiwanese cases, and reaches the following conclusions. First, before the control variable of country (Taiwan = 1, Korea = 0) is introduced into the equations, Christians tend to have higher levels of trust in NGOs, trust in people, interest in politics, and support for representation than all other religious believers do. However, second, Christians do not surpass all other religious believers in the variables of formal and private groups, trust in public institutions, and dislike strong leaders. Christians tend to join fewer formal and private groups than Buddhists and folk religion/Daoism believers do. Third, Buddhists are not significantly different from Christians in their democratic commitment. Lastly, although folk religion/Dao-ism believers rank significantly lower than Christians do in the variables of trust in NGOs, trust in news and televisions, trust in people, interest in politics, and support for representation, they rank significantly higher than Christians do in formal and private groups, trust in public institutions, and dislike of strong leaders.

These statistical comparisons among Taiwanese religions as well as between Taiwanese believers and Korean believers demonstrate that Christians tend to have higher democratic value and behavior than other religious believers do. However, there are more complicated stories underneath this general finding. Other religions also embed in their religious doctrines and lives strong elements of democratic value and behavior. Only after examining both the qualitative and quantitative data analyzed in previoius chapters can we generate balanced views about the relationship between religion and democracy in Taiwan. On this note, we turn to the concluding chapter of this book.

CHAPTER 6

Conclusion

At the beginning of this book, several theoretical and empirical questions were raised concerning the relationships between religion and democracy in Taiwan. Does religion matter in Taiwan's democracy? If religion matters at all in Taiwanese democracy, do Taiwanese religions contribute to or hinder the establishment and consolidation of democracy? Do different religions and religious groups support different political parties? Do various religions and religious groups have varying support for democratic values and behavior? And are Christians more democratic than other believers of traditional Chinese religions?

Based on the previous chapters, the general answers to these questions are: Religions do matter in Taiwan's democracy. However, their impacts on democracy are affected by the types of religions and religious organizations. Some contributed to the establishment and consolidation of democracy, some retarded it, and others did not matter. The explanations lie in their varying political theology, ecclesiology, and interaction with the state. Taiwanese Christians, particularly the Presbyterians, have made a disproportional contribution to the democracy.

This is not to argue that the establishment and consolidation of Taiwanese democracy is determined by religious factors alone. Other factors, such as U.S. pressure, the persistence of the opposition movement, the division within the KMT, and the rise of political consciousness of the middle class as a result of economic development might be more important than religious factors were. However, the findings of this book demonstrate that religions and religious groups in Taiwan continually influence the value base and the actual operation of democracy through their political theology, ecclesiology, and interaction with the state. These religious factors can be critical to democratic development in the short term (e.g., at such a competitive national

115

election like the 2000 and 2004 presidential elections) as well as in the long-term (e.g., citizen's support for democracy), as they had been in Latin American countries, Turkey, Algeria, South Korea, the Philippines, and even the United States in the twenty-first century.

SUMMARY AND COMPARISON

The Chinese heritage of Taiwanese Buddhist theology, ecclesiology, and interaction with the state has made a mixed contribution to democratization. With the exception of Ven. Zhaohui and a few liberal Buddhist scholars, Taiwanese Buddhists have developed a primitive democratic theology based on humanistic Buddhism mixed with Confucian ideals. Their religious organizations rely very much upon supreme mastership and clerical hierarchy. However, humanistic Buddhism has contributed to the establishment of vast nonclergy organizations, which create a hospitable milieu for believers to learn democratic values and behavior. During the martial law period, leaders of the major Buddhist organizations either actively supported the KMT government or took the extreme position of religion-state separation. However, political democratization has generated a significant impact on Buddhist organizations in terms of democratic theology, ecclesiology, and interaction with the state, again, to differing degrees.

During the early martial law period, Buddha Light Mountain (*Foguangshan*) was relatively weak in democratic theology because of its nonpolitical humanistic Buddhism. Its ecclesiology was based on supreme mastership, the superiority of clergy over laity, and a centralized decision-making system. It actively supported the KMT government. After the lifting of martial law, some democratic theological arguments were developed to allow positive interaction between Buddhism and the state. While the supreme mastership and centralization persisted, democratic reforms were introduced to the FGS system to reduce inequality among clergy and between clergy and laity. After the failure of supporting an independent candidate in the 2000 presidential election, FGS has gradually diversified its political connections with different political parties instead of concentrating on pan-blue parties.

Ciji did not exhibit significant differences in democratic theology and ecclesiology before and after the lifting of martial law. It takes an extremely isolationist view toward the relationship between Buddhism and the state. The ecclesiology is based on supreme mastership and centralized decision-making. Because Ciji has only a small number of clergy and lay believers dominate the organization, the controversy about equality between clergy and laity is not serious in this organization. To some extent, lay believers are able to learn some democratic values and behavior in this otherwise authoritarian organization.

Dharma Drum Mountain (*Fagushan*) followed the nonpolitical humanistic Buddhist theology and an isolationist practice toward the KMT government before 1987. Its ecclesiology was based on supreme mastership, the superiority of clergy over laity, and centralized decision-making. After 1987, some democratic theology has developed and more active interaction between the organization and the state has occurred. More than their counterparts at Ciji are, lay believers in Dharma Drum are able to learn democratic values and behavior through their leadership in the non-clerical organizations, where lay believers have an equal, if not superior, status over the clergy.

Zhongtai Zen Monastery did not develop any theological statement about democracy either before or after 1987. Its ecclesiology continues to build on supreme mastership, the superiority of the clergy over the laity, and a high degree of centralization. Its consistent support for the KMT, including in the 2000 and 2004 presidential elections, makes it unique among other Taiwanese Buddhist organizations, which have shifted toward political neutrality during the democratization process.

Although constituting a small percentage (about 5%) of the total population, Taiwanese Christians have exerted a disproportional influence on Taiwan's democratization process. This influence is built on their democratic theology, ecclesiology and interaction with the state, which distinguish them from other religious groups as well as among themselves. By the time Christianity was introduced to Taiwan by missionaries, their home countries had established democracies. Their theology and ecclesiology had incorporated various democratic elements, such as the priesthood of all believers, human rights, and checks and balances against the sinful nature of human beings. During the martial law era, most Christians, with the notable exception of the Presbyterians, were either supportive of the KMT government or abstained from political controversies. However, Christian theology and ecclesiology equipped them with differing degrees of exposure to democratic values and behavior. After the lifting of martial law, Taiwanese Christianity has further experienced rapid democratization in terms of its theology, ecclesiology, and interaction with the state. The well-articulated political theology, increased political activism, and organizational power of these Christian organizations enable them to continually contribute to Taiwan's democracy.

In the late 1960s, Presbyterians constructed a comprehensive democratic theology composed of human rights, political participation, democratic institutions and Taiwanese nationalism. They followed Western Presbyterians in establishing a democratic ecclesiology based on the relative equality between clergy and laity. Neither supreme mastership nor centralization existed in the religious system. Because of their close connection with the opposition movement, they were critical of the KMT government before 1987, but supportive of Taiwanese presidents afterward. The Presbyterians' devotion to Taiwan independence, however, has antagonized other Mandarin-speaking denominations.

Baptists adopted a passive isolationist view toward the state during the martial law period. Because of American influence, their ecclesiology revealed a high degree of local autonomy and different forms of clergy-laity relationships across local churches. In the post-1987 period, Baptists have developed a more democratic theology toward church-state relationships and the clergy have gradually lost their slim superiority over the laity. Since many of their members are public employees or mainland Chinese and their descendants, the Baptists tend to favor pan-blue parties.

Local Church has opted for an extremely isolationist view toward the state both before and after the lifting of martial law. It had supreme masters who also respected local autonomy and equality between clergy and laity. When the supreme leader passed away in 1997, the ecclesiology became even more democratic.

Daoism and folk religions are the most diversified of all Taiwanese religions. In many cases, the distinction between the two religions is hard to demarcate. However, they share many attributes in democratic theology, ecclesiology, and interaction with the state. Daoist political theology is built on the principle of cosmic harmony. Rulers are supposed to promote moral values and safeguard their subjects, while subjects should obey the rulers and perform assigned duties. Although seemingly a mutual obligation, Daoist political theology stresses the subject's loyalty more than the ruler's responsibility. Reinforcing its political conservatism is the Daoist ideal of the amalgamation of Daoism and the state. Although the Daoist eschatological theology provides a potential theological justification for revolution, its ultimate goal is to establish rule by a moral emperor rather than a democracy.

Taiwanese Daoism has developed rudimentary democratic elements in the past fifty years. Monastic Daoist clergy constitute a minority in Taiwanese Daoism, while nonmonastic clergy are not much different from ordinary people except when performing religious rituals. Except for a few Complete Perfection temples, most Daoist temples in Taiwan are not governed by clergy but by lay believers who acquire local social, economic, and political prestige. There is no central authority or sacred text to adjudicate new revelations or interpretations. The interpretive power of divine revelation falls into the hands of ordinary priests and lay believers. Daoist temples are autonomous from one another and have not established nationwide, centralized, religious empires as other Buddhist groups have. After 1949, Taiwanese Daoism escaped the government's attention due to its decentralized nature. Due to their conservative political theology, Taiwanese Daoists were supportive of the KMT before 1987. As the pace of democratization accelerated in the 1990s, however, many DPP politicians joined the governing committees of Daoist temples and rapidly reduced the KMT influence. Even with a DPP minority in the governing committees, most Daoist temples have decided to maintain political neutrality during elections in order to maximize donations and worshipers from both camps. Even when the governing committees of Daoist temples intend to influence the political attitude of believers, the effect is minimal at best. Worshipers at a particular temple are not equivalent to members at this temple. Worshipers come from all over Taiwan and tend to come only on specific occasions.

A representative case of the relationship between Daoism and democracy is Yiguandao (Way of Unity; YGD). YGD political theology is quite flexible toward changing political realities. It can be pro-government, antigovernment, or neutral, depending on the leaders' religious interpretation of the heavenly mandate. Although rich in political discourse, the YGD tribulation theology is far from a democratic theology. It does not address the importance of human rights, nor does it support checks and balances among governmental branches. Heavenly mandate plus a wise emperor is regarded as the best form of governance for both YGD and the nation.

The ecclesiology of YGD reveals both democratic and undemocratic elements. On the democratic side, YGD does not have the problem of the superiority of clergy over laity, because there are rarely any clergy. Each branch is highly independent from each other and from YGD headquarters. But on the undemocratic side, YGD ecclesiology indoctrinates its believers with authoritarian and theocratic values.

It has been a long march for YGD from a banned "evil cult" to a legalized religion with one of its believers becoming a two-term president of Taiwan. It has demonstrated the flexibility of YGD's political strategy under different political regimes. A close association with the dominant regime can generate religious dividends in the form of expanded religious organization (as in pre-1945 China), but it also invites political revenge once the authoritarian regime changes hands (from 1945 to 1987). Only when the regime becomes democratic after 1987 can YGD become a fully autonomous and self-reliant political force.

Another case of a Daoist relationship between religion and democracy is the Mazu belief, although it is often regarded as a folk religion as well. The Mazu belief says very little about politics. It does not address the issues of human rights, equality, and democratic decisions at the theological level. The Mazu belief could have developed a very democratic ecclesiology, if family elders, local elites, local factions, and gangsters had not intervened in their democratic structures. Lay believers hold an equal, if not higher, status than clergy in the liturgy and in major decisions of a temple. Temple leaders are usually elected according to a democratic procedure, but are guided by traditional, factional, or gangster norms. Most of the temples retain a high level of autonomy in relation to one another, but this autonomy does not necessarily impede large-scale cooperation on Mazu holidays. However, the loose connection between lay believers and temple leaders, as well as among Mazu temples, makes it extremely difficult for the Mazu belief to become a significant political force at the national level. In terms of interaction with the state, many large Mazu temples tend to support KMT candidates due to the close relationships between local factions and the KMT. During the democratization process, DPP politicians found their way onto the boards of trustees at Mazu temples and turned these temples toward political neutrality. Furthermore, due to the loose connection between temple leaders and worshipers, it is not clear whether worshipers would follow the political cues of temple leaders.

The preceding summary of Taiwan's major religions and religious groups offers a comprehensive and systematic description of the relationship between religion and the state during Taiwan's democratization. However, we do not know whether or not these case studies are representative of ordinary believers. Furthermore, we do not know the relative positions of these religions and religious groups compared to one another in terms of democratic values and behavior. Does one religion or religious group tilt toward one party or the other? Are believers in one religion or religious group more democratic than their counterparts in other religions or religious groups? Or, could each religion and religious group be more democratic in certain dimensions of democratic values and behavior but not in other dimensions?

Chapter 5 provided statistical answers to these questions. At both the belief (religion) and belonging (religious groups) levels of analysis, religion seems to have a significant impact on believers' party preference. In terms of both the 2000 and 2004 presidential elections, Daoists and folk religion believers tend to favor pan-green candidates, while Christians and Buddhists are divided between pan-green and pan-blue candidates. In terms of the 2001 legislative election, Daoists and folk religion believers still tend to favor pan-green candidates. These statistical findings are inconsistent with previous case studies that implied a pro-pan-blue orientation due to their conservative political theology and the KMT-dominated governing boards of these temples. The theoretical argument about the gap between the pulpit and the pew in a democratic environment is confirmed by the party preferences of ordinary adherents to Daoism and folk religions.

Among the religious groups, Other Christians, Ciji, and other Buddhists tend to favor pan-blue candidates in the 2000 and 2004 presidential elections. The coefficients of the Presbyterians, Mazu believers, Dharma Drum believers, and YGD believers reveal their pro-pan-green orientation and are not significantly different from the reference group of other Daoists and folk religion believers who strongly favor pan-green candidates. The coefficients of Buddha Light/Zhongtai do not support the general impression that their members are strongly pro-pan-blue. The party preference of their religious leaders does not necessarily dictate those of their believers—another example of the gap between the pulpit and the pew.

Chapter 5 also compares different religions and religious groups in terms of their democratic values and democratic behavior. As compared to atheists, Christians acquire the highest scores of democratic values and democratic behavior among all religions; Buddhists rank second; Daoists, third, and folk religion believers, last. These findings are consistent with previous case studies revealing the relatively high levels of democratic theology and democratic ecclesiology in Taiwanese Christianity, and low levels in Daoism and folk religions.

The relative high levels of Buddhist democratic values and behavior are somewhat inconsistent with the previous case studies. We attribute it to the dominance of the theology of humanistic Buddhism in Taiwanese Buddhism, which provides a large space for democratic learning in non-clerical organizations.

Among the religious groups, Presbyterians have the highest level of democratic values, followed by Buddha Light/Zhongtai members, while Mazu believers and other Buddhists have the lowest level of democratic values. For simplicity's sake, it is not necessary to compare other religious groups whose scores rank in the middle. The high scores of the Presbyterians are consistent with the case study that revealed their strong devotion to democratic theology and ecclesiology. The scores of the Mazu believers and other Buddhists are consistent with case studies as well, due to their low commitment to democratic theology and ecclesiology. Somewhat surprising are the cases of Buddha Light and Zhongtai members. We may attribute them to the political activism of these two religious groups, which provides opportunities to learn democratic values. Furthermore, the internal democratic reforms Ven. Xingyun introduced in the past two decades may have helped cultivate democratic values in his members.

In terms of democratic behavior, members of Buddha Light and Zhongtai rank first, trailed by Dharma Drum members and Presbyterians, while Mazu believers and Other Buddhists remain at the lowest level of democratic behavior. The cases of Buddha Light and Zhongtai, Presbyterians, Mazu believers, and other Buddhists are consistent with the discussion in the preceding paragraph. The relatively high scores of Dharma Drum members can be attributed to its large nonclerical organizations, which provide plenty of opportunity to learn democratic values and behavior.

Somewhat surprising are the relatively low scores of Other Christians, given the fact that Christians score higher than other religious believers in the upper half of Table 5.9. As explained in the case study, most non-Presbyterian Christians began to appreciate democratic values and behaviors only after 1987. Old values and behavior learned during the authoritarian rule may be hard to forget.

METHODOLOGICAL, THEORETICAL, AND PRACTICAL IMPLICATIONS

At the methodological level, this book points out the importance of combining both case study and statistical methods in studying Taiwanese religions. Most of the current studies on Taiwanese religions rely exclusively on case studies, including scripture study, document analysis, and interviews with clergy and lay leaders. Among these case studies, many concentrate on a particular religion or denomination. Although these case studies enrich our understanding of Taiwanese religions, they do not generate readymade comparisons among religions or denominations to give the reader a general picture of major Taiwanese religions. Furthermore, we are not sure whether the interview data or the documents produced by religious elites accurately reflect the thinking or behavior of the ordinary believers. Are we studying Taiwanese religions in the texts, in the minds of religious leaders, or in totality?

By combining both case study and statistical methods, this book suggests that these three research foci are not necessarily coherent; there can be important and surprising differences among them. For instance, despite the political neutrality position meticulously elaborated and enforced by Ciji supreme leader Ven. Zhenyan, Ciji members actually are strong supporters of pan-blue political candidates. By contrast, despite the clear pan-blue position of the leaders of Buddha Light and Zhongtai, their followers are divided between the two political camps. Finally, despite its exposure to Confucian authoritarian culture for two thousand years, Taiwanese Buddhism has cultivated relatively strong democratic values and behavior in its believers, sometimes even more than non-Presbyterian Christians have.

At the theoretical level, this book has demonstrated that the construction of both democratic theology and democratic ecclesiology is critical to the expansion of democratic values and behavior among believers. Current studies of the relationship between religion and democracy seem to put too much emphasis on theology and too little on ecclesiology in which believers can learn and practice (anti-)democratic values and behavior. Influenced by democratic theology and democratic ecclesiology when Christianity was imported to Taiwan, Taiwanese Christians rank the highest among all religious believers in terms of democratic values and democratic behavior. The native Chinese religions of Daoism and folk religion rank the lowest, due to their slow development of democratic theology and ecclesiology. Buddhism performs better than Daoism or folk religion in democratic values and democratic behavior because of Taiwanese Buddhism's emphasis on humanistic Buddhism and its heavy reliance on lay believers in its vast nonclerical organizations, where believers can learn democratic values and behavior.

At the practical level, the analysis of religious groups further highlights the importance of constructing both democratic theology and ecclesiology within religious organizations in order to contribute to the nation's democratic consolidation. Within the Taiwanese Christian community, Presbyterians perform much better than other Christians in democratic values and behavior. Within the Taiwanese Buddhist community, Buddha Light, Zhongtai, and Dharma Drum believers do better than other Buddhists and non-Presbyterian Christians in terms of democratic values.

Lastly, both the qualitative and quantitative studies of this book demonstrate that democracy is a multidimensional concept, which different beliefs and religious groups may partially integrate into their theology and ecclesiology. After the Second Vatican Council, Catholicism dramatically changed its political theology from one of antidemocratic to pro-democratic and inspired democratic movements in Eastern Europe and Latin America in the 1980s (Casanova 1994; Gill 1998). Specialists in Islam have provided both qualitative and quantitative data to reject the common impression that Muslims are intrinsically anti-democratic. Instead, they claim that the establishment of an Islamic democracy is a likely option for Muslim countries (Tessler 2002: 337–354; Tessler, Konold, and Reif 2004: 184–216). In the case of Taiwan, although Mazu and other Buddhists rank relatively low in democratic values and behavior, they are not the lowest all the time by all indicators. By contrast, Taiwanese Christians are more democratic than other Chinese religions on many, but not all, dimensions of democracy. The introduction of democratic theology and democratic ecclesiology could be tailored to the particular strengths and weaknesses of various religious groups. It can be initiated from the religious leaders (e.g., Buddha Light), from the lay believers (e.g., the Baptists), or from both (e.g., the Presbyterians). Either way, traditional religions will be able to make a significant contribution to the consolidation of a multireligious democracy in Taiwan.

In conclusion, both concepts of religion and democracy are multidimensional, allowing opportunities for mutual elucidation instead of mutual exclusion. Secularization theorists have underestimated the adaptability of religions to democratic values and behavior in different dimensions, while the modernization school assumes a naïve positive relationship between the existence of civic organization and democracy. This book demonstrates that the relationship is highly contingent upon the internal attributes of civic organizations. If civic organizations do not enthusiastically embrace democratic ideas, and if they do not practice democracy within the organization, they may be irrelevant or even harmful to democratization. As Vincent Ostrom (1997: 3) has correctly argued, "not only are democratic societies constructed around the essential place of citizens in those societies, but they cannot be maintained without the knowledge, moral integrity, skill, and intelligibility of citizens in the cultivation of those societies." The practical implication of this book is that Taiwan's democratic consolidation requires scholars, theologians, and activist laity to work with these religious groups to develop democratic theology and ecclesiology. Without a solid democratic foundation built up within these religious groups, which comprise about 90% of the population, the democratic consolidation process in Taiwan will likely be a bumpy and protracted one.

Notes

1. INTRODUCTION

1. Various reports from *Taiwan Daily News*, 10 March 2004; *China Times*, 10 March 2004, http://taiwantt.org.tw/books/cryingtaiwan8/200403/20040310 .htm, *BBC News*, 10 March 2004, http://news.bbc.co.uk/hi/chinese/news/newid_ 3497000/3497722.stm, 10 March 2004.

2. Various reports from the attendants of the convention, *ETtoday*, 27 May 2006, http://www.ettoday.com/2006/05/27/10844–19456671.htm; and *Central News*, 27 May 2006, http://www.gov.tw/news/cna/politics/news/2006, 27 May 2006.

3. One can argue that secularization does not necessarily lead to democracy, either. The separation of state and church from the 15th century to the mid-18th century helped establish and consolidate absolutist states. Not until after the Enlightenment was secularization regarded as a critical element of democracy (Casanova 1994: 15–21). Talal Asad (2003: 8) correctly points out that in the secularization history of Christianity and Islam, "a secular state does not guarantee toleration; it puts into play different structures of ambition and fear."

4. For counterarguments, see Hall and Ames (1987); Fox (1997); Fukuyama (1995); Moody (1996); Tu (2000).

5. For pioneering works on the role of Christians (particularly Presbyterians) in Taiwan's democratization, see Rubinstein (1991) and Cohen (1988, chap. 11). For the (weak) connection between Buddhists and democracy in Taiwan, see the masterful works by Jones (1999); Laliberté (1999) and his updated version, Laliberté (2001).

6. In this book, the terms "religious groups," "sects," and "denominations" are used interchangeably and in a strictly academic sense via Max Weber (1964). The common derogative meaning of "sect" is not implied here. The term "denomination" refers to a Christian sect, while "sect" refers to the denomination of other religions.

7. See Table 5.1 of this book.

8. *Jidujiao Luntanbao*, 25 June 2002, p. 1.

9. See Chapter 4 for details.

10. This book adopts the Chinese pinyin system for most Chinese words, except for well-known Taiwanese leaders, political parties, and places.

11. For the evolution of the relationship between religion and the state during Japanese colonial rule, see Jones (2003). Although Japanese rule left some legacy, Taiwan's postwar state-religion relations presented a dramatic break from the past, due to the migration of Chinese Buddhism, Christianity, Daoism, folk religions, and a Leninist state to Taiwan.

12. For a classic analysis of Taiwan's democratization, see Tien (1989) and Roy (2003).

13. Corporatist associations refer to social organizations that are organized according to the criteria of singularity, compulsion, government sponsorship, non-competitiveness, and functional differentiation (Schmitter, 1971). For instance, a textile firm had to join a state-approved textile association at the lowest level of administrative hierarchy. Then, the lower-level association had to be a member of a higher-level association. The peak association, the Chinese Textile Association, was the only one at the national level that represented the interests of all textile producers in Taiwan. All industrial producers' associations were members of the National Industry Association, which singularly represented the interests of all industrial producers.

14. For the few works (in Chinese) on the relationship between religion and the state in Taiwan, see Qü (1997), Y. Ye (2000), and B. Lin (1990).

15. Telephone interview with a KMT staff member, 26 June 2002.

16. Interviews with theologians at the Taiwan Theological Seminary and the Taiwan Baptist Seminary, 19 April 2002.

17. On domestic and external causes for the lifting of martial law, see Qi (1996).

18. On 17 March 1990, the Ministry of the Interior convened a religious conference in which sixty-two representatives from twelve state-recognized religions participated. Most participants agreed with the ministry to promulgate a law on religious groups. See Y. Ye (2000, 263).

19. President Jiang's wife, Song Mei-ling, was a Methodist. Her major contributions to Methodist evangelism in Taiwan included facilitating the establishment of a high school and the Souchou University sponsored by Methodist missions. However, the Methodist churches in Taiwan did not receive other special treatments from the govenrment. By 2001, this denomination consisted of only 27 churches, 19 pastors, and 2,416 believers (Ministry of the Interiors, 2001: 79).

2. TAIWANESE BUDDHISM

1. See Welch (1968: 29–33).

2. For the classic text on Chinese Buddhism from 1911 to 1949, see Welch (1968). For pioneering works on Taiwanese Buddhism in the Qing dynasty and Japanese colonial rule, see Jones (1999) and Laliberte (1999).

3. In an edited book by M. Zhang (1979), some Chinese Buddhists advocated political activism, but Taiwanese Buddhists ignored their views.

4. Taixü, *Rensheng foxue de shuoming* [The Elaboration of Secular Buddhism]. Jiechuang fouxue jiaoyüwang home page, http://www.jcedu.org/rsfj/Taixü/1/rsfx-dsm.htm; Yinshun, *Renjian fojiao yaolue* [The Major Summary of Secular Buddhism].

Buddhist Studies Society of Hong Kong University homepage, http://www.hku.hk/buddhist/yinshun/16/yinshun16–06.html, 7/5/02.

5. Yinshun, *Fo zai renjiang* [Buddha on Earth], 155; http://127.0.0.1/accelon/homepage.csp?db=yinshun&bk= 14&t=5776313&rr=1396#1, 7/5/02.

6. Yinshun, *Taixü dashi nianpu* [The Chronology of Master Taixü], 527–29, http://127.0.0.1/accelon/homepage.csp?db=yinshun&bk=13&toc=&rr=&t=628507, 7/5/02.

7. C. Jiang (1995a: 472–79); Ding (2004: 250–64).

8. Interview with Ven. Zhaohui, 27 May 2002.

9. The three gems refer to Buddha, Buddhist laws, and the clergy. The Buddhist ceremony of accepting the three gems is equivalent to a Christian baptism.

10. Chinese Buddhist tradition discredited the sermon by the laity (*baiyi shuofa*) as an ominous sign of the end of the world (*mofa*). In my interview (6 June 2002) with Buddhist scholar Yang Hui-nan, he mentioned that the *Book on Buddhist Fall* (*famiejing*) discussed this issue. But he suggested that the book's discussion has been quoted out of context and mixed up the causal relationships. The text's real intention was to attribute the fall of the Buddhist world and the sermon by the laity to the fall of the clergy.

11. The Japanese colonial government established the Nanying Buddhist association to monitor the activities of Taiwanese Buddhists in 1921. In 1946, the Association was renamed as the Taiwan Provincial Buddhist Association of China. After the BAROC was established in the following year, the Association was further renamed as the Buddhist Branch Association of the Taiwan Province (Shi Ruwu, 1990: 155).

12. A national Chinese Buddhist Layman's Association was established for lay believers in 1968. The BAROC severely attacked its legal and religious legitimacy. But since the founder was an influential retired official, the government granted its establishment. The Chinese Buddhist Layman's Association, however, attracted only a limited membership (Jones, 1999: 184–85).

13. "Zongjiao qifu zaocanhui bian fuxünhui," *China Nightly News*, 19 November 1997.

14. A senior KMT cadre accused Ven. Jingxin of political betrayal (interview with Wang Ming-cheng). But based on available news reports, what Jingxin and the BAROC have done reflects more a change toward political neutrality than a shift toward the Democratic Progressive Party.

15. According to American campaign finance law, a nonprofit organization (including religious organization) is not supposed to divert its funds to political activities. See *New York Times*, 14 April 1997, Editorial; http://www.cnn.com/ALLPO-LITICS/1997/01/24/gore.fundraiser, 27 May 2006; *Washington Post*, 23 February 1998, p. A01.

16. FGS membership numbers are probably more reliable than those of other Buddhist groups in the sense that members have to be at least twenty years old and complete the initiation ceremony of upholding the three gems (Jiang, 1997: 15).

17. Laliberté (1999: 99) cites another political speech by Xingyun in 1984, in which he espoused ethical democracy. Again, this idea is more Confucian than democratic.

18. Interviews with Ven. Zonggu, 5 May 2002, and with Ven. Nankin, 15 June 2002.

19. The following information is based on Foguangshan (2002, 12–15).

20. Interview with Ven. Zonggu, 5 May 2002.

21. *Fazongshibao*, 18 January 2005; *Renjianfubao*, 17 January 2005; *China Daily News*, 17 January 2005, p.A13; *Lianhebao*, 17 January 2005, p. A6.

22. Interview with a Dharma Teacher, 15 April 2003.

23. The Buddhist Association of the Republic of China home page. Available: http://www.baroc.org.tw/outwash.htm.

24. It was not clear whether or not Ven. Xinyun had urged Chen to run for the presidency. However, it seemed that Chen had approached all Buddhist organizations to support his campaign. Ven. Xinyun was the first one who publicly supported Chen; see *Lianhebao*, 16 September 1995, p.06; 3 March 1996, p.04.

25. They included legislators Pan Wei-gang and Huang Zhao-shun and KMT central committee members Zhao Li-yun and Li Zhong-gui. Wang Jing-ping has been the Speaker of the Legislature since 1999.

26. *China Times*, 10 March 2004, p. C3; interview with Wang Ming-cheng.

27. Douglass Shaw, ed., 1996, *Still Thoughts, Volume One*, by Cheng Yen, translated by Chia-hui Lin (Taipei: Still Thoughts Cultural Mission), p. 160, cited from Laliberté (1999, 126).

28. Ciji jijinhui mishuchu, "Xuanjü shijian aide dingning," [A Reminder during the Election Period] forwarded email, 19 December 2003.

29. Julia C. Huang, 2005. "Weeping, Silent Melody, and Discipline: Embodying Charisma, the Collective, and the State in the Compassion Relief Movement of Taiwan." Paper delivered at the International Conference on Religion, Modernity, and the State in China and Taiwan, UC Santa Barbara, October 28–30, 2005, p. 21.

30. Interview with Professor Chen, 2005.

31. Interview with Professor Chen, 12 June 2002.

32. Telephone inquiry with the Ciji Taipei office, 3 July 2002.

33. Interview with Professor Jiang, 13 June 2002.

34. *Ciji daolü banyuekan* [Ciji Biweekly]. No. 309. (1998, December 1). Tsu Chi Humanitarian Center home page, http://taipei.tzuchi.org.tw/taolu/309/p309-lf.htm; and No. 338/339 (2000, March 1); http://taipei.tzuchi.org.tw/taolu/338/p338-le.htm.

35. Interview with Yao Chong-zhi, 14 May 2002.

36. *Ibid.*

37. *Ibid.*

38. *Dharma Drum Monthly*, 1 May 2002, p. 2.

39. Interview with a high-ranking lmember of the laity of the DDM, 14 May 2002.

40. Interview with Ven. Jianzi, 14 May 2002.

41. Ven. Jianzi claimed that the slogan referred only to a spiritual status. But one senior lay believer admitted that the slogan was very misleading.

42. Interview with Ven. Jianzi, 14 May 2002.

43. Ibid.

44. Interviews with Zhongtai lay believers, 28 August 2002.

45. The Buddhist Association of the Republic of China main page, http://www.baroc.org.tw/outwash-1.htm.

46. Zhongtai mobilized against James Song, the presidential candidate of the People First Party, which was a KMT splinter party. Therefore, it was easier for Zhongtai to establish a new relationship with the DPP. See *Lianhebao*, 29 May 2001, p. 20.

47. *Lianhebao*, 2 September 2001, p. 3.

48. *Lianhebao*, 5 June 2002, p. 18.

49. In 1990, Ven. Weijue was sentenced to four months with two years of probation for his illegal appropriation of public land. In 1997, in a similar case, he was acquitted, but his disciples were found guilty. See *Lianhebao*, 16 March 2001, p. 10. In 1996, Ven. Weijue hastily conducted the tonsure ceremony for one hundred thirty-two college students without the consent of their parents.

50. *Ziyushibao* (The Liberty Times), http://www.libertytimes.com.tw/2004/new/mar/today/today-p1.htm; http://www.libertytimes.com.tw/2004/new/mar/today/today p2.htm, 3/12/2004

51. *Ziyushibao* (The Liberty Times), 5/24/2002.

52. Interview with Ven. Zhaohui, 27 May 2002.,

53. Ibid.

54. *Lianhebao*, 18 October 1991, p. 3; 21 March 1992, p. 4; 21 November 1992, p. 5; 21 August 1994, p. 7; 26 December 1994, p. 3; 18 March 1995, p. 7; 17 May 1995, p. 5; 26 October 1995, p. 2; interviews with Ten Thousand Buddha Association, 8 July 2002 and 5 November 2002.

3. CHRISTIANITY

1. See Chen Nanzhou (1991: 116–118).

2. Some foreign missionaries and theologians, such as Michael Thornberry, Donald J. Wilson, David Gelzer, and Daniel Keeby supported the PCT's Taiwan independence cause and were expelled by the KMT government (Zheng, 1999: 71; Huang, 1986: 304–309).

3. The membership of the Presbyterians includes not only baptized adults but also baptized infants, absentee members, and unbaptized churchgoers. The latter three categories constitute about half of the total membership. See Taiwan jidu zhanglao jiaohui zonghui yianjiu fazhang zhongxin (1999).

4. *Christian Tribune News*, 25 June 2002, p. 1.

5. Interviews with C. S. Song from 2004 to 2005.

6. The most representative works include N. Chen (1991) and Luo (2001). See also a similar conclusion reached by Wachman (1994, 231).

7. Interview with K.T. Kiao, 18 March 2002.

8. Taiwan Jiduzhanglaojiaohui, Taiwan Zhuquanduli Xuanyan (Declaration of Taiwan's Sovereignty Independence), August 20, 1991.

9. Interview with Rev. Z.F. Beng, 19 March 2002.

10. Interview with Rev. Lo Rong-guang, 22 March 2002; interview with Rev. C.I. Guang, 25 March 2002.

11. PCT, "Church Statistics," http:/www.pct.org.tw/stat, 8 July 2005.

12. *Jidujiao Luntanbao* (Christian Tribune), 5–7 November 2005, p. 1; 1–2 December 2005, p. 3.

13. Interview with Rev. Z. F. Yeng, 19 Marh 2002. A representative work is H. Lin (1994).

14. In the 1970s, the speaker served a one-year term, and the general secretary served a three-year term. See Hu (2001: 222).

15. Interview with Rev. T. R. Chen, 14 March 2002; interview with Rev. Y. X. Zhu, 15 March 2002.

16. Interview with Rev. T. Y. Kiao, 18 March 2002; interview with Rev. Z. C. Ko, 19 March 2002.

17. Interview with Rev. Z. C. Ko, 19 March 2002.

18. Interview with Rev. Z. C. Ko, 19 March 2002; interview with Rev. C. I. Guang, 25 March 2002.

19. Interview with X. G. Zhao, 16 August 2005.

20. Interview with Y. X. Zhu, 15 March 2002.

21. The phrase "critical support" (*pipingxin de zhichi*) was coined by Rev. Huang Zhang-hui, former president of the Presbyterian Seminary in Tainan.

22. http://acts.pct.org.tw/bulletin/ab_doc_asp.asp, 8 December 2006.

23. Our telephone inquiries of the assistants of all legislators, conducted in May 2002.

24. Since the Baptists insist on adult baptism, the membership number does not include children and nonbaptized churchgoers as the Presbyterian census does.

25. Interviews with theologians at the Taiwan Baptist Seminary, 19 April 2002.

26. Interview with deacon SD Xie, 13 March 2002.

27. Interview with Rev. ZC Mi, 14 September 2002.

28. Interview with Rev. NH Yue, 7 March 2002.

29. Rev. Zhou recalled his heated debate with American evangelists about changing English sermons to Mandarin ones (Zhou, 1994: 166–68).

30. American evangelists had occupied the deans of the Baptist Seminary until 1982, when a Chinese pastor succeeded to the post.

31. Interview with Deacon TM Zin, 8 March 2002; interview with Rev. NH Yue, 7 March 2002.

32. Zhou (2006: 34).

33. Interview with Rev. XR Wang, 19 April 2002. Rubinstein (1991: 89–90) might have misinterpreted Rev. Zhou's and the Baptist Church's political role when he labeled them as strong supporters of the KMT government.

34. In 1985, about 80% of Baptist churches used Mandarin as their church language. See D. Huang (1993: 48).

35. In the past decade, I have given lectures on relations between church and state in more than a dozen Baptist churches and organizations. Most of time, I would ask believers and pastors about their political party preferences.

36. Interview with Rev. KD Van, 19 April 2002.

37. In the early history of the Local Church, the name of their hymn book included the words "Little Flock." Western evangelists thus called them the Little Flock. The Local Church repeatedly objected to such a title (C. Li 2001, 145). Rubinstein (1991, 109–112) translates the church's name as the "Assembly Hall Church." The church is called "local" church because each branch shares the name of the city in which it is located, for example, Taipei Church, Gaoxion Church. They are differentiated by numerical orders according to their sequence of establishment, for example, the Eleventh Assembly Hall of the Taipei Church.

38. *Christian Tribune News*, 25 June 2002, p. 1. The Local Church accepts teenagers for baptism. Thus, the age qualification for Local Church members is higher than for Presbyterians but lower than for Baptists.

39. Interview with Zhang Aiwha, 7 December 2006.

40. Interview with YE Riu, 27 March 2002.

41. Interview with IR Yang, 14 March 2002.

42. *Ibid.*

43. After the lifting of martial law, some aboriginal TJC churches went public in their support for political parties and candidates. The TJC headquarters discouraged this trend to little avail. Interview with SA Yang, 22 April 2002.

44. Interview with ZS Dai, 11 March 2002; interview with SA Yang, 22 April 2002.

45. Interview with Rev. IR Xü, 14 March 2002.

46. The BLC was representative of most Mandarin churches, which became active supporters of the New Party and the People First Party. Interview with theologian YY You, 5 March 2002.

47. Interview with Rev. IR Xü, 14 March 2002; interview with deacon GM Gu, 18 March 2002.

48. *Christian Tribune News*, 19 August 2006 and 22 August 2006.

49. "Profile of Chinese Regional Bishop's Conference" (15 April 2002). Chinese Regional Bishop's Conference home page, http://ww.catholic.org.tw/bishops/profile/profiles.htm.

50. See Leung (1992).

51. Interview with Rev. AZ Xü, 18 April 2002.

52. Ibid.

53. Cardinal Paul Shan Kuo-his, guest speaker's speech delivered at the International Conference on Religion and Politics: A Holy but Controversial Affiliation, cosponsored by the National Sun Yat-sen University and the Taiwanese Political Science Association, Gaoxion, Taiwan, 15–16 August, 2005.

54. Interview with Rev. AZ Xü, 18 April 2002.

4. DAOISM AND FOLK RELIGIONS

1. "Daojiao." (13 April 2001). Taiwan, China home page, http://big51.chinataiwan.org/web/webportal/W2001317/A2042027.html, 7 May 2006; interview with Zhang Sheng and Gao Zhong-xin. Daoism conducts a formal membership ceremony for new believers, called Chuandu. However, few Daoist believers in Taiwan go through this ceremony. Therefore, the number of Daoist believers is exaggerated according to this strict standard.

2. Interview with Zhang Sheng, 7 July 2004.

3. Kohn (2000: xii) points out that the popular view of Hong Ge being the founder of religious Daoism is wrong.

4. Interview with Abbot Xü.

5. "Zhengyidao" is translated as Orthodox One, Orthodox Unity, or the Way of the Celestial Master. Priests from other denominations, like the Maoshan and Sannai, also performed these rituals, but Orthodox One was the major denomination (Qing 1996: 541–42). Jones (2003: 13–15) argues that Daoism and Buddhism were not very active during the rule of Zheng Cheng-gong. Regional temples hosting local deities were the major religious foci.

6. See Cai (1990: 236–239); Jones (2003: 22–27).

7. This is consistent with the teaching of another Daoist classic, the Daodejing, which says that "the Way is great, Heaven is great, the Earth is great, and the emperor is equally great."

8. http://www.jht.com.tw/html/5.htm, 30 December 2000.

9. This definition extends the boundary of Daoism to the worship of prominent people but excludes the worship of nonhumans in folk religions.

10. One exception can be found in the Scripture of the Great Peace, which says that man, representing yang, is superior to woman, who is ying, and it is better for each man to have two women because yang is an odd number and ying is an even number (Yü 2001, 47, 314).

11. Interview with Lee Fong-mao, 9 July 2004.

12. Ibid.

13. Ibid. http://group.kitde.com.tw/index_2.asp?Page=5&class=%A4%BA%ACF%B3%A1%AA%C0%B9, 3/3/05.

14. Interview with Zhang Sheng, 7 July 2004.

15. Interviews with Wang Ming-cheng and Lee Fong-mao, 9 July 2004.

16. Caituan faren cangying hongdao jijinhui home page, http://home.pchome.com.tw/society/hongdao/start1.html, 3 March 2005.

17. Interview with Lee Fong-mao, 9 July 2004.

18. Interview with Zhang Sheng, 7 July 2004.

19. Interview with Gao Zhong-xin, 13 July 2004.

20. Interviews with Gao Zhong-xin, 13 July 2004, and You Yuan-shun, 17 August 2004.

21. Interview with Gao Zhong-xin, 13 July 2004.

22. From the late Ming dynasty to the end of the Qing dynasty, YGD theology combined only the three traditional Chinese religions, and called it "Three Religions in One" (*sanjiaoheyi*), or "The One Integrates the Three Extremes" (*sanjiyiguan*) (see Lin, 2001: 345–48). The inclusion of Christianity and Islam was an innovation by the last Great Master Zhang, who started collecting "divine revelations" from Jesus and Mohammad in 1938 (Fu, 1999: 424–29).

23. "CPWR vs. World Yiguandao Headquarters." (28 January 2005). World Yiguandao Headquarters home page, http://www.with.org/activities-en.htm, 28 January 2005; telephone interview with YGD headquarters, 29 March 2005.

24. Interview with Lin Zhi-xiang.

25. Ibid.

26. Ibid.

27. Zhang Tian-ran's "Yitiao Jinxian" (A Golden Line), cited from Fu (1999, 732).

28. The use of children was stipulated by Zhang Tian-ran's work, *Yiguandao wenti jieda*. However, some YGD branches use three persons of older ages or adults due to the difficulty of recruitment and training (interview with Lin Chin-chi, 10 December 2004).

29. Li Wen-si was released from prison in 1980 by a special pardon.

30. Song (1983, 127) recognizes eight Way Masters.

31. Interview with Liu Xi-xiang, 20 August 2004.

32. The three treasures consist of pointing the mystic portal (*dianxuanguan*), the hand seal (*baohetong*), and the true sutra (*koujue*) of five wordspassed on only orally, see Wang (2000,77–79); Taiwanzonglan/Kejiwenjiao/Xinxingzongjiao/Yiguandao (一), http://big5.chinataiwan.org/web/webportal/W2001318/A2030656.html, 14 January 2005; Derek Lin. "Three Treasures of Yiguandao." True Tao homepage, http://www.truetao.org/ikuantao/treasures.htm.

33. "Introduction to Yiguandao." True Tao home page, http://www.truetao.org/ikuantao/i-kuan.htm.

34. Interview with Tiantaishenggong.

35. Interview with Lin Zhi-xiang; "Yiguandao (II)." (10 April 2001). Taiwan, China home page, http://big5.chinataiwan.org/web/webportal/W2001318/A2030657.html.

36. "Yiguandao (II)." (10 April 2001). Taiwan, China home page, http://big5.chinataiwan.org/web/webportal/W2001318/A2030657.html.

37. Interviews with Tiantaishenggong and Lin Zhi-xiang.

38. Interview with Lin Zhi-xiang. Before 1949 in China, the major competitor of YGD was the Li religion (*Lijiao*), which had a very similar theology and rituals to YGD. In 1945, the Li religion reported YGD to the KMT government for the latter's alleged crime of conspiracy during the anti-Japanese war (Qin and Yan, 2000, 290–91). However, there is no evidence that the Li religion participated in the prosecution of YGD in Taiwan, but another similar religion, the Chinese Confucius society *(Zhongguo kongxuehui)*, was involved in the prosecution.

39. The Daoist opposition was from a disgruntled Daoist leader and probably did not represent the whole religion.

40. In 1983, former minister of interior affairs Lin Yang-gang, also a relative of the Way then, chaired an interagency meeting to discuss YGD's legalization. But due to opposition from the secret police, the legalization proposal was rejected. Nevertheless, he ordered the police department not to harass YGD meetings (see Song, 1996: i–ii).

41. Chen's YGD membership was confirmed by our telephone interview with the Chongde division, 31 January 2005.

42. *China Times*, 28 February 2000; *China Nightly News*, 17 March 2000; *Xinxinwen Weekly*, 14–18 March 2000, p. 16, pp. 110–11.

43. Interview with Lin Zhi-xiang; *China Times*, 23 March 2004, p. C4.

44. Interview with Tiantaishenggong.

45. *China Times*, 22 October 2004, C5; 29 November 2004, A9; Central Election Commission of ROC home page, http://210.69.23.140/cec/vote3.asp?pass1=B2004A0000000000aaa, 14 January 2005.

46. *Gongshang Daily*, 15 September 2002, p. O8; *China Times*, 15 June 2003, p. O2.

47. Interview with Lin Zhixiang; *China Times*, 11 March 2004, p. A5; *China Times*, 15 June 2004, p. A8.

48. *China Times*, 10 March 2004, p. C3; interview with Wang Ming-cheng.

49. Sangren (1993, 565) estimated the number of religious pilgrims to the Beigang Chaotiangong alone to be four to five million.

50. L. Li (1995, 90–94) categorizes it as a folk religion, Beigang Chaotiangong (2003, 4–5) regards it as a Buddhist religion, but the DARC leaders insist that it is a Daoist belief (Daojiaohui 2000, 6; Daojiao zongmiao 2003, 5).

51. *Haixiapinglun*, no. 74, 1997, pp. 62–63.

52. Interviews with Zhang Xun and Paul Katz, 24 June 2004; Lee Fong-mao, 5 July 2004; and Zheng Zhi-ming, 28 June 2004.

53. Interview with Zhang Xun, 24 June 2004.

54. Interview with Lin Mei-rong, 8 June 2004. Some temple chairpersons are directly elected by the assembly of believers, for example, the Luermen Tianhougong in Tainan (interview with Lin Chuan-xian, 20 August 2004).

55. Interview with Liu Yü-lin.

56. Interview with Ji Ren-zhi, 1 July 2004.

57. Interview with Ji Ren-zhi, 1 July 2004.

58. Interview with Guo Jin-lun, 1 July 2004.

59. *Xinxinwen Weekly*, 22–28 April 1999, p. 10–12.

60. *Xinxinwen Weekly*, 14–18 March 2000, p. 111.

61. Central Election Commission of ROC home page, http://www.cec.gov.tw; interview with Manager Guo.

62. *China Times*, 28 February 2001; *China Times*, 1 September 2004, p. A5.

63. Central Election Commission of ROC home page, http://210.69.23.140/cec/cechead.asp, 14 January 2005.

64. *China Times*, 30 September 2004, p. A10.

65. Interview with Liu Yü-lin, 15 July 2006.

5. STATISTICAL ANALYSIS

1. Kuan Ping-yin and Wang Yong-ci (2005) traced the evolution of religious attitudes in Taiwan from 1984 to 2000, crosstabulated by gender, age, and education.

2. The TSCS 2004 did not include any Muslims or members of Falungong, despite their proclaimed memberships of four hundred thousand (including foreign workers) and one million, respectively. Because Falungong teaches its members that it is not a religion but a Qigong club, we introduced the question "Have you practiced Falungong before?" in the survey. No respondent gave a positive answer to this question.

3. Tudigong is an earth god and is ranked the third most popular god in Taiwan, after Wanyie and Mazu. Because he blesses the earth, many farmers, morticians (providers of funeral services), miners, loggers, construction workers, and realtors regularly worship him. Guan-gong was a warrior of the Three Kingdom era (A.D. 220–280). As a symbol of justice, credibility, and strength, he became a popular god worshiped by business people, police, and gangsters.

4. Calculated by the author from the American National Election Survey 2000 data set, collected by the ICPSR. The following US statistics also came from this source.

5. In the TEDS 2003, we asked the respondents to provide the name of their religious organizations. It turned out to be a research disaster. Not only were there many more religious groups than we could handle, the membership of major religious groups was also under-represented due to the respondents' inability to remember the organization's exact name. Based on our prior knowledge of Taiwan's religious profile, the TSCS 2004 was able to include the major religious groups with a sufficient number of cases for meaningful statistical study.

6. Department of Statistics, Ministry of the Interior, "Population by Age in Taiwan-Fujian Area," http://www.moi.gov.tw/stat, 8/2/05.

7. We do not include party identification in the control variable list because it overlaps with our theoretical assumption that some religions tend to favor pan-blue parties while other religions favor pan-green. Nor do we control for religious behavior variables. In our various trials, a composite variable of these behavioral variables does not generate significant results, while it reduces the religion variable to an insignificant level.

8. We do not conduct more comparisons than what is included in this section due to the large number of religious groups and insignificant coefficients.

9. The East Asia Barometer Project (2000–2004) was co-directed by Profs. Fu Hu and Yun-han Chu and received major funding support from Taiwan's Ministry of Education, Academia Sinica, and National Taiwan University. The Asian Barometer Project office (www.asianbarometer.org) is solely responsible for the data distribution. I appreciate the assistance in providing data by the institutes and individuals aforementioned. The views expressed herein are my sole responsibility.

Glossary

Baisheng 白聖

Baiyang 白陽

Banshiyuan 辦事員

Beigang Chaotiangong 北港朝天宮

Bian'e 匾額

Chan (Zen) 禪

Chen, Lü-an 陳履安

Chen, Shui-bian 陳水扁

Chen, Yi-shen 陳儀深

Chuan sanbao 傳三寶

Dadi 大帝

Dajia Zhenlangong 大甲鎮瀾宮

Dangtuan 黨團

Daodeyuan 道德院

Daojiao jüshihui 道教居士會

Daojiao lianhehui 道教聯合會

Daojiaohui 道教會

Daoqin 道親

Daotong 道統

Daozhang 道長

Dari rulai 大日如來

Dashi 大士

Dejiao 德教

Dianchuanshi 點傳師

Dicai 地才

Dongchu 東初

Dongshihui 董事會

Dui guoshi de shengming yü jianyi
　　對國是的聲明與建議

Fenling 分靈

Fenxianghuo 分香火

Fengshan 封山

Foguangshan zuzhi zhangcheng
　　佛光山寺組織章程

Fojiao jiuguo jiuxian yundong
　　佛教救國救憲運動

Fojiao kenan ciji gongdehui
　　佛教克難慈濟功德會

Fotang 佛堂

Fulu 符籙

Gao, Zhong-xin 高忠信

Gong, Peng-cheng 龔鵬程

Gongren 工人

137

Guanli weiyuanhui 管理委員會

Guanlihui 管理會

Guanyin 觀音

Guiyi sanbao 皈依三寶

Guoshi 國師

Guoyü jiaohui 國語教會

Hongyang 紅陽

Huichai 會差

Huifuben shengjing 恢復本聖經

Huineng 慧能

I-Kuan Tao zonghui 一貫道總會

Jiandu simiao tiaoli 監督寺廟條例

Jiang, Can-teng 江燦騰

Jiang, Jie-shi (Chiang, Kai-shek)
    蔣介石

Jiang, Jing-guo (Chiang, Ching-kuo)
    蔣經國

Jiangshi 講師

Jiaohui jühuisuo 教會聚會所

Jiaoqü 教區

Jie 劫

Jigongfo 濟公佛

Jihui youxingfa 集會遊行法

Jingsi yülu 靜思語錄

Jingxin 淨心

Lanyishe 藍衣社

Laoqianren 老前人

Lee, Feng-mao 李豐楙

Li, Deng-hui (Lee, Teng-hui) 李登輝

Li, Chang-shou 李常受 (Witness Li)

Li, Wan-jü 李萬居

Li, Wen-si 李文斯

Lian, Zhan 連戰

Lizhang 里長

Lin, Feng-zheng 林豐正

Lin, Mo-niang 林默娘

Lingliangtang 靈糧堂

Lishihui 理事會

Liu, Shuai-zhen 劉率真

Lu, Zhong-yi 路中一

Ma, Yong-chang 馬永常

Mazu 媽祖

Meinan jinxinhui Taiwan chaihui
    美南浸信會臺灣差會

Ni, Tuo-sheng 倪柝聲 (Watchman Nee)

Nongchansi 農禪寺

Pipanxing zhichi 批判性支持

Putidamo 菩提達摩

Qianren 前人

Qingyang 青陽

Qiu, Chu-ji 邱處機

Rencai 人才

Renjian fojiao 人間佛教

Renmin tuanti zuzhifa 人民團體組織法

Renquan xuanyan 人權宣言

Sancai 三才

Sannai furen 三奶夫人

Sanqi mojie 三期末劫

Sanqinggong 三清宮

Sengshi sengjue 僧事僧決

Shangren 上人

Shanshu 善書

Shen 神

Shengyan 聖嚴 (Sheng Yen)

Shimupai 師母派

Shixiongpai 師兄派

Song, Ze-lai 宋澤萊

Songhuizong 宋徽宗

Songshan Ciyougong 松山慈祐宮

Su, Dong-qi 蘇東啟

Sun, Su-zhen 孫素真

Sun, Hui-ming 孫慧明

Taipei Guandugong 台北關渡宮

Taipingjing 太平經

Taiwan zhuquan duli xuanyan
台灣主權獨立宣言

Taixü 太虛

Tan jianshi/jiangshi 壇教師/講師

Tanzhu 壇主

Tao-tsang (Dao-Cang) 道藏

Tiancai 天才

Tianzhujiao zhongguo zhujiaotuan
天主教中國主教團

Wanfohui 萬佛會

Wang, Shou 王壽

Weihuang shangdi 維皇上帝

Weijue 惟覺 (Wei Chueh)

Weiyuan 委員

Wenzheng buganzhi 問政不干治

Women de huyü 我們的呼籲

Wu, Bo-xiong 吳伯雄

Wujilaomu 無極老母

Wuming 悟明

Wutong chengfa 五統乘法

Wuye youmin 無業遊民

Xian 仙

Xiaohui 小會

Xinding 心定

Xingyizu 興毅組

Xingyun 星雲 (Hsing Yun)

Xü, Jun-xi 徐俊熙

Xü, Xun 許訓

Yang 陽

Yang, Hui-nan 楊惠南

Yaochi jinmu 瑤池金母

Yin 陰

Yinshun 印順

Yuehuipusa 月慧菩薩

Zengcai, Mei-zuo 曾蔡美佐

Zhaijiao 齋教

Zhang, Dao-ling 張道陵

Zhang, En-pu 張恩溥

Zhang, Guang-bi (Zhang, Tian-ran)
張光璧 (張天然)

Zhang, Rong-fa 張榮發

Zhang, Ying-yü 張英譽

Zhaofoguidao 詔佛歸道

Zhaohui 昭慧

Zheng, Zhi-ming 鄭志明

Zhengyan 證嚴 (Cheng Yen)

Zhengyixian 正義線

Zhenjun 真君

Zhenlidang 真理黨

Zhenyesu jiaohui 真耶穌教會

Zhinangong 指南宮

Zhongguo daojiaohui 中國道教會

Zhongguo fojiaohui 中國佛教會

Zhongguo kongxuehui 中國孔學會

Zhongguo rujiaohui 中國儒教會

Zhonghua fosi xiehui 中華佛寺協會

Zhonghuaminguo daojiaohui
    中華民國道教會

Zhonghuaminguo daojiaozonghui
    中華民國道教總會

Zhonghuaminguo fojiao qingnianhui
    中華民國佛教青年會

Zhonghuaminguo xiandai fojiao xiehui
    中華民國現代佛教協會

Zhonghui 中會

Zhongjun 忠君

Zhongsheng pingdeng 眾生平等

Zhongtai chansi 中台禪寺

Zhou, Lian-hua 周聯華

Zhou, Shen-zhu 周神助

Zhu, Wu-xian 朱武獻

Zong guanli zhongxin 總管理中心

Zongsheng 宗聖

Zongwu weiyuanhui 宗務委員會

Zushi 祖師

Bibliography

Almond, Gabriel A., R. Scott Appleby, and Emmanuel Sivan. 2003. *Strong Religion: the Rise of Fundamentalisms around the World*. Chicago, IL: University of Chicago Press.

Asad, Talal. 2003. *Formations of the Secular: Christianity, Islam, Modernity*. Stanford, CA: Stanford University Press.

Berkowitz, Peter. 1999. *Virtue and the Making of Modern Liberalism*. Princeton, NJ: Princeton University Press.

Berger, Peter L. 1967. *The Sacred Canopy: Elements of a Sociological Theory of Religion*. New York: Anchor Books.

———. ed. 1999. *The Desecularization of the World: Resurgent Religion and World Politics*. Grand Rapids, MI: William B. Eerdmans Publishing Company.

Bosco, Joseph. 2003. "Tianhougong zhi chongjian yü huoli: Taiwan yü Xianggang bijiao yanjiu" (The Restructuring and Liveliness of Tianhougong). In *Ma-zu xinyang de fazhan yü bianqian: Ma-zu xinyang yü xiandai guoji shehui yantaohui lunwenji* (International Symposium on the Development and Transition of the Folk Belief of Mazu: The Folk Belief of Ma-zu and Contemporary Society), ed. M. Lin, X. Zhang, and X. Cai. Taipei: Taiwan zongjiao xuehui.

Bourdieu, Pierre. 1986. "The Forms of Capital." In *Handbook of Theory and Research for the Sociology of Education*, ed. L. C. Richardson. New York: Greenwood Press, S241-S258.

Buddha's Light International Association (BLIA). 2001. *World Headquarters 10th Anniversary Special Edition*. Hacienda Heights, CA: BLIA.

Buddhist Association of the Republic of China (BAROC). 1983. *Zhongfo huikan* (BAROC Newsletter) 18: 1.

Cai, Xiang-hui. 1994. "Yi ma-zu xinyang weili: lun zhengfu yü minjian xinyang de guanxi" (On the Relationship between Government and Folk Belief: The Case of Ma-zu). In *Minjian xinyang yü zhongguo wenhua guoji yantaohui lunwenji* (International Symposium on Folk Beliefs and Chinese Culture). Taipei: Hanxue yanjiu zhongxin.

Caituanfaren Zhongtaishan fojiao jijinhui bianjizu. 1998. *Zhontai xingchu* (The Zhongtai Journey). Puli, Nantaoxian: Caituan faren Zhongtaishan fojiao jijinhui.

Calvin, John. 1989. *Institute of the Christian Religion.* Trans. Henry Beveridge. Grand Rapids, MI: William. B. Eerdmans Publishing Company.

Casanova, José. 1994. *Public Religions in the Modern World.* Chicago, IL: University of Chicago Press.

Chen, Hui-jian. 2000. *Zhengyan fashi de ciji shijie* (Ven. Zhengyan and Her Tzu Chi World). Hualian: Ciji zhiye zhongxin.

Chen, Nan-zhou. 1991. *Taiwan jidu zhanglao jiaohui de shehui zhengzhi lunli* (Social and Political Ethics of the Taiwan Presbyterian Church). Taipei: Yongwang Press.

———. 2000. "Rentong de shenxue" (Identified Theology). In *Jidu zongjiao yanjiu xueshu yantaohui lunwenji* (Symposium on the Study of Christian Belief), ed. Taiwan zongjiao xuehui. Taipei: Taiwan zongjiao xuehui.

Chen, Qiu-lin, Jia Li, and Aman Lü. 1990. "Fojiao jiuguo jiuxian yundong" (A Buddhist Movement of Safeguarding the Nation and Constitution). *Fojiao wenhua* (Buddhist Culture) 4: 9–11.

Chen, Yi-shen. 1990. "Taixü fashi de zhengzhi sixiang chutan" (The Preliminary Probing to Ven Taixü's Political Thoughts). *Zhongyangyanjiuyuan jindaishi yanjiusuo jikan* (Bulletin of the Institute of Modern History, Academia Sinica) 19: 279–298.

Cheng-tian Kuo and Ping-yin Kuan. 2005. "Religious Factors in Taiwanese Democracy." Paper presented at the International Conference on Religion and Politics: A Holy but Controversial Affiliation, co-sponsored by the National Sun Yat-sen University and the Taiwanese Political Science Association, Gaoxion, Taiwan, 15–16 August, 2005.

Chin, Ko-lin. 2003. *Heijin: Organized Crime, Business, and Politics in Taiwan.* Armonk, NY: M. E. Sharpe.

Ching, Julia. 1993. *Chinese Religions.* Maryknoll, NY: Orbis Books.

Clark, J. C. D. 1994. *The Language of Liberty 1660–1832: Political Discourse and Social Dynamics in the Anglo-American World.* Cambridge, UK: Cambridge University Press.

Clart, Philip. 1997. "The Phoenix and the Mother: The Interaction of Spirit Writing Cults and Popular Sects in Taiwan." *Journal of Chinese Religions* 25 (Fall): 1–32.

Cohen, Marc J. 1988. *Taiwan at the Crossroads: Human Rights, Political Development and Social Change on the Beautiful Island.* Washington, DC: Asia Resource Center.

Coleman, James S. 1990. *Foundations of Social Theory.* Cambridge, MA: Harvard University Press.

Dahl, Robert A. 1989. *Democracy and Its Critics.* New Haven, CT: Yale University Press.

Daojiao zongmiao sanqinggong weiyuanhui. 2003. *Women dui Daojiao yingyou de renshi* (The Knowledge of Daoism). Yilan: Daojiao zongmiao sanqinggong weiyuanhui.

Daojiaohui. 2000. *Daojiao zhushen shengji* . 道教會。2000。道教諸神聖紀。台北: 台北市道教會。(A Holy Documentation of Daoist Deities). Taipei: Taipei Daoist Association.

Davie, Grace. 1999. "Europe: The Exception That Proves the Rule?" In *The Desecularization of the World: Resurgent Religion and World Politics*, ed. Peter L. Berger. . Grand Rapids, MI: William B. Eerdmans Publishing Company.

Diamond, Larry, and Marc F. Plattner. eds. 2001. *The Global Divergence of Democracies*. Baltimore, MD: Johns Hopkins University Press.

Ding, Ren-jie. 2004. *Shehui fenhua yu zongjiao zhidu bianqian: Dangdai Taiwan xinxing zongjiao xianxiang de shehuixue kaocha* (Social Differentiation and the Transformation of Religious Institutions: A Sociological Study of Contemporary New Religious Phenomena in Taiwan). Taipei: Lianjing.

Djupe, Paul A., and Christopher P. Gilbert. 2000. "Are the Sheep Hearing the Shepherds?" Paper presented at the APSA annual meeting. Washington, DC. 2–5 September.

Dong, Fang-yuan. 1986. *Renshi Taiwan minjian xinyang* (Understanding Taiwanese Folk Belief). Taipei: Changqing wenhua.

Education Committee of Chinese Baptist Church. 1985. *Jinxinhui jiaohui shouce* (Baptist Church Manual). Taipei: Chinese Baptist Church.

Eidsmoe, John. 1987. *Christianity and the Constitution: The Faith of Our Founding Fathers*. Grand Rapids, MI: Baker Books.

Esposito, John L. 1996. *Islam and Democracy*. New York: Oxford University Press

Filali-Ansary, Abdou. 2001. "Muslims and Democracy" In *The Global Divergence of Democracies*, Larry Diamond and Marc F. Plattner, eds., Baltimore, MD: Johns Hopkins University Press.

Foguangshan. 2002. *Foguangshan kaishan jinian sanshiyi zhounian nianjian* (A Special Issue Commemorating the Thirty-First Anniversary of Foguangshan). Kaohsiung: Foguang Press.

Fong, Shiaw-Chian. 1996. "The Politics of Narrative Identity in the Ma-zu Cult." *Issues and Studies* 32 (11): 103–125.

Fox, Russell Arben. 1997. "Confucian and Communitarian Responses to Liberal Democracy." *Review of Politics* 59 (3): 561–592.

Fu, Zhong. ed. 1999. *Yiguandao fazhanshi* (The Historical Development of I-Kuan Tao). Taipei: Zhengyi shanshu chubanshe.

Gill, Anthony James. 1998. *Rendering unto Caesar: The Catholic Church and the State in Latin America*. Chicago, IL: University of Chicago Press.

———. 2001. "Religion and Comparative Politics." *Annual Review of Political Science* 4: 117–138.

Gong, Peng-cheng. 1998. *Daojiao xinlun erji* (New Study on Daoism). Jiayi: Nanhua College of Management.

Gong, Xue-zeng. 2000. *Zongjiao wenti ganbu duben* (Cadre's Manual of Religious Issues). Beijing: Zhonggong zhongyang dangxiao chubanshe.

Greenberg, Anna. 1999. "Political Communication in the Church." Paper presented at the APSA annual meeting. Atlanta. 2–5 September.

Gutiérrez, Gustavo. 1988. *A Theology of Liberation*. 2nd ed. Maryknoll, NY: Orbis Books.

Hardacre, Helen. 1989. *Shinto and the State, 1968–1988*. Princeton, NJ: Princeton University Press.

Hatch, Nathan O. 1989. *The Democratization of American Christianity*. New Haven, CT: Yale University Press.

He, Feng-jiao. 1996. *Taiwansheng jingwu dangan huibian—minsu zongjiao pian* (The Collection of Taiwan Police Works). Taipei: Guoshiguan.

Hofmann, Steven Ryan. 2004. "Islam and Democracy: Micro-Level Indications of Compatibility." *Comparative Political Studies* 6 (6): 652–676.

Hong, Jin-lian. 1995. Taixudashi Fojiaoxiandaihua Zhi Yanju (*Research on Taixü-dashi's Buddhist Modernization*. Taipei: Dongchu.

Hou, Kun-hong. 2003. "Zhanhou Taiwan fojiao yü zhengzhi guanxi zhi yanjiu" (The Study on the Relationship between Buddhism and Politics in Taiwan after WWII). Paper delivered at Ershi shiji Taiwan minzhu fazhan xueshu taolunhui (Symposium on the Development of Democracy in Taiwan in the Twentieth Century). Guoshiguan. Taipei. 24–26 September.

Hu, Hui-lin. 2001. *Shizijia zhilu: Kao jun-ming mushi huiyilu* (The Way to Cross: Memoir of Rev. Chunming Kao). Taipei: Wangchunfong Press.

Huang, Chien-yu Julia. 2005. "Tiawanese 'Grassroots Globalization': The Cultural Politics of a Global Buddhist Nongovernmental Organization in Taiwan." Manuscript.

Huang, Chien-yu Julia, and Robert P. Weller. 1998. "Merit Mothering: Women and Social Welfare in Taiwanese Buddhism." *Journal of Asian Studies* 57 (2): 379–396.

Huang, Dong-zhu. 1993. *Zhonghua jidujiao jinxinhui zaitai budao yü jiaohui zengzhang zhi tantao* (A Study of the Evangelism and Church Growth of the Chinese Baptists). Taipei: Taiwan jinxinhui chubanshe.

Huang, Mei-ying. 1994. *Taiwan ma-zu de xianghuo yü yishi* (The Fire and Cults of the Folk Belief of Ma-zu in Taiwan). Taipei: Ziliwanbaoshe.

Huang, Wu-dong. 1986. *Huang wudong huiyilu* (The Memoirs of Huang Wu-dong). Irvine, CA: Taiwan Publishing Company.

Huntington, Samuel P. 1991. *The Third Wave: Democratization in the Late Twentieth Century*. Norman: University of Oklahoma Press.

———. 1993. "The Clash of Civilizations?" *Foreign Affairs* (Summer): 22–49.

———. 1996. *The Clash of Civilizations and the Remaking of World Order*. New York: Simon & Schuster.

Hwang, Kwang-Kuo. ed. 1988. *Zhongguoren de quanli youxi* (The Chinese Power Game). Taipei: Jüliu.

Jelen, Ted Gerard, and Clyde Wilcox. 2002. Religion and Politics in Comparative Perspective: The One, the Few, and the Many. New York: Cambridge University Press.

Jiang, Can-teng. 1995a. *Ershi shiji Taiwan fojiao de zhuanxing yü fazhan* (The Transformation and Development of Taiwan's Buddhism in the 20th Century). Kaohsiung: Jingxin wenjiao jijinhui.

———. 1995b. "Jieyanhou de Taiwan fojiao yü zhengzhi" (Buddhism and Politics in Taiwan after the Lifting of Martial Law). In *Fojiao yü zhongguo wenhua guoji xueshuhuiyi lunwenji: zhongji* (International Symposium on Buddhism and Chinese Culture). Taipei: Zhonghua wenhua fuxing zonghui zongjiao yanjiu weiyuanhui.

———. 1997. *Taiwan dangdai fojiao: Foguanshan, Ciji, Fagushan, Zhongtaishan* (Contemporary Taiwanese Buddhism). Taipei: Nantian shujü.

Jones, Charles B. 1999. *Buddhism in Taiwan: Religion and the State, 1660–1990.* Honolulu: University of Hawaii Press.

———. 2003. "Religion in Taiwan at the End of the Japanese Colonial Period." In *Religion in Modern Taiwan: Tradition and Innovation in a Changing Society*, ed. Philip Clart and Charles B. Jones. Honolulu: University of Hawaii Press.

Jordan, David K., and Daniel L. Overmyer. 1986. *The Flying Phoenix: Aspects of Chinese Sectarianism in Taiwan.* Taipei: Caves Books.

Kang, Bao (Paul R. Katz). 1995. "The Worship of Lüdongbin: the Example of Zhinangong." Xinshixue, 6(4). 21–41. 康豹 (Paul R. Katz)。1995。「台灣呂洞賓信仰: 以指南宮為例」。新史學, 6(4): 21–41.

Kang, Wi-jo. 1997. *Christ and Caesar in Modern Korea: A History of Christianity and Politics.* Albany: State University of New York Press.

Katz, Paul. 1995. "Taiwan lüdongbin xinyang: yi zhinangong weili" (The Folk Belief of Lüdongbin in Taiwan: The Case of Zhinangong). *Xinshixue* (New Historiography) 6 (4): 21–41.

———. 2003. "Religion and the State in Postwar Taiwan." *China Quarterly* 174: 395–412.

Kirkland, Russell. 2004. *Taoism: The Enduring Tradition.* New York: Routledge.

Kohn, Livia. ed. 2000. *Daoism Handbook.* Netherlands: Koninklijke Brill NV.

Kramnick, Isaac, and R. Laurence Moore. 1996. *The Godless Constitution: The Case against Religious Correctness.* New York: W. W. Norton & Company.

Kuan, Ping-yin, and Wang Yong-ci. 2005. "Ningjinggeming" (Silent Revolution). In *Ningju Taiwan Shengmingli* (Converging Vitality in Taiwan), ed. Wang Zhenhuan and Zhang Ying-hua. Taipei: Juliu.

Kuo, Cheng-tian. 2001. *Zhengjiao de fenli yü zhiheng* (The Separation, Checks, and Balances of Politics and Religions). Taipei: Chinese Evangelical Seminary.

———. 2006. "Christianity and Democracy in Asian Pluralist Religious Markets: Taiwan and South Korea." Prepared for delivery at the 2006 Annual Meeting of the American Political Science Association, Philadelphia, PA, 30 August–3 September 2006.

Lai, Zong-xian. 1999. *Taiwan daojiao yuanliu* (The Origin of Daoism in Taiwan). Taipei: Zhonghuadaotong chubanshe.

Laliberté, André. 1999. *The Politics of Buddhist Organizations in Taiwan, 1989–1997.* Ph.D. dissertation. University of British Columbia.

———. 2001. "Buddhist Organizations and Democracy in Taiwan." *American Asian Review* 19 (4): 97–129.

Lancaster, Lewis R., and Richard K. Payne. eds. 1997. *Religion and Society in Contemporary Korea*. Berkeley: Institute of East Asian Studies, University of California.

Lee, Fong-mao. 1993. "Ma-zu yü ru shi dao sanjiao" (Ma-zu and Confucianism, Buddhism, and Daosim). *Lishiyuekan* (History Monthly) 63: 34–42.

———. 1997. "Daojiao jielun yü dangdai dujie zhishuo: yige kuayue ershi shiji dao ershiyi shiji de zongjiao guancha" (The Study on Tribulation and Modern Statement of Passing the Tribulation in Daoism: Observation from a Religious Perspective across the Twentieth Century to the Twenty-First Century). In *Xinbie shenge yü Taiwan zongjiao lunshu* (Gender, Godhood, and Statement of Taiwanese Religions), ed. F. Lee and R. Zhu. Taipei: Institute of Chinese Literature and Philosophy, Academia Sinica.

———. 2003. "The Daoist Priesthood and Secular Society: Two Aspects of Postwar Taiwanese Daoism." In *Religion in Modern Taiwan: Tradition and Innovation in a Changing Society*, ed. P. Clart and C. Jones. Honolulu: University of Hawaii Press.

Leonard, Bill J. 2003. *Baptist Ways: A History*. Valley Forge, PA: Judson Press.

Leung, Beatrice. 1992. *Sino-Vatican Relations: Problems in Conflicting Authority 1976–1986*. New York: Cambridge University Press.

Li, Chang-shou. 2001. *Lishi yu qishi (II)* (History and Revelation ([II]). Taipei: Taiwan Gospel Books.

Li, Jia-fu. 2001. *Nichaisheng yü zhongguo difang jiaohui yundong* (Watchman Nee and the Chinese Local Church Movement). Masters thesis. History Institute of Taiwan Normal University.

Li, Lu-lu. 1995. *Ma-zu xinyang* (The Folk Belief of Ma-zu). Taipei: Hanyang chubanshe.

Li, Shi-yü. 1975. *Xianzai huabei de mimi zongjiao* (Modern Secret Religions in North China). Taipei: Gutingshuwu.

Li, Yi-dao. 2000. *Dianchuanshi yü zibenjia: zongjiao yü laodong kongzhi de guanxi, yi yiguandao weili* (Dian-Chuan-Shi and Capital: The Relationship between Religion and Labor Control, An Example by I-Kuan-Tao). Masters thesis. National Chengchi University.

Liao, Wu-zhi, and Lian-fu Huang. ed. 2003. *Guandugong*. Taipei: Caituanfaren taibeishi guandugong.

Lieberman, Evan S. 2005. "Nested Analysis as a Mixed-Method Strategy for Comparative Research." *American Political Science Review* 99 (3): 435–52.

Lin, Ben-xuan. 1990. *Taiwan de zhengjiao chongtu* (Church-State Conflicts in Taiwan). Taipei: Daoxiang.

———. 1997. "Meizhou ma-zu dailai de xinyang rechao yü Zhenyi" (The Passionate Belief and Discussion of Meizhou Ma-zu). *Guojia Zhengce Shuangzhoukan* (National Policy Research Biweekly) 157: 14–15.

———. 2004. 'Taiwanmingzhong De Zongjiaoliudong Yu Dililiudong" (Religious Fluidity and Geographical Fluidity of the Taiwanese People) *Conference Proceedings of Religion and Social Change*. Institute of Sociology, Academia Sinica.

Lin, Hong-xin. 1994. *Jiaerwen shenxue* (Theology of John Calvin). Taipei: Liji Press.

Lin, Mei-rong. 1991. "Taiwan qüyüxing zongjiao zuzhi de shehui wenhua jichu" (The Social and Cultural Bases of Regional Religious Institutions in Taiwan). *Dongfang zongjiao yanjiu* (Oriental Religious Studies) 2: 345–364.

Lin, Mei-rong, and Xü Gu-ming. 2003. "Guandu ma-zu de xinyangquan" (The Circle of the Folk Belief of Guandu Ma-zu). In *Ma-zu xinyang de fazhan yü bianqian: Ma-zu xinyang yü xiandai guoji shehui yantaohui lunwenji* (International Symposium on the Development and Transition of the Folk Belief of Mazu: The Folk Belief of Ma-zu and Contemporary Society), ed. M. Lin, X. Zhang, and X. Cai. Taipei: Taiwan zongjiao xuehui.

Lin, Rongze. 1993. "Yiguandao Fayilingyin" (The Lingyin Division of the Fayi Branch of Yiguandao). *Dongfang zongjiao yanjiu* 3: 269–295.

Lin, Wan-chuan. 1985. *Xiantiandao yanjiu* (A Study of the Xiantiandao). Tainan: Qijushuju.

———. 2001. "Yiguandao" (I-Kuan Tao). In *Zongjiao jianjie* (Introduction to Religions), ed. Ministry of the Interior. Taipei: Department of Civil Affairs, Ministry of the Interior.

Ling, L. H. M., and Shih Chih-yü. 1998. "Confucianism with a Liberal Face: The Meaning of Democratic Politics in Postcolonial Taiwan." *Review of Politics* 60 (1): 55–82.

Locke, John. 1683, 1993. *Two Treatises of Government*. Rutland, VT: Charles E. Tuttle.

Lu, Hui-xin. 1997. "Xingbie, jiating yü zongjiao: yi fojiao ciji gongdehui weili" (Gender, Family, and Buddhism: The Case of Buddhist Tsu Chi Gongdehui). In *Xinbie shenge yü Taiwan zongjiao lunshu* (Gender, Godhood, and Statement of Taiwanese Religions), ed. F. Lee and R. Zhu. Taipei: Institute of Chinese Literature and Philosophy, Academia Sinica.

Lu, Zhen-ting, and Liu Fang. eds. 1987. *Women Renshide Xingyundashi* (Xingyundashi Whom We Know). Taipei: Caifeng Publications.

Lu, Zhong-wei. 1998. *Yiguandao neimu* (The Confidentiality of I-Kuan Tao). Nanjing: Jiangsu renmin chubanshe.

Luo, Rong-guang. 2001. *Wei Taiwan qidao: Luo rong-guang mushi wenji* (Prayers for Taiwan: The Collection of Rev. Luo Rong-guang). Taipei: Wangchunfeng Press.

Marty, Martin E. and R. Scott Appleby. eds. 1991. *Fundamentalisms Observed*. Chicago: University of Chicago Press.

———. 1993a. *Fundamentalisms and Society: Reclaiming the Sciences, the Family, and Education*. Chicago, IL: University of Chicago Press.

———. 1993b. *Fundamentalisms and the State: Remaking Polities, Economies, and Militance*. Chicago, IL: University of Chicago Press.

———. 1994. *Accounting for Fundamentalisms*. Chicago: University of Chicago Press.

———. 1995. *Fundamentalisms Comprehended*. Chicago: University of Chicago Press.

McHale, Shawn. 2004. *Print and Power: Confucianism, Communism, and Buddhism in the Making of Modern Vietnam*. Honolulu: University of Hawaii Press.

Miller, James. 2003. *Daoism: A Short Introduction*. Oxford: Bell & Bain.

Ministry of the Interior. 2000. *Neizheng tongji fenxi zhuanji* (Special Report of Interior Affairs Statistical Analysis). Taipei: Ministry of the Interior.

———. 2001. *Zongjiao jianjie* (Brief Introduction to Religions). Taipei: Department of Civil Affairs, Ministry of the Interior.

Mio, Yu-ko. 2003. "Cong liangan mazumiao de jiaoliu lai tan Taiwan de minzuzhuyi" (The Analysis of Taiwanese Nationalism Based upon the Interaction between Ma-zu Temples across the Taiwan Strait). In *Ma-zu xinyang de fazhan yü bianqian: Ma-zu xinyang yü xiandai guoji shehui yantaohui lunwenji* (International Symposium on the Development and Transition of the Folk Belief of Mazu: The Folk Belief of Ma-zu and Contemporary Society), ed. M. Lin, X. Zhang, and X. Cai. Taipei: Taiwan zongjiao xuehui.

Monsma, Stephen V., and J. Christoper Soper. 1997. *The Challenge of Pluralism: Church and State in Five Democracies.* Lanham, MD: Rowman & Littlefield.

Moody, Peter R., Jr. 1996. "Asian Values." *Journal of International Affairs* 50 (1): 166–92.

Morgan, Edmund S. ed. 1965. *Puritan Political Ideas 1558–1794.* New York: Bobbs-Merrill.

Mu, Yü. 2002. *Yiguandao gaiyao* (A Digest of I-Kuan Tao). Taipei: Zhonghuaminguo yiguandao zonghui.

Nettels, Curtis P. 1963. *The Roots of American Civilization: A History of American Colonial Life.* 2nd ed. New York: Appleton-Century-Crofts.

Ostrom, Vincent. 1997. *The Meaning of Democracy and the Vulnerability of Democracies: A Response to Tocqueville's Challenge.* Ann Arbor, MI: University of Michigan Press.

Paine, Thomas. 1776, 1995. *Rights of Man, Common Sense, and Other Political Writings*, ed. Mark Philp. New York: Oxford University Press.

Paper, Jordan. 1996. "Mediums and Modernity: The Institutionalization of Ecstatic Religious Functionaries in Taiwan." *Journal of Chinese Religions* 24: 105–130.

Park, Andrew Sung. 1993. *The Wounded Heart of God: The Asian Concept of Han and the Christian Doctrine of Sin.* Nashville, TN: Abringdon Press.

Przeworski, Adam, and Henry Teune. 1970. *The Logic of Comparative Social Inquiry.* Malabar, FL: Krieger Publishing.

Putnam, Robert D. 1993. *Making Democracy Work: Civic Traditions in Modern Italy.* Princeton, NJ: Princeton University Press.

Pye, Lucian W. 1985. *Asian Power and Politics: The Cultural Dimensions of Authority.* Cambridge, MA: Belknap Press.

Qi, Guan-gyu. 1996. *Zhonghuaminguo de zhengzhi fazhan: minguo sanshiba nian yilai de bianqian* (The Political Development of the Republic of China: The Transformation since 1949). Taipei: Yangzhi.

Qin, Bao-qi, and Le-bin Yan. 2000. *Dixia shenmi wangguo yiguandao de xingshuai* (Underground Secret Kingdom: The Rise and Fall of I-Kuan Tao). Fujian: Fujian renmin chubanshe.

Qing, Xi-tai. ed. 1996. *Zhongguo daojiaoshi* (History of Daoism in China). Vol. 4. Chengdu, Sichuan: Sichuan renmin chubanshe.

Qü, Hai-yuan. 1997. *Taiwan zongjiao bianqian de shehui zhengzhi fenxi* (A Sociopolitical Analysis of Taiwan's Religious Transformation). Taipei: Guiguan.

Queen, Christopher S., and Sallie B. King. eds. 1996. *Engaged Buddhism: Buddhist Liberation Movements in Asia.* Albany: State University of New York Press.

Rozman, Gilbert. 2002. "Can Confucianism Survive in an Age of Universalism and Globalization?" *Pacific Affairs* 75 (1): 11–37.

Rubinstein, Murray A. 1991. *The Protestant Community on Modern Taiwan: Mission, Seminary, and Church.* Armonk: M. E. Sharpe.

———. 2001. "The Presbyterian Church in the Formation of Taiwan's Democratic Society, 1945–2001." *American Asian Review* 19 (4): 63–96.

Sangren, P. Steven. 1993. "Power and Transcendence in the Ma Tsu Pilgrimages of Taiwan." *American Ethnologist* 20 (3): 564–82.

Schlesinger, Arthur M. 1968. *The Birth of the Nation: A Portrait of the American People on the Eve of Independence.* Boston, MA: Houghton Mifflin Company.

Schmitter, Philippe C. 1971. *Interest Conflict and Political Change in Brazil.* Stanford: Stanford University Press.

Shengyan. 1979. *Fojiao rumen* (Introduction to Buddhism). Taipei: Fagu wenhua.

———. 1995. *Dingning* (Exhort). Taipei: Huangguan Press.

———. 1999. *Mingri de fojiao* (Buddhism of the Future). Taipei: Fagu wenhua.

———. 2001a. *Xuefou qunyi* (Questions and Doubts on Learning Buddhism). Taipei: Fagu wenhua.

———. 2001b. *Zhengxin de fojiao* (The Orthodox Belief of Buddhism). Taipei: Fagu wenhua.

Shi, Nengrong. 2003. *Lüzhi, qinggui ji qi xiandai yiyi zhi tanjiu* (The Study on Rules, Regulations, and Their Modern Meaning). Taipei: Fagu wenhua.

Shi, Ruwu. 1990. *Guangfu qianhou Taiwan Fojiao zhi bijiao* (A Comparison of Taiwanese Buddhism before and after the Retrocession). In *The Second International Symposium on Politico-Religious Relations in China*, ed. Liangsheng Zheng, Taipei: Department of History, Tamkan University.

Shi, Tianjian. 2000. "Political Culture: A Prerequisite for Democracy?" *American Asian Review* 18 (2): 53–83.

———. 2001. "Cultural Values and Political Trust: A Comparison of the People's Republic of China and Taiwan." *Comparative Politics* 33 (4): 401–419.

Shi, Zhaohui. 1995. *Fojiao Lunlixue* (Buddhist Ethics). Taipei: Fajie Publications.

———. 1992. *Foxue Jinquan* (Contemporary Interpretation of Buddhism). Taipei: Fajie Publications.

Shiding Wulucaishenmiao Xinjianweiyuanhui. 2002. *Wulu wucaishenmiao* (The Temple of Five Military Fortune Gods). Taipei County: Shiding Wulucaishenmiao Xinjianweiyuanhui. 石碇五路財神廟興建委員會。2002。五路武財神廟。台北縣: 石碇五路財神廟興建委員會。

Shields, Currin V. 1958. *Democracy and Catholicism in America.* New York: McGraw-Hill.

Sigmund, P.E. 1990. *Liberation Theology at the Crossroads: Democracy of Revolution?* New York: Oxford University Press.

Song, Ze-lai. 1989. *Bei beipan de foutuo* (Buddha Betrayed). Taipei: Ziliwanbaoshe.

————. 1990. *Bei beipan de foutuo xüji* (Buddha Betrayed [II]). Taipei: Ziliwanbaoshe.

Song, Guang-yü. 1983. *Tiandao gouchen* (The Tribulation of the Heavenly Way). Taipei: Self-published.

————1996. *Tiandao chuandeng* (The Continuation of the Heavenly Way). Taipei: Zhengyi shanshu chubanshe.

Steigmann–Gall, Richard. 2003. *The Holy Reich: Nazi Conceptions of Christianity, 1919–1945.* Cambridge, NY: Cambridge University Press.

Suh, David Kwang-sun. 2001. *The Korean Minjung in Christ.* Eugene, OR: Wipf & Stock Publishers.

Taiwan Association of University Professors. 1997. *Newsletter* 13: 1–11.

Taiwan jidu zhanglao jiaohui zonghui. 2002. *Yi Taiwanguo min, xing Taiwan lu: Taiwan guojia zhengming, jiaru lianheguo xunyan* (In the Name of Taiwan, On the Way of Taiwan: The Declaration on Joining the United Nations in the Name of Taiwan). Taipei: Taiwan jidu zhanglao jiaohui zonghui.

Taiwan jidu zhanglao jiaohui zonghui bianji xiaozu. 2000. *Renshi Taiwan jidu zhanglao jiaohui* (Introduction of the Presbyterian Church in Taiwan). Taipei: The General Assembly of the Presbyterian Church in Taiwan.

————. 2002. *Taiwan jidu zhanglao jiaohui jiaohui yilanbiao* (The Directory of the Presbyterian Churches in Taiwan, 2001–2002). Taipei: The General Assembly of the Presbyterian Church in Taiwan.

Taiwan jidu zhanglao jiaohui zonghui fagui weiyuanhui. 2000. *Jiaohui fagui* (Church Law). Taipei: The General Assembly of the Presbyterian Church in Taiwan.

Taiwan jidu zhanglao jiaohui zonghui yianjiu fazhan zhongxin. 1999. *Taiwan jidu zhanglao jiaohui yijiujiuba niandu jiaoshi tongji ziliao shouce* (Annual Report of the Presbyterian Church in Taiwan, 1998). Taipei: The General Assembly of the Presbyterian Church in Taiwan.

Tamadonfar, Mehran. 2002. "Islamism in Contemporary Arab Politics: Lessons in Authoritarianism and Democratization." In *Religion and Politics in Comparative Perspective: The One, the Few, and the Many,* ed. Ted Gerard Jelen and Clyde Wilcox. New York: Cambridge University Press.

Tang, Chong-rong. 1991. *Congrenlun tan ziyou minzhu renquan fazhi* (Freedom, Democracy, Human Rights, Sovereignty). Taipei: CMI Publishing Company.

Tang, You-zhi. 1996. *Yuan nideguo jiangling: Zhengzhi shengxue yu lunli* (Thy Kingdom Come: Political Theology and Ethics). Hong Kong: Baptist Press.

Tessler, Mark. 2002. "Islam and Democracy in the Middle East: The Impact of Religious Orientations on Attitudes Toward Democracy in Four Arab Countries." *Comparative Politics* 34 (April): 337–354.

Tessler, Mark, C. Konold, and M. Reif. 2004. "Political Generations in Developing Countries: Evidence and Insights from Algeria." *Public Opinion Quarterly* 68 (Summer): 184–216.

Thompson, Laurence G. 1996. *Chinese Religion: An Introduction.* 5th ed. New York: Wadsworth Publishing Company.

Tien, Hung-Mao. 1989. *The Great Transition: Political and Social Change in the Republic of China.* Stanford, Ca.: Hoover Institution Press.

Tocqueville, Alexis de. 1969. *Democracy in America,* ed. J. P. Mayer. Garden City, NY: Anchor Books.

Tu, Wei-ming. 2000. "Implications of the Rise of 'Confucian' East Asia." *Daedalus* 129 (1): 195–218.

Wachman, Alan M. 1997. *National Identity and Democratization.* Armonk, NY: M. E. Sharpe.

Wang, Jian-chuan. 1996. *Taiwan de zhaijiao yü luantang* (Vegetarian Religion and Luan Temples in Taiwan). Taipei: Nantian shujü.

Wang, Reizhen. 2000. *Disanzhiyan kan yiguandao* (An Alternative Perspective on Yiguandao). Taipei: Xiaoyuan Shufang,

Weber, Marx. 1964. *The Sociology of Religion.* Boston: Beacon Press.

———. 1978. *Economy and Society,* ed. Guenther Roth and Claus Wittich. Berkeley: University of California Press.

Weijue. 1994. *Jianxin chengfou* (Knowing Self and Becoming Buddha). Taipei: Zhongtai Cultural Foundation.

Welch, Holmes. 1968. *The Buddhist Revival in China.* Cambridge, MA: Harvard University Press.

Weller, Robert P. 2000. "Living at the Edge: Religion, Capitalism, and the End of the Nation-State in Taiwan." *Public Culture* 12 (2): 477–498.

Witte, John, Jr. 2000. *Religion and the American Constitutional Experiment: Essential Rights and Liberties.* Boulder, CO: Westview Press.

Wu, Wen-ren. ed. 1998. *Cong bianjiang dao formosa: Jinxinhui zaitai wushie nianshi, 1948–1998* (From Frontier to Formosa: The Fifty Years' History of the Baptist Church in Taiwan, 1948–1998). Taipei: The Chinese Baptist Press.

Wuthnow, Robert. 2002. "Religious Involvement and Status-Bridging Social Capital." *Journal for the Scientific Study of Religion* 41: 669–684.

Xingyun. 2001. "Renjian fojiao de lantu (II)" (A Blueprint of Secular Buddhism [II]). *Pumen xuebao* (Universal Gate Buddhist Journal) 6: 28–32.

———. "Guanyuan de zunyan" (The Dignity of the Officials). *Miwu zhijian (III)* (Between Ignorance and Enlightment [III]). Taipei: Xianghai wenhua.

Yang, C. K. 1961. *Religion in Chinese Society: A Study of Contemporary Social Functions of Religion and Some of Their Historical Factors.* Berkeley, CA: University of California Press.

Yang, Hui-nan. 1993. *Dangdai fojiao sixiang zhanwang* (The Perspectives of Contemporary Buddhism's Thoughts). Taipei: Dongda Books.

Yang, Yü-mei, and Zhang, Shu-juan. 1989. *Zhenlangong wuchennian qingcheng qian qingjiao zhuanji* (. . .) Taichung: Caituanfaren dajia zhenlangong.

Ye, Lun-hui. 2003. *Songshan Ciyougong.* Taipei: Caituanfaren taibeishi songshan ciyougong.

Ye, Yong-wen. 2000. *Taiwan zhengjiao guanxi* (Taiwan's State-Church Relations). Taipei: Fengyun Luntan.

Yü, Bo-le. 1994. *Lun zongjiao zuzhi zhi kecenghua qingxiang: yi jiaohui jühuisuo weili* (The Bureacratization Trend of Religious Organizations: An Example of the Local Church). Masters thesis. Soochow University.

Yü, Guang-hong. 1994. "Lugang tianhougong de yingxiang fanwei" (Spheres of Influence of Lugang Tianhougong). In *Minjian xinyang yü Zhongguo wenhua guojiyantaohui lunwenji* (International Symposium on Folk Beliefs and Chinese Culture). Taipei: Hanxue yanjiu zhongxin.

Yü, Li-ming. 2001. *Taipingjing zhengdu* (Study on the Scripture of the Great Peace). Chengdu: Bashushushe.

Zhang, Hao. 1990. *Youan yizhi yu minzhu chuantong* (Dark Consciousness and Democratic Tradition). Taipei: Lianjing.

Zhang, Man-tao. 1979. *Fojiao yü zhengzhi* (Buddhism and Politics). Taipei: Dasheng wenhua chubanshe.

Zhang, Mau-gui and Lin Ben-shuan. 1992. "Zongjiao de shehuiyixiang" (The Social Image of Religion). *Bulletin of the Institute of Ethnology, Academia Sinica*, 74:95–124.

Zhang, Sheng. 2001. "Daojiao" (Daoism). In *Zongjiao jianjie* (Introduction to Religions), ed. Ministry of the Interior. Taipei: Department of Civil Affairs, Ministry of the Interior.

Zhang, Tian-ran. 1942, 1993. "Yiguandao yiwenjieda" (Answers to the Questions about Yiguandao). *Daxue Baihuajiesho, Yiguandao Yiwenjieda* (Vernacular Annotations of Daxue: Answers to the Questions of Yiguandao). Taipei: Tianbindaomaitan.

Zhang, Xün. 1995. "Fenxiang yü jinxiang: Ma-zu xinyang yü renqun de zhenghe" (The Distribution of Incense Powder and the Pilgrimage: The Folk Belief of Mazu and the Integration of People). *Si yü Yan* (Thoughts and Words) 33 (4): 83–105.

Zheng, Ding-wang. 2002. *Feiyingli zuzhi fazhan ji yunzuo zhi yanjiu* (Study of Nonprofit Organizations). Taipei: Caituanfaren DDM renwen shehui jiangzhu xueshu jijinhui.

Zheng, Yan-gen. 1999. *Lishi yu xinyang: Cong jidujiao guandian kan Taiwan he shijie* (History and Belief: A Christian Perspective of Taiwan and the World). Tainan: Jiaohui Gongbao.

Zheng, Zhi-ming. 1991. "Dangdai luanshu de zhengjiao lichang" (The Church-State Views of Contemporary Luan Books). In *Dierjie zhongguo zhengjiao guanxi guoji xueshu yantaohui lunwenji* (Second International Symposium on Relationship between Politics and Religions in China), ed. Zheng Liang-sheng. Taipei: Danjiang daxue lishixi.

———. 1994. "Taiwan wanfouhui de zhengjiao lichang" (The Political and Religious Positions of Wanfouhui in Taiwan). In *Zongjiao yü wenhua guanxi xueshu yantaohui lunwenj* (Symposium on the Relationship between Religions and Cultures in China), ed. Zongxian Zhou. Taipei: Danjiang daxue lishixi.

———. 1997. "Taiwan ma-zu jidian de xianxiang fenxi" (The analysis of the the Ma-zu Ceremony in Taiwan). *Zongjiao Zhexue Jikan* (Journal of Religious Philosophy) 3 (1): 155–168.

Zhinangong. 1998. *Lingshan yüxiu zhinangong muzha xiangongmiao* (Sacred and Spirited Zhinangong: Fairy Temple in Muzha). Taipei: Zhinangong guanli wei-yuanhui.

Zhong, Qiu-yü. 2001. "Mingshi zunchong xinyang yü xintu de xiuxing zhilu" (The Belief-Devoted Masters and the Road of Discipleship). Paper delivered at the Zongjiao de shenshengxing: xianxiang yü quanshi (Conference of the Sacrament of Religion: The Phenomena and Interpretations, Institute of Religious Studies). National Chengchi University. Taipei. 1–2 July.

Zhonghua jidujiao jinxinhui lianhui. 2000. *Zhonghua jidujiao jinxinhui lianhui de sishiqijie huiyuan dahui dahui shouce* (The Manual of the 47th Conference of Chinese Baptist Church Association). Tainan. 24–26 September.

Zhongtai fojiao xueyuan. 2001. *Zhongtai shijie* (The Zhongtai World). Puli, Nantouxian: Zhongtai fojiao xueyuan.

Zhou, Lian-hua. 1994. *Zhou Lian-hua huiyilu* (The Memoir of Zhou Lian-hua). Taipei: Lianhe Wenxue.

———. 2006. *Shidaidchusheng* (The Call of the Epoch). Taipei: Taiwan Jidujiao Wenyichubanshe.

Index

Note: Page numbers with an *f* indicate figures; those with a *t* indicate tables.

Zhonghuaminguo Daojiaohui, 10, 56, 58, 63–64
Zhongtai Chansi. *See* Zhongtai Zen Monastery
Zhongtai Zen Monastery, 7, 16, 30–33, 89f, 93, 121
  democratization and, 101–106, 103t, 105t, 110–112, 111t

ecclesiology of, 31, 117
party preferences and, 100, 101, 117, 129n46
presidential elections and, 20
theology of, 31, 117
Zhou Lian-hua, Rev., 11, 49–50
Zhou Shen-zhu, Rev., 53
Zhu Wu-xian, 79